APPROXIMATE REASONING
in
INTELLIGENT SYSTEMS,
DECISION
and
CONTROL

APPROXIMATE REASONING in INTELLIGENT SYSTEMS, DECISION and CONTROL

Edited by

E. SANCHEZ

Université Aix-Marseille II, Marseille, France

and

L. A. ZADEH

University of California, USA

PERGAMON PRESS

OXFORD · NEW YORK · BEIJING · FRANKFURT
SÃO PAULO · SYDNEY · TOKYO · TORONTO

U.K.	Pergamon Press plc, Headington Hill Hall, Oxford OX3 0BW, England
U.S.A.	Pergamon Press Inc, Maxwell House, Fairview Park, Elmsford, New York 10523, U.S.A.
PEOPLE'S REPUBLIC OF CHINA	Pergamon Press, Room 4037, Qianmen Hotel, Beijing, People's Republic of China
FEDERAL REPUBLIC OF GERMANY	Pergamon Press, Hammerweg 6, D-6242 Kronberg, Federal Republic of Germany
BRAZIL	Pergamon Editora, Rue Eça de Queiros, 346, CEP 04011, Paraiso São Paulo, Brazil
AUSTRALIA	Pergamon Press Australia, P.O. Box 544, Potts Point, N.S.W. 2011, Australia
JAPAN	Pergamon Press, 8th Floor, Matsuoka Central Building, 1-7-1 Nishishinjuku, Shinjuku-ku, Tokyo 160, Japan
CANADA	Pergamon Press Canada, Suite No. 271, 253 College Street, Toronto, Ontario, Canada M5T 1R5

First edition 1987
Reprinted 1988

Library of Congress Cataloging in Publication Data
Approximate reasoning in intelligent systems,
decision and control.
1. Artificial intelligence. 2. Reasoning.
3. Fuzzy systems. 4. Expert systems (Computer
science) I. Sanchez, Elie, 1944– . II. Zadeh,
Lofti Asker.
Q335.A68 1987 006.3 86–30497

British Library Cataloguing in Publication Data

Approximate reasoning in intelligent systems,
decision & control.
1. Expert systems (Computer science)
2. Fuzzy sets
I. Sanchez, Elie II. Zadeh, L.A.
006.3′3 QA76.76.E95
ISBN 0–08–034335–X

In order to make this volume available as economically and as rapidly as possible the author's typescript has been reproduced in its original form. This method unfortunately has its typographical limitations but it is hoped that they in no way distract the reader.

Printed in Great Britain by
Antony Rowe Ltd, Chippenham, Wiltshire

Preface

It is a long-standing tradition in science to accord respect to what is quantitative, precise and rigorous, and view with disdain what is not. We are impressed by results which require long proof and deep reasoning even in fields in which the systems are much too complex to admit of precise analysis. As a case in point, the von Neumann–Morgenstern theories have spawned a vast and mathematically sophisticated literature aimed at constructing a rigorous foundation for decision analysis, game playing and econometric modeling. And yet, it is widely agreed at this juncture that such normative theories have failed to reflect the remarkable human ability to act in situations in which the underlying information is ill-defined, incomplete or lacking in reliability, and thus are of little predictive value in the analysis of human behavior.

In effect, what is missing in such theories are the bridges to the real world. These bridges are not there because the precision of mathematical models of human reasoning on which such theories are based is much too high considering the ways in which humans reason and make decisions in realistic settings. What this implies is that the development of theories of approximate — rather than precise — reasoning is a prerequisite for the development of theories of human behavior which can provide realistic models of rational thinking in ill-defined environments.

The papers presented in this volume are aimed at this objective. Many, but not all, of the papers make use of the conceptual framework of the theory of fuzzy sets. In this theory classes are not required to have sharply defined boundaries as they do in classical set theory. As a result, the theory of fuzzy sets provides a better model for human concepts and serves as a more expressive language for the representation of knowledge — especially commonsense knowledge.

An important advantage of fuzzy logic — which is based on the theory of fuzzy sets — is that it subsumes both multivalued logic and probability theory. By providing a single framework for both logical and probabilistic inference, fuzzy logic makes it possible to develop rules of inference in which the premises as well as the probabilities are lexically imprecise, i.e., contain predicates and probabilities exemplified by *small, large, much larger than, usually, most, likely, very unlikely,* etc. This facility plays a particularly important role in the representation of uncertainty in expert systems.

The emergence of expert systems as one of the major areas of activity in information science and technology is providing a strong impetus to the development of theories of approximate reasoning as a basis for representing — and reasoning with — expert knowledge. It would be unrealistic to expect that such theories will be easy to develop, since human reasoning is much too complex to admit of simple formalization. Nevertheless, significant progress is being made, as is demonstrated by the papers presented in this volume — papers which address a wide range of issues in approximate reasoning and represent a broad variety of viewpoints and countries of origin. What is particularly important about these papers is that they point the way to applying approximate reasoning to realistic problems which do not lend themselves to analysis by conventional techniques. Through such applications, approximate reasoning will eventually establish itself as a powerful system of reasoning for dealing with the pervasive imprecision of the real world and approaching the human ability to manipulate commonsense knowledge.

The Editors

Publisher's Note

Most of the papers appearing in this volume were presented at the International Conference on BUSINESS APPLICATIONS OF APPROXIMATE REASONING, Paris, 8–10 January 1986, sponsored by Générale de Service Informatique and organised by Georges Attard (GSI) and Elie Sanchez.

Contents

Fuzzy Hardware Systems of Tomorrow

T. YAMAKAWA

Department of Electrical Engineering and Computer Science, Faculty of Engineering, Kumamoto University, Kumamoto 860, Japan

ABSTRACT

Nine basic fuzzy logic circuits employing p-ch and n-ch current mirrors are presented, and the fuzzy information processing hardware system design at a low cost with only one kind of master slice (semicustom fuzzy logic IC) is described. These intrinsic fuzzy logic circuits have the following distinctive features; (1) Electrical characteristics are insensitive to wafer process parameters. (2) The circuits exhibit good linearity, robustness against the thermal and supply voltage fluctuations, and very high operation speed. (MIN and MAX circuits can normally operate with supply voltage of 4V ~ 8V under the temperature range of -55°C ~ +125°C and respond enough within 20 nsec.) (3) They don't need resistors nor isolation, etc. These circuits will be building blocks of "fuzzy computer". Finally, the prospect and situation of fuzzy hardware systems are discussed.

KEYWORDS

Fuzzy computer; current mode circuit; MOS current mirror; basic logic cell; post-binary machine; fuzzy integrated circuit; ratioless circuit; decimal computer; semicustom IC.

I. INTRODUCTION

Two-state operation of digital hardware systems based on boolean algebra naturally exhibits high noise immunity and low sensitivity to the variance of transistor characteristics used in the systems. This means the robustness and extensibility of binary digital hardware systems. It is the reason why digital computers have been popularized nowadays. Since the binary digital hardware systems are based on crisp sets, they are suitable for the exact calculations of large numbers and processing of deterministic informations, but not for the intuitive and/or synthetic decision making and processing of ambiguous informations.

Fuzzy sets and theory proposed by Prof. L. A. Zadeh admirably compensates for this weak point of binary systems (Zadeh, 1965). Various applications of fuzzy sets to engineering, medical science, civic science, social science and other fields have been proposed and realized. The applications up to the present are confined to utilizing digital computers in any case, because there are no other tools useful for fuzzy information processing. Generation of membership functions, and calculations of MAX, MIN, Summation, Division and other functions are executed with numbers 0.0 through 10.0 or so instead of 1.0 . Although the fuzzy information processing employing a digital computer is useful for many purposes according to programming, it is not so effective with respect to the speed of processing, the power dissipation, the functional density, the design and fabrication cost and so on. Fuzzy reasoning with hundreds of fuzzy implications or rules in that manner is not easy to accomplish in the real-time mode. To be able to be used and to be suitable for use are different from each other. Fuzzy information processing requires exclusive hardware systems that deal with fuzzy signals but not binary signals.

II. WHAT IS DESIRED FOR FUZZY HARDWARE SYSTEMS?

In evaluating hardware systems we usually use the measures such as operating speed (response time), reliability, power dissipation, functional density, cost and so forth. Fuzzy reasoning, pattern recognition and other information processing require fast operations. Therefore, hardware systems should be considered from the viewpoint of the operation speed.

An usual digital computer consists of the CPU, its external memories and other peripheral devices organized with buses. The operation speed in this case is limited by the rate of data transfer through buses, but not by response times of logic gates involved in the CPU. Thus the system on chip rather than off chip is desirable for high speed operation.

Response times of a synaptic junction and a nerve fiber are much longer than binary logic gates which are typical building blocks in a binary digital computer. The information processing of the whole nervous system, however, exhibits much higher speed than that simulated by a digital computer. It is caused by the differences in the architecture, algorithm, operations of gates and so forth. When the hardware was very expensive, a stored-program concept proposed by John von Neumann was evaluated to be an excellent concept, because this concept produces simple hardware systems. The integrated circuit technology allows us to get complicated hardware systems at very low price in recent years. Therefore, we should adopt the parallel architecture for higher speed even at the sacrifice of system complexity.

The hardware system of parallel architecture is in need of much more logic gates than that of von Neumann concept. An implementation of fuzzy logic with binary devices (switches) forces hardware designers to mount a large number of active devices and a large area of interconnection region on the silicon chip, and results in higher power dissipation, lower yield (thus higher cost), lower functional density and some other demerits. Therefore, the electronic circuits peculiar to fuzzy logic gates should be designed on the basis of linear operation or an alternative but not binary operation (intrinsic fuzzy logic gates). Needless to say, fuzzy logic devices (not fuzzy logic circuits) will be the most suitable for fuzzy hardware systems, if possible.

Accordingly, the fuzzy information processing in parallel, on chip and by using exclusive fuzzy logic gates or fuzzy logic devices are desired for fuzzy hardware systems. The following sections describe nine basic fuzzy logic function circuits, which were designed in current mode to work in linear operation and consisted of much smaller amount of devices than those implemented with binary devices.

III. BASIC FUZZY LOGIC FUNCTIONS

Basic fuzzy logic functions are defined in terms of membership functions μ_X and μ_Y ($0 \leq \mu_X, \mu_Y \leq 1$) in the following, where $\vee, \wedge$, + and - denote max, min, algebraic sum and algebrainc difference, respectively.

Bounded-Difference

$$\mu_{X \ominus Y} \triangleq 0 \vee (\mu_X - \mu_Y) \quad (1)$$

$$= \mu_X \ominus \mu_Y \quad (1')$$

Fuzzy Complement

$$\mu_{\overline{X}} \triangleq 1 - \mu_X \quad (2)$$

$$= 1 \ominus \mu_X \quad (2')$$

Bounded-Product

$$\mu_{X \odot Y} \triangleq 0 \vee (\mu_X + \mu_Y - 1) \quad (3)$$

$$= (\mu_X + \mu_Y) \ominus 1 \quad (3')$$

Fuzzy Logic Union (MAX)

$$\mu_{X \cup Y} \triangleq \mu_X \vee \mu_Y \quad (4)$$

$$= (\mu_X \ominus \mu_Y) + \mu_Y \quad (4')$$

$$= (\mu_Y \ominus \mu_X) + \mu_X \quad (4'')$$

Bounded-Sum

$$\mu_{X \oplus Y} \triangleq 1 \wedge (\mu_X + \mu_Y) \tag{5}$$

$$= 1 \ominus (1 \ominus (\mu_X + \mu_Y)) \tag{5'}$$

Fuzzy Logic Intersection (MIN)

$$\mu_{X \cap Y} \triangleq \mu_X \wedge \mu_Y \tag{6}$$

$$= \mu_X \ominus (\mu_X \ominus \mu_Y) \tag{6'}$$

$$= \mu_Y \ominus (\mu_Y \ominus \mu_X) \tag{6"}$$

Implication

$$\mu_{X \rightarrow Y} \triangleq 1 \wedge (1 - \mu_X + \mu_Y) \tag{7}$$

$$= 1 \ominus (\mu_X \ominus \mu_Y) \tag{7'}$$

Absolute-Difference

$$\mu_{|X - Y|} \triangleq \begin{cases} \mu_X - \mu_Y & (\mu_X \geq \mu_Y) \\ \mu_Y - \mu_X & (\mu_X < \mu_Y) \end{cases} \tag{8}$$

$$= (\mu_X \ominus \mu_Y) + (\mu_Y \ominus \mu_X) \tag{8'}$$

Equivalence

$$\mu_{X \leftrightarrow Y} \triangleq \mu_{X \rightarrow Y} \wedge \mu_{Y \rightarrow X} \tag{9}$$

$$= 1 \ominus ((\mu_X \ominus \mu_Y) + (\mu_Y \ominus \mu_X)) \tag{9'}$$

All of the basic fuzzy logic functions presented here can be expressed only with the Bounded-Difference and the Algebraic Sum, as described above. Thus, each basic fuzzy logic function circuit is implemented with the Bounded-Difference circuit and the Algebraic Sum circuit. In the current mode circuits, the Algebraic Sum is implemented only by connecting two lines to be summed (Wired Sum). Therefore, the Bounded-Difference arrays can be adapted to many kinds of fuzzy information processing hardware systems, the design of which should be directed only to wiring between the Bounded-Difference circuits (ie. basic logic cells).

IV. BASIC FUZZY LOGIC FUNCTION CIRCUITS AND MULTIPLE-FANOUT CIRCUIT EMPLOYING CURRENT MIRRORS

A current mirror necessary for constructing the Bounded-Difference circuit or the basic logic cell is implemented with bipolar transistors or MOS FETs.

A bipolar current mirror produces two types of significant errors. One is caused by the base current or the finite forward current gain of transistors. Fig. 1 (a) illustrates its aspect. Assuming that the electrical characteristics of two transistors Q_1 and Q_2 are identical to each other, the input current I_i and the output current I_o are obtained from Fig. 1 (a) at a glance as

$$I_i = I_c + \frac{2}{\beta} I_c = I_c(1 + \frac{2}{\beta}) \tag{10}$$

$$I_o = I_c \tag{11}$$

where β and I_c are the forward current gain and the collector current of Q_1 and Q_2, respectively. Eqs. (10) and (11) give the current mirror factor (or current mirror ratio) G_I as follows.

$$G_I = \frac{I_o}{I_i} = \frac{I_c}{(1 + 2/\beta)I_c} = \frac{1}{(1 + 2/\beta)} \tag{12}$$

Eq. (12) shows that the current mirror factor G_I is exactly equal to unity only if $\beta = \infty$. However, in ordinary case of $\beta \simeq 100$, G_I is obtained to be 0.98, and in case of the standard I^2L, the lower value of $\beta = 2 \sim 20$ (Möllmer and Müller, 1978; Flocke, 1978; Koopmans and van der Meij, 1982) inadequately gives $G_I \simeq 0.5 \sim 0.9$. In contrast with the bipolar current mirror, a MOS current mirror has the input and output current paths separated, so that no error nominally appears as shown in Fig. 1 (b). The other error in bipolar current mirror is caused by the effect of saturation of one collector on the other collectors. It is shown in Fig. 2. The more collectors saturate, the more another collector current is reduced, while drain currents of a MOS current mirror are independent of each other. Since these significant errors are not permissible for fuzzy logic circuits, the multivalued I^2L family (Dao, McCluskey and Russell, 1977) is not suitable for fuzzy logic.

On the other hand, a MOS current mirror produces little error even in case of multiple output current mirror. Akiya and Nakashima (1984) presented a higher matching accuracy of a MOS current mirror with matching error of less than 0.5 % even in lower current regions and a smaller pattern area than similar bipolar current mirrors. Therefore, a MOS current mirror is adopted in this paper and represented as Fig. 1 (c) which is equivalent to Fig. 1 (b).

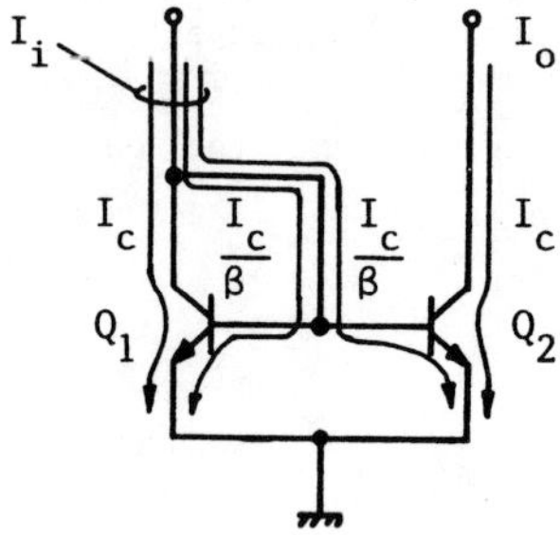

$$I_o = I_c = \frac{1}{1 + \frac{2}{\beta}} I_i$$

(a)

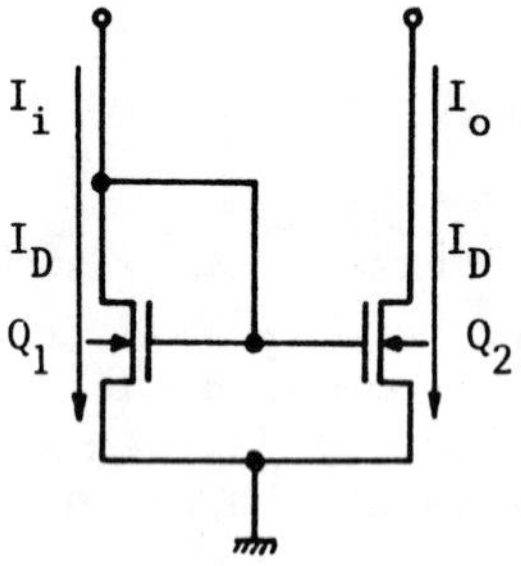

$$I_o = I_D = I_i$$

(b)

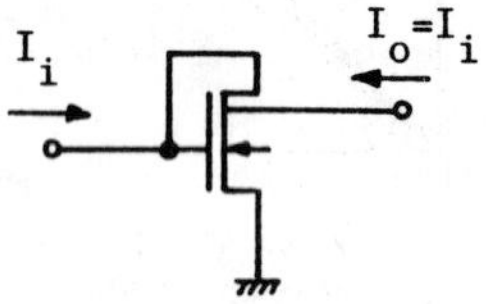

(c)

Fig. 1 (a) Current mirror circuit employing NPN transistors. (b) Current mirror circuit employing n-ch MOS FETs. (c) Symbol of n-MOS current mirror cirucit.

The combination of this current mirror and the diode, which is easily obtained from an FET with gate connected to drain, give the basic logic cell shown in Fig. 3. It forms all of the basic fuzzy logic function circuits and thus the various complicated fuzzy hardware systems. In Fig. 3, if the input current I_{i1} flows into the input terminal of the n-MOS current mirror, the same amount of current $I_D = I_{i1}$ flows into the output terminal of the current mirror. When $I_{i2} \geqq I_{i1}$, the output current of the basic logic cell I_o is equal to $I_{i2} - I_{i1}$. When $I_{i2} < I_{i1}$, the output current I_o is equal to 0 A , because the reverse current is blocked by the diode D. Thus

$$I_o = \begin{cases} I_{i2} - I_{i1} & (I_{i2} \geqq I_{i1}) \\ 0 & (I_{i2} < I_{i1}) \end{cases} \qquad (13)$$

$$= 0 \vee (I_{i2} - I_{i1}) \qquad (13')$$

The use of an FET of diode-connectoin D facilitates zero error operation under the conditions discussed later on (V.). In this circuit,

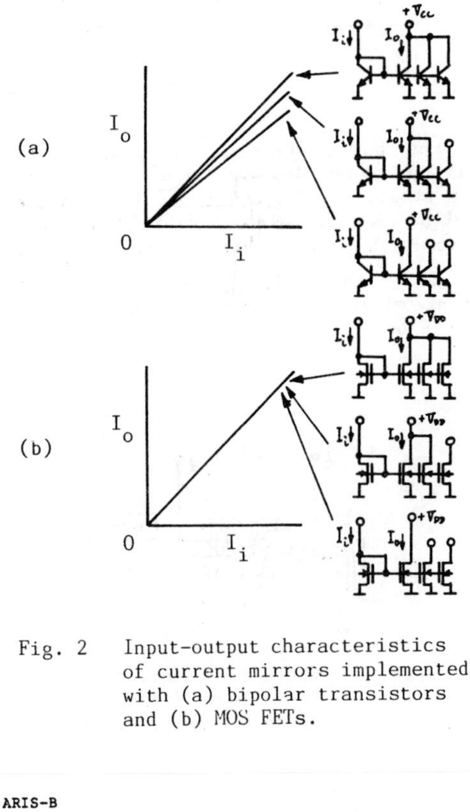

Fig. 2 Input-output characteristics of current mirrors implemented with (a) bipolar transistors and (b) MOS FETs.

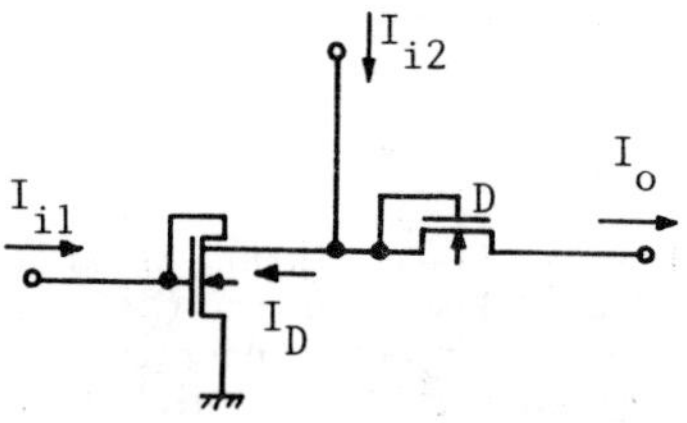

Fig. 3 Basic logic cell circuit.

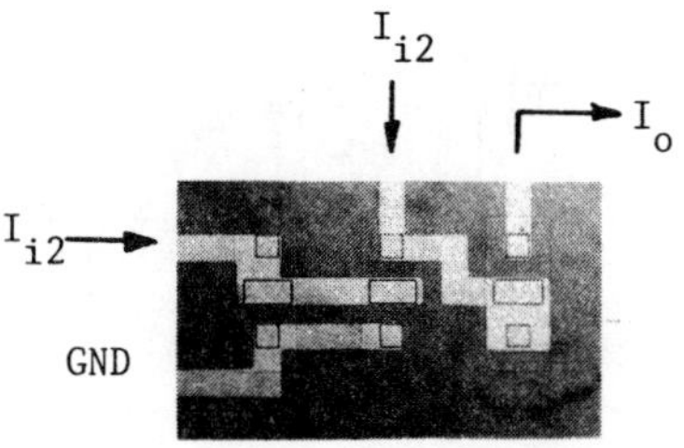

Fig. 4 Microphotograph of the basic logic cell.

replacing the input current I_{i1} and I_{i2} by μ_Y and μ_X, respectively, we can obtain the output current $I_o = \mu_X \Theta \mu_Y = \mu_{X\Theta Y}$. Therefore the basic logic cell shown in Fig. 3 operates as the Bounded-Difference circuit. This circuit exhibits multiple functions according to the assignment of the input current I_{i1} and I_{i2}, as shown in TABLE 1. Fig. 4 shows a microphotograph of the basic logic cell circuit which is composed of only three MOS FETs. It is fabricated in the standard Al-gate MOS technology.

TABLE 1 Functions of the Basic Logic Cell

Functions	Input		Output
	I_{i1}	I_{i2}	I_o
Bounded-Difference	μ_Y	μ_X	$\mu_X \Theta \mu_Y$
Complement	μ_X	1	$\mu_{\bar{X}} = 1 \Theta \mu_X$
Bounded-Product	1	$\mu_X + \mu_Y$	$\mu_{X\odot Y} = (\mu_X + \mu_Y) \Theta 1$

Adding only one input terminal to the basic logic cell brings it to the Fuzzy Logic Union (MAX) cirucit as shown in Fig. 5. It needs two input currents identical to each other. Fig. 6 shows the cascade connection of two basic logic cells. It also exhibits multiple functions according to the assignment of the input currents I_{i1}, I_{i2} and I_{i3}, as shown in TABLE 2. In this circuit, the input characteristics of the second current mirror exhibits a rectification, so that the diode in the first stage can be eliminated.

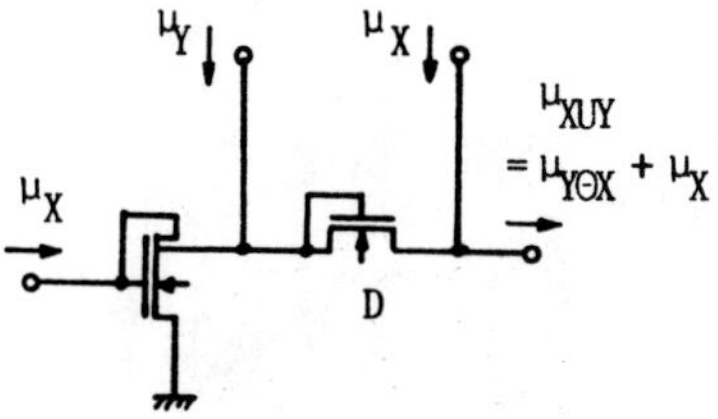

Fig. 5 Union (MAX) circuit.

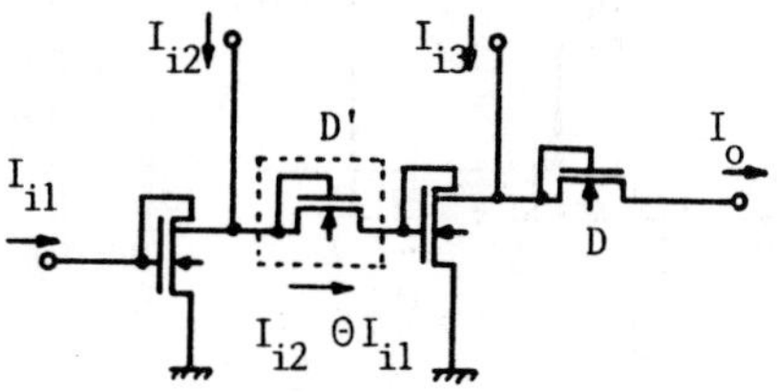

Fig. 6 Cascade connection of basic logic cell. The diode D' can be eliminated.

TABLE 2 Functions of the Cascade-Connected Basic Logic Cells

Functions	Input			Output
	I_{i1}	I_{i2}	I_{i3}	I_o
Bounded-Sum	$\mu_X + \mu_Y$	1	1	$\mu_{X \oplus Y} = 1 \ominus (1 \ominus (\mu_X + \mu_Y))$
Intersection	μ_Y	μ_X	μ_X	$\mu_{X \cap Y} = \mu_X \ominus (\mu_X \ominus \mu_Y)$
Implication	μ_Y	μ_X	1	$\mu_{X \to Y} = 1 \ominus (\mu_X \ominus \mu_Y)$

Wired Sum of two basic logic cells gives us the Absolute-Difference circuit as shown in Fig. 7. The cascade connection of this Absolute-Difference circuit and the basic logic cell implements the Equivalence circuit as shown in Fig. 8. In this circuit, the diode D' can be eliminated, because the current flowing through the diode can not be negative.

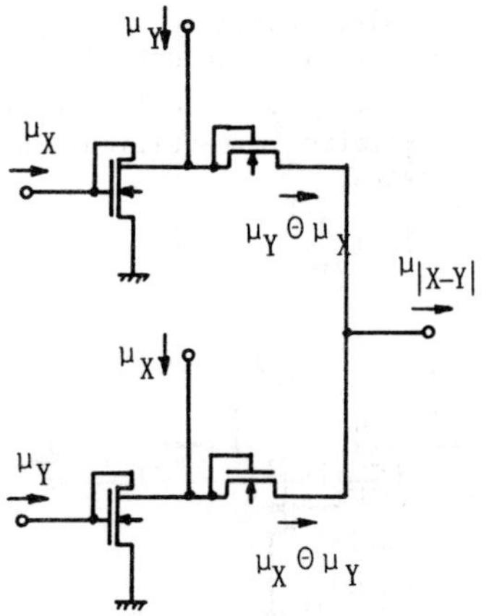

Fig. 7 Absolute-Difference circuit.

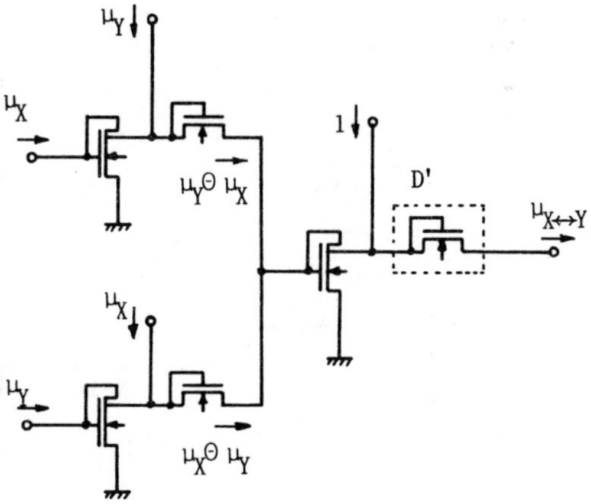

Fig. 8 Equivalence circuit. The diode D' can be eliminated.

Among the basic fuzzy logic function circuits described above, the Fuzzy Logic Union (MAX), Bounded-Sum, Fuzzy Logic Intersection (MIN), Absolute-Difference and Equivalence circuits are in need of one or two current sources which supplies two currents identical to each other. In the large scale fuzzy information processing hardware systems, much more identical current sources should be disposed.

Moreover, in the current mode circuit systems, every circuit must have some output terminals, the number of which is identical to that of the following circuits to be driven. Therefore, the circuit which supplies many identical currents is necessary. This is the multiple-fanout circuit which is made up of a single-output n-MOS current mirror and a multiple-output p-MOS current mirror as shown in Fig. 9. This circuit produces many identical currents from one input current and thus allows a single-fanout circuit to drive many following circuits. The single-output n-MOS current mirror can be extracted from the basic logic cell and thus the multiple-output p-MOS current mirror is the basic circuit as well as the basic logic cell, which are essentially necessary for the fuzzy information processing hardware systems.

Accordingly a master slice, which includes the basic logic cell and multiple-output p-MOS current mirror arrays, can be adapted to the arbitrary fuzzy logic semicustom ICs as shown in Fig. 10. It contains two test devices, nine basic fuzzy logic function circuits and other test circuits.

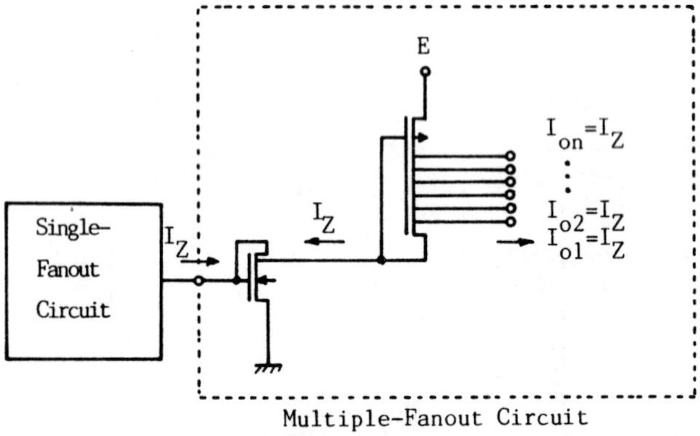

Fig. 9 Multiple-fanout circuit.

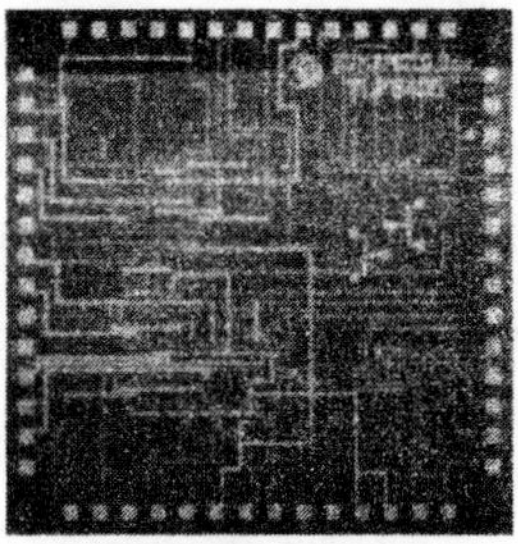

Fig. 10 Fuzzy logic semicustom IC.

V. DESIGN CRITERIA

The sufficient conditions for reasonable operation of the basic logic cell are obtained in the following on the assumption that the short-chunnel effect is negligible. Fig. 11 (a) shows the typical configuration of the basic logic cell driven by two current sources Q_1 and Q_2 . Q_4 is the input portion of the next stage, which acts as the diode in the basic logic cell as described above.

The output characteristics $V_D - I_o$ of the circuit A and the input characteristics $V_D - I_o$ of the circuit B are concurrently illustrated in Fig. 11 (b), naming each curve A and B, respectively. The curve C represents the drain characteristics of Q_2 , and the curve D the locus of the saturation drain voltage of Q_3 , below which the drain current I_{D3} is smaller than I_{i1} . V_D and I_o in Fig.11 (a) are obtained from the cross point p in Fig. (b). The reasonable output current I_o (Eq.(13)) of the basic logic cell can be obtained only if the cross point p is on the flat portion of the curve A. Thus the following conditions are obtained.

$$\sqrt{I_{i1}/\beta_3} \leqq V_{TN} \tag{14}$$

$$V_{TN} + \sqrt{I_o/\beta_4} \leqq E - \sqrt{I_{i2}/\beta_2} \tag{15}$$

where β_2, β_3, β_4 : β of MOS FETs Q_2, Q_3 and Q_4, respectively

$$\beta = \frac{1}{2}\cdot\frac{\mu\varepsilon_o\varepsilon_{ox}}{t_{ox}}\cdot\frac{W}{L}$$

μ : surface carrier mobility

$\varepsilon_o = 8.86 \times 10^{-14}$ F/cm, permitivity of free space

$\varepsilon_{ox} = 3.9$, relative permitivity of gate oxide

t_{ox} : thickness of gate oxide

W, L : width and length of channel

V_{TN} : threshold voltage of an enhancement mode n-ch MOS FET (absolute value)

E : supply voltage

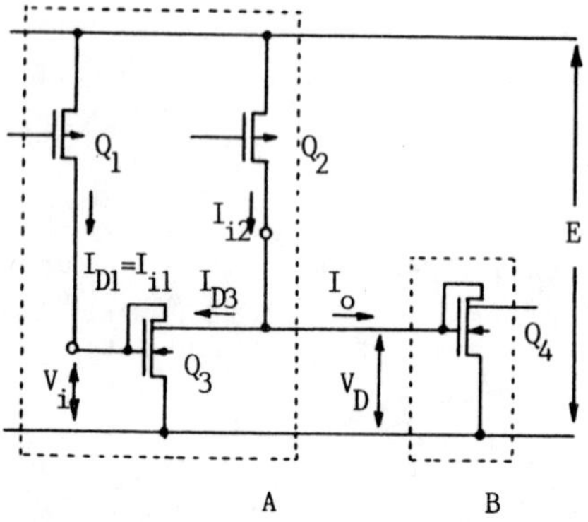

(a)

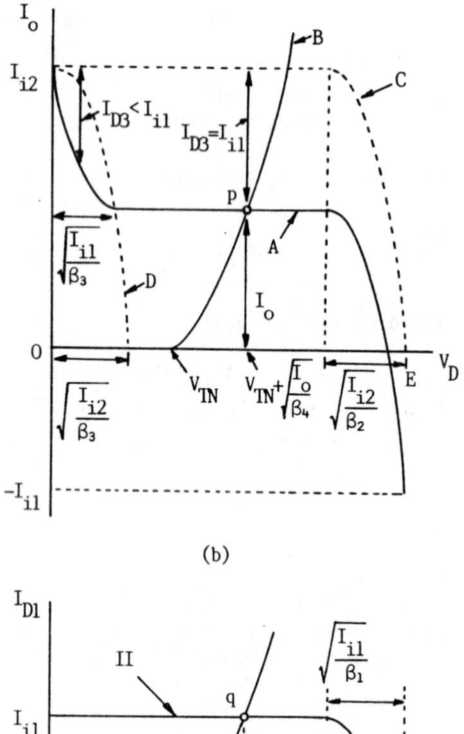

(b)

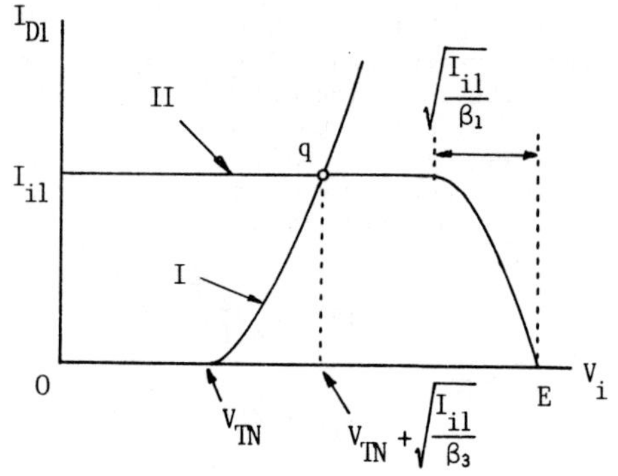

(c)

Fig. 11 (a) Typical configuration of the basic logic cell for design criteria.
(b) V_D - I_o characteristics of the circuits A and B to get the operating point p.
(c) The input characteristics of Q_3 (curve I) and the drain characteristics of Q_1 (curve II) to get the operating point q.

The conditions for the reasonable operation within the range of $0 \leq I_{i1}, I_{i2} \leq I^*$ is obtained by substituting $I_{i1} = I_{i2} = I_o = I^*$ to Eqs.(14) and (15) as

$$I^* \leq \beta_3 V_{TN}^2 \tag{16}$$

$$V_{TN} + \sqrt{I^*}(1/\sqrt{\beta_2} + 1/\sqrt{\beta_4}) \leq E \tag{17}$$

where I^* represents the maximum corresponding to the fuzzy truth value (or grade) of 1.0 .

Moreover, the basic logic cell should be properly driven by the current source Q_1 . Fig. 11 (c) shows the $V_i - I_{D1}$ characteristics where curves I and II illustrates the input characteristics of Q_3 and the drain characteristics of Q_1 , respectively. The cross point q gives the input current and voltage of the basic logic cell. Q_1 can supply an input current of nominal value I_{i1} only if the cross point q is on the flat portion of the curve II in Fig. 11 (c). Thus the following condition is obtained.

$$V_{TN} + \sqrt{I_{i1}/\beta_3} \leq E - \sqrt{I_{i1}/\beta_1} \tag{18}$$

where β_1 is β of Q_1.

The condition for Q_1 to drive Q_3 properly within the range of $0 \leq I_{i1} \leq I^*$ is obtained by substituting $I_{i1} = I^*$ to Eq.(18) as follows.

$$V_{TN} + I^*(1/\sqrt{\beta_1} + 1/\sqrt{\beta_3}) \leq E \tag{19}$$

Eqs. (16), (17) and (19) are the sufficient conditions for the reasonable operation of the basic logic cell. These conditions show that the current mode fuzzy logic circuits described here are ratioless circuits. Therefore, they can be fabricated with a master slice of CMOS transistor array and thus the least area of active region is assured. When all circuits are implemented with p-ch and n-ch MOS FET arrays of the same dimension, conditions (16), (17) and (19) can be simplified to

$$I^* \leq \beta_N V_{TN}^2 \tag{20}$$

$$V_{TN} + \sqrt{I^*}(1/\sqrt{\beta_P} + 1/\sqrt{\beta_N}) \leq E \tag{21}$$

where β_P and β_N are β of p-ch and n-ch MOS FETs, respectively.

The threshold voltage V_{TN} and β_N are expressed as

$$V_{TN} = -\frac{Q_B + Q_{ss}}{\varepsilon_o \varepsilon_{ox}} t_{ox} + (\phi_{MS} - 2\phi_F) \tag{22}$$

$$\beta_N = \frac{1}{2} \cdot \frac{\mu_e \varepsilon_o \varepsilon_{ox}}{t_{ox}} \cdot \frac{W}{L} \tag{23}$$

where $Q_B = -\sqrt{2\varepsilon_o \varepsilon_{Si} q N_A (2\phi_F)}$, depletion-layer charge in p-well

$\varepsilon_{Si} = 11.7$, relative permitivity of Si

$q = 1.60218 \times 10^{-19}$ C, electron charge

N_A = acceptor concentration in p-well

ϕ_F (<0 for n-ch) : potential difference between the fermi level and the intrinsic level

Q_{ss} : fixed oxide charge

$\phi_{MS} = \phi_M - \phi_S$ (<0) : metal-silicon work function difference

μ_e : surface electron mobility

W/L : width-length ratio of all transistors

Substituion of Eqs. (22) and (23) to Eq. (20) gives

$$I^* \leqq \frac{1}{2}\mu_e \varepsilon_o \varepsilon_{ox} \frac{W}{L}\left(\left(\frac{Q_B + Q_{ss}}{\varepsilon_o \varepsilon_{ox}}\right)^2 t_{ox} - \frac{2(Q_B + Q_{ss})(\phi_{MS} - 2\phi_F)}{\varepsilon_o \varepsilon_{ox}} + \frac{(\phi_{MS} - 2\phi_F)^2}{t_{ox}}\right) = f(t_{ox}) \tag{24}$$

When

$$t_{ox} = \frac{\varepsilon_o \varepsilon_{ox}(\phi_{MS} - 2\phi_F)}{Q_B + Q_{ss}} \tag{25}$$

the function $f(t_{ox})$ exhibits the minimum value

$$f(t_{ox})\big|_{min} = 2\mu_e (Q_B + Q_{ss})(\phi_{MS} - 2\phi_F)\frac{W}{L} \tag{26}$$

Substituting Eq. (26) to Eq. (24), we can get the following condition.

$$I^* \leqq 2\mu_e (Q_B + Q_{ss})(\phi_{MS} - 2\phi_F)\frac{W}{L} \tag{20'}$$

It is interesting that this condition is independent of the gate oxide thickness t_{ox} . Accordingly the sufficient conditions for the reasonable operation of the basic logic cell and the derivatives composed with the p-ch and n-ch transistor array are found to be

$$\begin{cases} I^* \leqq 2\mu_e (Q_B + Q_{ss})(\phi_{MS} - 2\phi_F)\frac{W}{L} & (20') \\ V_{TN} + \sqrt{I^*}(1/\sqrt{\beta_P} + 1/\sqrt{\beta_N}) \leqq E & (21) \end{cases}$$

In order to design whole systems, the following condition, which is obtained by the condition of a multiple-fanout circuit, should be added to two conditions (20') and (21)

$$V_{TP} + \sqrt{I^*}(1/\sqrt{\beta_P} + 1/\sqrt{\beta_N}) \leq E \qquad (27)$$

where V_{TP} is the threshold voltage of an enhancement mode p-ch MOS FET (absolute value).

VI. SPICE II SIMULATION

It is very effective to make use of a digital computer for designing and estimating electronic circuit systems or integrated circuits. The most famous and authorized software system for circuit simulation would be SPICE II which was developed in University of California. Here MIN circuit and MAX circuit, which are the typical building block of fuzzy system, are examined by SPICE II simulation. The circuit configuration under test are shown in Fig. 12 (a) and (b), where two identical input currents are supplied by a multiple-fanout circuit. The device model used here is "level 2" and device parameters are listed in TABLE 3. Those values of parameters are reasonable and easily accomplished in standard CMOS technology.

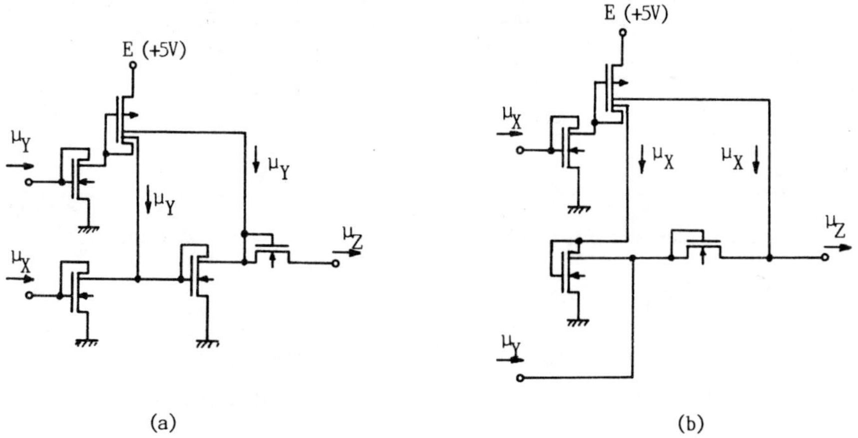

Fig. 12 Circuit configuration of (a) MIN and (b) MAX circuits for SPICE II simulation.

The input-output characteristics of MIN circuit and MAX circuit are shown in Fig. 13 (a) and (b), respectively. Fuzzy truth values or grade of 0 and 1 are represented by currents of 0A and 100 μ A, respectively. These two figures show us that output errors of MIN and MAX circuits are 5 %F.S. (full scale) at most, that is, the ratio of output error current to 100 μA (corresponding to 1) is within 5 % . This error is permissible in designing fuzzy hardware systems.

TABLE 3 Device Parameters Used in SPICE II Simulation

Parameter	Value	Unit
Thickness of Gate Oxide	700	Å
Channel Length	7	μm
Channel Width	20	μm
Threshold Voltage (n-ch)	1.0	V
Threshold Voltage (p-ch)	-1.0	V
B-D Junction Capacitance at Zero-Bias	0.032	pF
B-S Junction Capacitance at Zero-Bias	0.032	pF
Impurity Concentration of n-Substrate	$4x10^{15}$	$atoms/cm^3$
Impurity Concentration of p-Well	$1x10^{17}$	$atoms/cm^3$

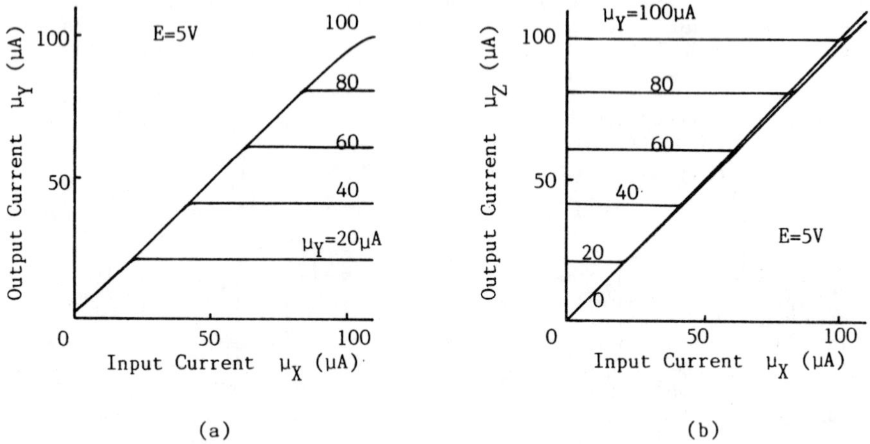

Fig. 13 Input-output characteristics of (a) MIN and (b) MAX circuits.

The dependence of input-output characteristics upon the supply voltage is examined and the results are shown in Fig. 14 (a) and (b). The fluctuation between 4V and 6V in supply voltage causes 3 %F.S. in both cases of MIN and MAX circuits. If the signal error of 6 %F.S. can be permitted, then the fluctuation of supply voltage between 4V and 8V is permissible. This insensitiveness to supply voltage is one of the distinctive features of the circuits described here, which can not be achieved by an ordinary digital system or digital computer in voltage mode. It allows us to use a noisy power supply or a decaying battery.

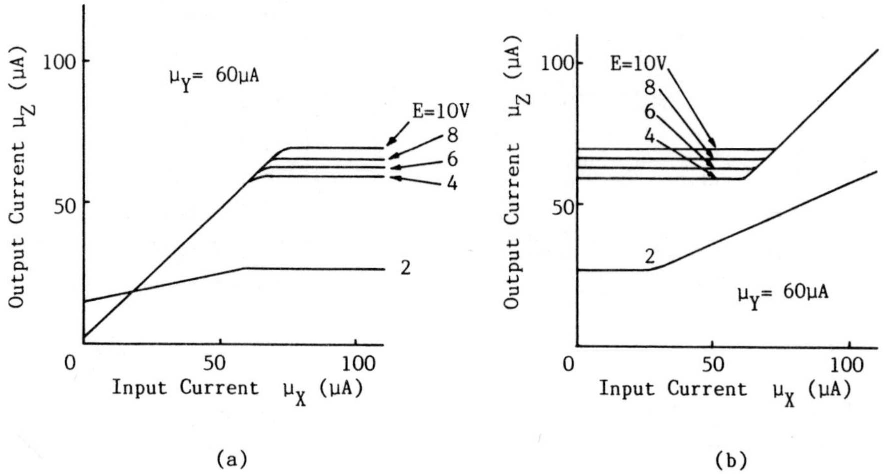

Fig. 14 Dependence of input-output characteristics of (a) MIN and (b) MAX circuits upon the supply voltage.

A temperature characteristics is also important, because a hardware system should be normally operate anywhere in the world, e.g., very cold places as the polar regions and very hot or heated circumstances. The military standard constrains hardware systems to operate normally in the temperature range of −55 °C ∿ +125 °C which is a very severe condition. The MIN and MAX circuits described here admirably pass the military standard, which is easily understood by Fig. 15 (a) and (b). A change of temperature from −55 °C to +125 °C causes the output current deviation of only 0.74 %F.S. which is none of the problem in the fuzzy hardware systems.

The most significant point of hardware systems is the operating speed or response time as described previously. Fig. 16 (a) and (b) show the operating speed of MIN circuit and MAX circuit shown in Fig.12 (a) and (b), respectively. In both cases, one input current μ_Y is a constant value (50 μA) and the other input current μ_X is a rectangular wave changing from 10 μA to 100 μA . Therefore the output currents of MIN circuit and MAX circuit must change from 10 μA to 50 μA and from 50 μA to 100 μA , respectively. Simulated results show that these circuits constructed with ten transistors or so can respond enough within 20 nsec. It is very difficult to achieve by using ordinary digital hardware systems, if not impossible. MIN and MAX circuits shown in Fig. 12 can be regarded as intrinsic fuzzy logic gates.

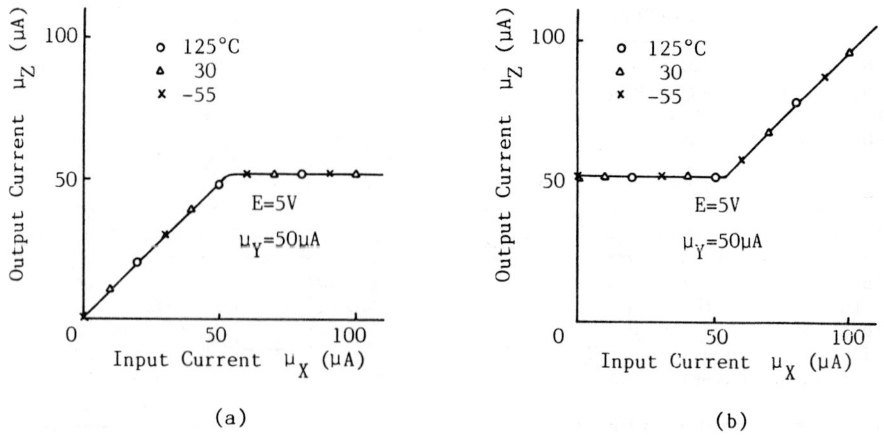

Fig. 15 Temperature characteristics of (a) MIN and (b) MAX circuits.

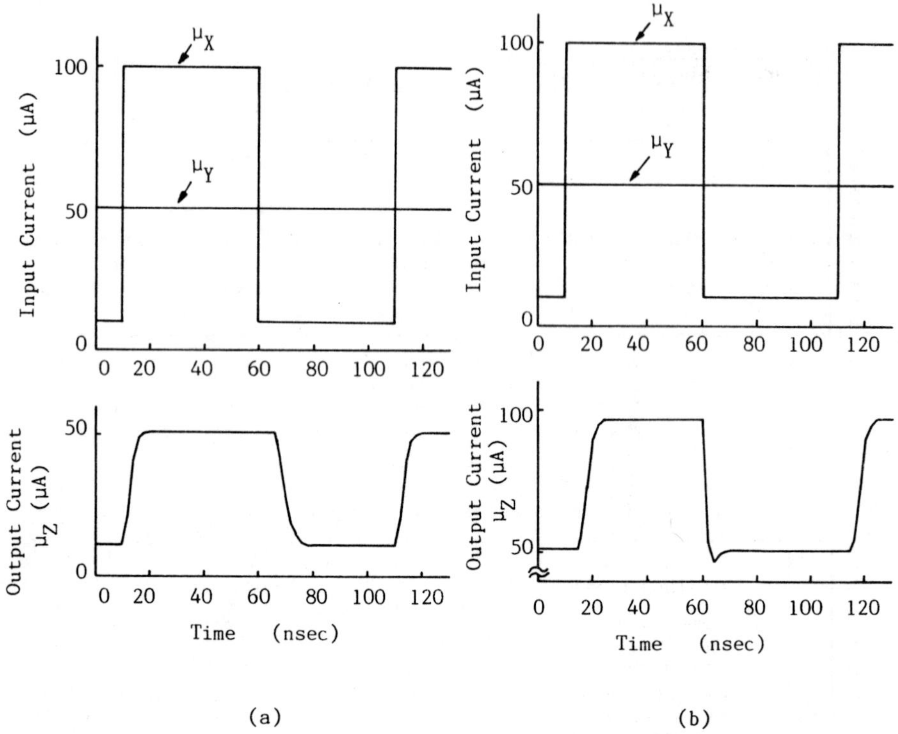

Fig. 16 Operating speed of (a) MIN and (b) MAX circuits.

VII. PROSPECT AND SITUATION OF FUZZY HARDWARE SYSTEMS

The first step of the fuzzy hardware systems will be a fuzzy controller chip or a microprocessor. Because many applications of fuzzy reasoning to controller have already been accomplished and the usefulness of them has been proved.

A fuzzy reasoning or a fuzzy decision making is specified with the definitions of membership functions, fuzzy logic functions, defuzzification functions and so forth which are defined innumerably. It forces the designers into the heuristic method of designing the fuzzy hardware systems. The simulations, which are now achieved with a digital computer, are indispensable to the system design. Thus a fuzzy simulator for the general purpose will appear. It will be advanced to a fuzzy computer which accomplishes fuzzy information processing instantaneously though it is weak in the exact calculation.

The exact calculation and the deterministic processing will be accomplished by a decimal computer (ten-valued logic) (Yamakawa, 1985) in place of a binary digital computer as shown in Fig. 17. A decimal computer is, of cource, one of the digital machines and based on crisp sets, while a fuzzy computer is based on fuzzy sets. The operations of these two types of computers are more similar to that of a human brain than a binary digital computer is. The curtain of the post-binary age will be raised by the harmony of the fuzzy computer and the decimal computer.

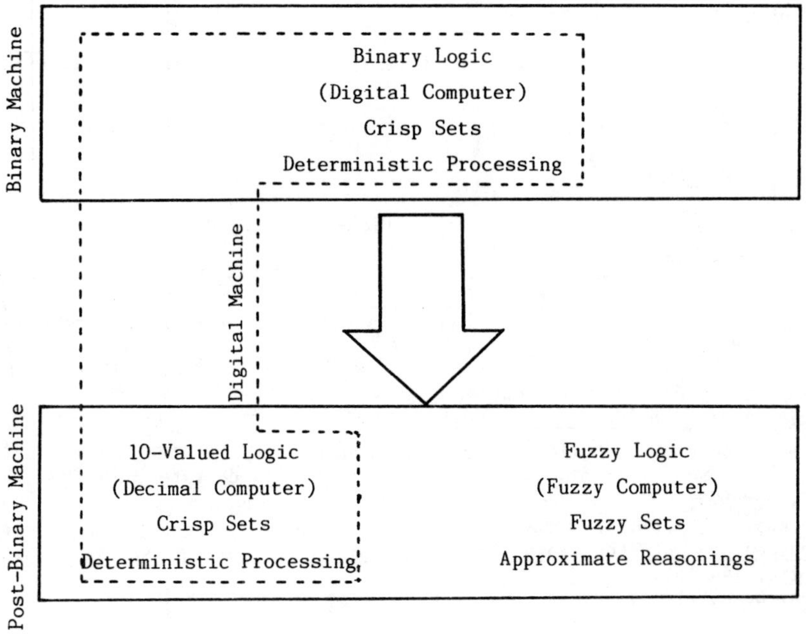

Fig.17 Situation of fuzzy hardware systems.

VIII. CONCLUSIONS

Nine basic fuzzy logic functions are all expressed only with the Bounded-Difference and the Algebraic Sum. The Algebraic Sum is implemented only by wiring in current mode circuits. Thus the Bounded-Difference circuit is regarded as s basic logic cell. Any complicated fuzzy hardware systems made up of nine basic fuzzy logic functions can be realized with only one kind of master slice including the Bounded-Difference (basic logic cell) and multiple-output p-MOS current mirror array.

CMOS fuzzy logic semicustom IC presented here exhibits the following distinctive features. (1) The effect of the variation in V_{TH} and g_m on the electrical characteristics of the hardware systems can be cut off by adjusting the supply voltage to the appropriate value. Thus the expensive ion implanter is not needed. (2) The basic logic cell exhibits good linearity, robustness against the thermal and supply voltage fluctuations, and very high operation speed, which can not be easily achieved in voltage mode. (MIN and MAX circuits can normally operate with supply voltage of 4V ∿ 8V under the temperature range of -55 °C ∿ +125 °C, and respond enough within 20 nsec.) (3) Since it does not need resistors nor isolation, it is suitable for a large scale fuzzy hardware system. (4) Circuits presented here can be appropriated to a binary logic and even to a 10-valued logic. (5) It exhibits the advantage over fuzzy information processing by using binary circuits, which arises from the ability to provide much more "functions per unit area". (6) It presents a low cost and a short term of design and fabrication.

Lastly, the prospect and situation of fuzzy hardware systems are discussed.

REFERENCES

Akiya, M. and S. Nakashima (1984). High-precision MOS current mirror. IEE Proceedings, 131, Pt.I, 170-175.

Dao, T. T. , E. J. McCluskey and L. K. Russell (1977). Multivalued integrated injection logic. IEEE Trans. Comput., C-26, 1233-1241.

Flocke, H. H. (1978). I^2L design in a standard bipolar process. IEEE J. Solid-State Circuits, SC-13, 914-917.

Koopmans, J. M. and C. J. van der Meij (1982). Base resistance in I^2L structures: Its determination and its influence on upward current gain. IEEE J. Solid-State Circuits, SC-17, 783-786.

Möllmer, F. and R. Müller (1978). A simple model for the determination of I^2L base current components. IEEE J. Solid-State Circuits, SC-13, 899-905.

Yamakawa, T. (1985). CMOS multivalued circuits in hybrid mode. IEEE Proceedings of the 15th International Symposium on Multiple-Valued Logic, 144-151.

Zadeh, L. A. (1965). Fuzzy Sets. Inf. Control, 8, 338-358.

Functional Requirements for a Fuzzy Expert System Shell

W. SILER, J. BUCKLEY* and D. TUCKER

Carraway Medical Center, Birmingham, AL 35234, USA

ABSTRACT

There are several general-purpose fuzzy expert system shells now in existence. However, experience with our system FLOPS indicates that several hurdles must be overcome before widespread successful use of the full power of such fuzzy reaoning systems can be confidently expected. Many of these hurdles confront non-fuzzy systems as well.

Major developments needed include advances in appropriate fuzzy systems theory in several areas; abstract definitions of problem domain which transcend particular fields of application; standardization of blackboard architecture; standardized interfaces to blackboards and data bases; standardized interfaces to procedural languages; a sharp increase in production system computational efficiency; and software tools for development and debugging of rules.

Theoretical developments badly needed include use of prior associations in fuzzy logic, i.e. dealing with the problems that have plagued Bayes' theorem for over a hundred years; development of a theory of nonmonotonic fuzzy logic; further development of the theory of fuzzy numbers, especially in set-theoretic operations and inequalities; narrowing the field of set-theoretic operations on fuzzy sets by tieing particular operators to their sphere of usefulness, and extending them to fuzzy sets of higher levels and types; creating theories of automated fuzzy reasoning, deductive and inductive; and refining a theory of fuzzy logic which takes account of the special role of expert system rules as replacement operators rather than logical propositions.

KEYWORDS

Fuzzy expert systems, production systems, non-monotonic logic, fuzzy systems theory, parallel systems, inductive reasoning.

*Dr. Buckley's mailing address:
University of Alabama at Birmingham, Birmingham, AL 35294, USA

INTRODUCTION

After the development of the first crude fuzzy reasoning system FUZZY (LeFaivre, 1974) a lapse of about ten years occurred before true fuzzy expert system shells were reported. Then, almost explosively, the systems REVEAL (Jones, 1985), CADIAG (Adlassnig, Kolarz and Schweithauer, 1985), ARIES (Applebaum and Ruspini, 1985) and FLOPS (Siler and co-workers, 1985) appeared almost simultaneously, together with the first book on the subject (Negoita, 1985). REVEAL and FLOPS are now comercially marketed, and Ruspini has offered to supply ARIES to interested persons. While CADIAG was somewhat of a special-purpose tool its concepts are quite generally applicable. Several additional systems are in various stages of development, including SPII (Martin-Clouaire and Prade, 1984) and SPHINX (Fieshi and colleagues, 1982). The fuzzy data base system FRIL (Baldwin, 1983) is reportedly being extended to include performance as a fuzzy expert system. Still other systems are currently in development at a few universities. This list is far from exhaustive, and is presented as a sampling of current work rather than as a complete list.

The systems all bear the signs of their originator's interest; there has been too little time for a consensus to develop as to how such systems should be written. ARIES employs interval logic and gives the user an option as to what version of fuzzy logic he wishes to use. SPII and FLOPS make use of fuzzy numbers; FLOPS provides a complete set of fuzzy inequality operators. REVEAL is designed to run on a large-scale main-frame computer in the administrative world. Each system is idiosyncratic, as is to be expected at this stage of development.

Unfortunately, we know too little of other fuzzy expert systems and their applications to be able to discuss them with authority. Accordingly, the major part of this chapter is based primarily on our experience with our own system FLOPS, and only in part of what we know of other systems. However, we find no contradiction between our experience and what we know of the experience of others.

We should acknowledge that fuzzy expert systems are based on a great amount of important work by the Artificial Intelligence community in non-fuzzy expert systems, with several of these handling uncertainties using Bayes' theorem. The most interesting and stimulating non-fuzzy systems to us are OPS5 (Forgy, 1984) whose syntax FLOPS has adapted; MYCIN (Shortliffe, 1976) which attaches single confidence levels to data; and PROSPECTOR (Duda, Hart and Nilsson, 1980) which uses dual upper and lower confidence levels.

CURRENT DESIGN OF FLOPS

Since the current state of FLOPS has been described elsewhere (Buckley, Siler and Tucker, 1986) we will discuss FLOPS as it now exists only minimally in this chapter; instead, we will concentrate on how it came to be what it is, and where it should go from here.

The Application

FLOPS did not come about because we were interested in expert systems or fuzzy systems theory; we had a problem to solve and existing tools were inadequate to solve it. The problem and its solution are discussed elsewhere (Siler and colleagues, 1985; Buckley, Siler and Tucker, 1986; Tucker and colleagues, 1986) and will be outlined only briefly here. We think it important to note that the development of FLOPS, and the theoretical work reported here, have been application-driven from the start.

The problem was to process echocardiogram images of the heart by computer, unsupervised by humans, to yield chamber volumes and meaures of regional heart muscle function. Source data were time sequences of 24 noisy two-dimensional ultrasound heart images. Low-level image processing programs had been written to segment the images into regions of interest. Unfortunately, the noise in the images and the constraint of unsupervised processing meant that many of these "regions of interest" were artifacts; some regions were artifactually split, and other regions were artifactually merged. We had to identify the regions to be what an experienced cardiologist would perceive them to be. We used fuzzy numbers and fuzzy inequalities to cluster the regions in the 24 frames in each image sequence before developing the expert system. FLOPS was developed so that we could classify the region clusters by (in effect) having the computer look at the images in the same way as a cardiologist.

FLOPS' Rules

FLOPS is a production system whose syntax is derived from the non-fuzzy system OPS5 (Forgy, 1984). A typical rule in FLOPS is:

```
rule small 1000 2 ( region ^area ~>= 100,10,0.1
                    ^area ~<= 400,10,0.1
                     ^size.SMALL 0 )
                   -->
                   modify 1 ^size.SMALL ;
```

This **rule**, named **small**, is one in which we place complete confidence (**1000**), and is in rule block **2**. Its antecedent requires that in some instance of memory element **region** the **area** be fuzzily greater than or equal to (~>=) a fuzzy number with central value **100**, absolute uncertainty of **10**, and a relative error of 10% (**0.1**). The net uncertainty is the root mean square value of the absolute uncertainty and the product of the central value and the relative error. The antecedent also requires that the **area** be fuzzily less than or equal to a fuzzy number with central value **400** and the same error specifications, and that the grade of membership of member **SMALL** in fuzzy set **size** be zero. If the fuzzy AND of the confidences of all data and comparison operators in the predicate is above a confidence threshold, by default 500 (0.5 on a 0-1 scale), the rule is fireable. When fired, the rule will store the fuzzy AND of the antecedent confidence and the rule confidence as the grade of membership of member **SMALL** in its fuzzy set **size**.

Discussion of FLOPS' Features:

In designing FLOPS for utility in the problem of classification of multiple objects characterized by multiple fuzzy numeric features, we often found either too much fuzzy systems theory (a multiplicity of operators) or not enough. The following discussion of some of FLOPS special features will illustrate this point.

Fuzzy numbers. Since FLOPS arose from a problem involving fuzzy numbers and their comparison, it is not surprising that explicit provision is made for both fuzzy numbers as data types and for operators for their comparison. The membership functions of fuzzy numbers are normally distributed about their central values, since this is to be expected when a measurement is subject to a large number of small disturbances. Using two terms to describe their uncertainty usually permits the error specification to be invariant for many types of measurements, an important advantage.

We had no problem with fuzzy arithmetic; existing theory was well developed and well suited to our application.

Theoretical problems first emerged when defining comparison operators for fuzzy numbers. Several different ways of obtaining a confidence for equality of fuzzy numbers exist in the literature, with no guidelines as to the circumstances under which each might be useful. We used the simple max-min rule for equality of two fuzzy numbers because in practice it worked well; this is an extension of the Willaeys and Malvache (1976) rule for consistency of discrete fuzzy sets. Another problem arose when defining the fuzzy comparison 'less than OR equal to'; the Bellman-Zadeh OR simply didn't work. The theoretical solution to this problem was furnished by Ruspini (1982), a paper which has had a great impact on our work. Ruspini noted that the Bellman-Zadeh rules for fuzzy AND and OR assume implicitly that the two operands are maximally positively associated, and that the Lukasiewicz operators assume the operands to be maximally negatively associated. Obviously, the conditions 'less than' and 'equal to' are incompatible and maximally negatively associated; hence the Lukasiewicz OR should be used. Now our combined comparisons worked very well.

Eventually, this train of thought led us to the notion that since fuzzy numbers are fuzzy sets, we should be able to use them as operands with the set theoretic operations AND, OR and NOT as well as operands for fuzzy arithmetic (no problem here). Unary inequality operators were defined such as <fuzzily less than> and <fuzzily greater than> which convert one fuzzy number (say fuzzy 2) to another (say fuzzily less than fuzzy 2). Given these three types of operators, set theoretic, arithmetic and inequality conversions, a single max-min test of consistency of fuzzy numbers suffices for decision making. A paper on this point is now in preparation.

Production rules, implication and modus ponens. Our next problem arose when deciding how a rule should modify data. It was easy to decide that the net confidence in the rule and all the elements of its antecedent was the proper confidence to store with any data modified by the rule when the previous confidence in the data was zero. It was harder to decide what to store when we realized that values other than the one a rule wanted to store might previously exist, and that the old data might have confidence greater than the new! We finally decided that new data could replace old if the confidence in the new data were greater than or equal to the old confidence, but that the system would reject replacement of old data by new data of lesser confidence. We called this "weakly monotonic fuzzy logic" because confidences could (by default) never decrease, and in recognition of a related problem considered by those building automated Aristotelian logic systems (Bobrow, 1980). We then developed the beginnings of a theory of monotonic and nonmonotonic fuzzy logic (Siler, Buckley and Tucker, 1985).

Although the syntax of production rules closely resembles the syntax of the implication connective (A --> B) or the modus ponens (if A then B), the same difficulty which led us to define monotonic and nonmonotonic fuzzy logics now led us to examine whether a production rule is a modus ponens, as generally assumed by logicians. It dawned upon us that the consequent of a rule is not a proposition (in the sense of a statement whose truth can be examined) but is instead a set of actions to be taken, contingent on the confidence in the truth of the antecedent, which is a logical proposition. The most interesting rules are those which modify memory:

(x = A) --> (y = B),

or equivalently

if (x = A) then (y = B).

The rule is neither an implication nor a modus ponens, just as the often-seen computer instruction

x = x + 1

is not an equation, in spite of the resemblances. The rule is instead a conditional instruction to replace any current value of y with a new value B. Obviously, any current value of y and its current truth value must be considered before deciding what to do. Automated logic through production rules is in this sense qualitatively different from classical logic, fuzzy or non-fuzzy; we call it "replacement logic", and questions of monotonicity are of critical importance. In FLOPS' default "weakly monotonic fuzzy logic" the replacement is allowed to take place if the new truth value is greater than or equal to the current truth value, otherwise the replacement called for by the rule is denied.

Deductive and inductive reasoning and rule-firing mode. We had been for some time aware of the important developments taking place in hardware for parallel computation (Uhr, 1984) and the distinction between computer and brain architecture drawn by von Neumann (19xx). In a production system, all rules are examined for fireability on all data, effectively simultaneously. Although FLOPS (like all productions systems) was implemented on a conventional sequential computer, it became obvious in programming certain real problems, and especially the driving problem of echocardiogram analysis, that this sequential rule firing was often awkward; was often not the way we really think; was contrary to the inherent parallelism of a production system; and could be easily gotten around.

We then built a new version of FLOPS, which fired all fireable rules effectively in parallel. In certain respects, this made life easy; we no longer had to maintain a stack of fireable but unfired rules, no longer needed an algorithm to decide which of several fireable rules we would actually fire (the rule conflict algorithm), and backtracking was no longer an applicable concept. Instead of a rule conflict algorithm, we now needed a memory conflict algorithm in case more than one rule tried to modify the same datum.

Fortunately, the memory-conflict algorithm was already at hand; our default weak fuzzy monotonicity worked just fine. Further, for the proper problem rule writing became simpler, and to our great joy systems overhead (always a problem with production systems) was greatly reduced. We now tend to equate sequential rule firing with logical deductive reasoning, and parallel rule firing with pattern-matching inductive reasoning. These two different styles strongly remind us of right-brain and left-brain function.

File access methods. The very first pilot version of FLOPS could read FLOPS programs from a disk file. At first, all data were included in the program file, but two factors made this unfeasible. First, it seemed undersirable to include a mish-mash of rules, expert factual data and run-specific data in the same file. Secondly, for general use FLOPS has to be able to write files as well as read them.

Accordingly, two types of FLOPS files were designed. Type I, FLOPS command files, can include data and/or rules, and can be nested to any depth so that a Type I file opened for reading can open another Type I file for reading. Type II data files are "flat" files of simple structure which can be both read and written by FLOPS. Type II files are a primary mode of communication with non-FLOPS programs such as data base systems or BASIC programs. Since Type II files are difficult to read, a special syntax-oriented full-screen text editor is provided for them which first reads the FLOPS program file to which the data are destined, and the reads the data file itself.

Communication with other programs. While Type II files provide some communication with other programs, we felt that more flexible communication was necessary with both utility programs such as word processors and with procedural language programs which would process data used by the FLOPS programs. Two types of program calls are provided. The first type of call includes a command string which is transmitted to the called program. This type of call is most often used manually from the keyboard when FLOPS is in command mode. The second call is usually executed in the consequent of a rule, and transmits the addresses of FLOPS attributes to the called program. This "call by reference" permits the called program to receive attribute values from FLOPS, and also to return attribute values. This call type places some restrictions on the language and calling conventions of the called program; we generally call programs written in the C language, although others (such as PASCAL) should be suitable.

Recursion. The fact that all rules in a production system are examined for fireability on all data at every program step means that production systems possess an inherent recursivity. However, this is not always utilized, or for that matter not often discussed. PROLOG, of course, is as easily recursive as C or PASCAL. FLOPS also is recursive, but a little care must be taken to save key memory elements under some circumstances. The Tower of Hanoi problem when solved in OPS5, an important non-fuzzy production system, does not make use of recursivity; the program takes over twenty rules. The core of the Tower of Hanoi problem takes three statements in PROLOG, and three rules in FLOPS. Clearly it is highly desirable for an expert system to have recursivity available for those problems that require it.

Systems overhead and computational efficiency. Since production systems were first implemented they have been plagued by computational inefficiency due to systems overhead. The RETE algorithm invented by Forgy (1984) for OPS5 was an important step in reducing overhead, but the problem, while reduced in size, remained. FLOPS employs the RETE algorithm, but well over half the run time for a typical sequential FLOPS program is used up in systems overhead. This is especially annoying when working a large problem on a slow computer, such as the IBM PC without an 8087 math coprocessor.

We were pleased to discover that the reduction in systems overhead realized with parallel FLOPS can result in a substantial improvement in run time for problems suitable for parallel computation. The echocardiogram analysis program can involve lengthy runs. When using an IBM PC, a speed improvement of a factor of four in program execution time can be gained by adding an 8087 math coprocessor. An additional factor of four can be gained by going to an AT or compatible with an 80286 microprocessor. Going from sequential to parallel FLOPS gains an additional speed factor of four or five. (These factors apply to program execution, exclusive of compilation and I/O.) Clearly, substantially faster times can be gained by using the faster computers; since application programs are very likely to increase in complexity, it is well to weight computation speed heavily when evaluating computers for running production systems. But also, the gain realized by parallel operation can be almost as great as by changing computers! For a given computer, it is important to identify those problems suited for parallel computation early in the game, so that the potential gain in speed can be realized.

Desirable Features Not Provided:

Entire fuzzy sets as operands in rules. Alas, our report on FLOPS must also include some things it cannot as yet do. While we can specify an entire fuzzy number as an operand in a single rule, to the best of our knowledge no system currently available can specify entire discrete fuzzy sets as operands in a single rule. For that matter, there is no concensus as to what operators should be made available in addition to the Bellman-Zadeh AND, OR and NOT, and even here there are problems. As mentioned earlier, Ruspini (1982) has pointed out the importance of prior associations between the operands on the definition of these fundamental operators. Zimmerman (1980) reports a most interesting operator, the compensatory AND, useful when multiple goals are to be met, a quite general problem. We have not yet gained experience with the Zimmerman operator, but it includes cases which we are sure must be included as special cases of a general operator, and we intend to test it in the next major version of FLOPS; this will include entire fuzzy sets as operands, with extensions to cover dual-valued confidences.

Dual-valued confidences. While we have gotten along quite well so far with a single confidence level, we believe that dual values will shortly displace the single confidence values. Ruspini has already implemented them in ARIES; the Dempster-Shafer theory requires them; and there is the hard fact that with single-value confidences, one cannot distinguish between something about which we have absolutely no knowledge at all (confidence 0) and something which we know not to be true (confidence 0) except to be very careful in our programming. This led us to work out a theory of dual valued operators (Siler and Buckley, 1986) for incorporation in the next major revision of FLOPS.

Once dual confidences are implemented, the problem of prior associations can scarcely be avoided, and we will have problems of estimation of priors similar to those which have plagued Bayes' theorem for well over a century and which plague writers of non-fuzzy expert systems which attach confidences to values (Shortliffe, 1976; Duda, Hart and Nilsson, 1980).

Software Tools for Building Applications Programs. FLOPS currently provides a number of commands for debugging FLOPS programs, but not for building them. The problem of painlessly acquiring expert knowledge is also addressed by FLOPS through its use of rule-generating rules and its data base edit program FLEDIT, but these tools are not really adequate to the task. Plaza and Lopez de Mantaras (1985) have been working on a concept-based system for acquisition and refinement of uncertain knowledge. We badly need tools like TEREASIS (Davis, Buchanan and Shortliffe, 1977).

Useful Goodies for Producing User-Friendly Programs. Finally, if fuzzy expert systems are to find widespread use, tools must be provided to those who develop the application programs so that the finished product will show the signs of professional competence and user-friendliness which users and professional programmers have come to expect. This means that simple features like the ability to build a user screen must be present. The expert system shell writer must make available features like control of cursor position and video attributes, string manipulation, function keys and menus, and the like.

DISCUSSION

While fuzzy expert systems have come a long way in the last few years, and have reached the stage of practical application, much more work remains to be done on the theoretical and practical level to make such systems commonly-accepted working tools for solution of a large number of real-world problems. The power already demonstrated by existing fuzzy systems makes it clear that undertaking their further development is eminently worth while. For example, flexible communication between the fuzzy system and procedural programs, and between the fuzzy system and data files, is obviously needed. Existing fuzzy theory should be screened to identify those techniques useful in practice, and new theoretical developments oriented toward automated fuzzy reasoning should receive a high priority. Computer science tools need overhauling, and new tools need developing. A good review article on existing fuzzy expert systems and directly applicable theoretical work is badly needed as a guide to those actively engaged in system development and refinement.

Finally, the time has come to subject those tools already developed to the test of significant real-world applications. Feedback from these applications should favorably influence future theoretical developments as well as construction of actual systems.

REFERENCES

Adlassnig, K.-P., G. Kolarz and W. Schweithauer (1985). Present state of the medical expert system CADIAG-2. Meth. Inform. Med. 24, 13-20.

Applebaum, L. and E. H. Ruspini (1985). ARIES: a tool for inference under conditions of imprecision and uncertainty. Proc. SPIE - Soc. of Photo-optical Engineers 548,

Baldwin, J. F. (1983). A Fuzzy relational inference language for expert systems. Intl. Symp. on Multi-valued Logic, Japan.

Bobrow, D. G. (ed) 1980. Special issue on non-monotonic logic. Artificial Intelligence 13 (1, 2).

Buckley, J., W. Siler and D. Tucker (1986). FLOPS, a fuzzy expert system: applications and perspectives. Fuzzy Expert Systems: Theory and Applications (Negoita and Prade, Eds). Verlag T.U.V. Rheinland, Cologne, Fed. Rep. Germany (In press).

Davis, R., B. G. Buchanan and E. H. Shortliffe (1977). Production rules as a representation for a knowledge-based consultation system. Artificial Intelligence 8, 15-45.

Duda, R. O., Hart, P. and Nilsson, N. (1980). Subjective Bayesian methods for rule-based inference systems. Technical Note 124. Artificial Intelligence Center, Stanford Research International, Menlo Park, CA.

Fieschi, M., M. Joubert, D. Fieschi and M. Roux (1982). SPHINX: a system for computer aided diagnosis. Meth. Inform. Med. 21, 143-148.

Forgy, C. L. (1982). RETE: a fast algorithm for the many pattern/many object pattern match problem. Artificial Intelligence 19, 17-37.

Jones, P. (1985). A model of organization dynamics. In M. Small, Ed. Policy Evaluation Using REVEAL. Internation Computers Ltd., Manchester, England.

LeFaivre, R. (1974). FUZZY: a programming language for fuzzy problem solving. Technical Report 202, Computer Sciences Dept., University of Wisconsin, Madison, WI 53706.

Martin-Clouaire, R. and H. Prade (1984). SPII-1: a simple inference engine for accomodating both imprecision and uncertainty. To appear in Computer-Assited Decision Making. North-Holland, Amsterdam.

Negoita, C. (1985). Fuzzy Systems and Expert Systems. Benjamin Cummings Press, Menlo Park, CA.

Plaza, E. and Lopez de Mantaras, R. (1985). Knowledge acquisition and refinement using a fuzzy conceptual base. Proc. Workshop on Fuzzy Expert Systems and Decision Support, Atlanta, GA. North Amer. Fuzzy Inform. Processing Soc.

Ruspini, E. H. (1982). Possibility theory approaches for advanced information systems. Computer 15, 83-91.

Shortliffe, E. (1976). Computer-based medical consultation: MYCIN. Elsevier North-Holland, New York.

Siler, W., J. Buckley and D. Tucker (1985). Non-monotonic fuzzy logic: experience with FLOPS. Proc. Workshop on Fuzzy Expert systems and Decision Support, Atlanta, GA. North Amer. Fuzzy Inform. Processing Soc.

Siler, W., D. Tucker, J. Buckley and V. G. Powell (1985). Artificial intelligence in processing a sequence of time-varying images. Proc. SPIE - Soc. of Photo-optical Engineers 548,

Siler, W. and J. Buckley (1986). Fuzzy operators for possibility interval sets. Fuzzy Sets and Systems (in press).

Tucker, D., W. Siler, V. G. Powell and A. W. H. Stanley Jr. FLOPS: A fuzzy expert system for unsupervised echocardiogram anaylsis. In Computers in Cardiology 1985, IEEE Computer Society, Silver Springs, MD.

Uhr, L. (1984). Algorithm-Structured Computer Arrays and Networks. Academic Press, New York.

von Neumann, J. (1958). The Computer and the Brain. MIT press, Cambridge, Massachusetts.

Willaeys, D. and N. Malvache (1976). Utilization d'un referentiel de sous-ensemble flous, application a un algorithme flou. International Conference on Systems Science, Wroclaw, Poland.

Zimmerman, H.-J. and P. Zysno (1980). Latent connectives in human decision making. Fuzzy Sets and Systems 4, 37-51.

An Uncertainty Calculus for Expert Systems

J. F. BALDWIN

Information Technology Research Centre and Engineering Mathematics Department, University of Bristol, UK

ABSTRACT

This paper, written in tutorial style, describes a form of knowledge representation and inference suitable for the design of Expert Systems. It is based on a theory of Support Logic Programming which uses support pairs to model various forms of uncertainty, including those of a probabilistic and fuzzy nature. What constitutes an Expert System is first discussed before providing a more detailed look at a possible form of knowledge representation and inference under uncertainty suitable for many application domains.

Knowledge representation is in the form of facts and rules of a prolog style. Support pairs are associated with each fact and rule providing support measures for them. Facts not in the knowledge base are assumed to be uncertain so that a closed world assumption is not used. Something which is known to be false can be so represented by suitable choice of the support pair associated with it.

Evidence is central to all branches of knowledge engineering. An inquiry seeks evidence to support a given hypothesis or choose between several possible decisions or decide on what plan of action to take. The data collected to provide the information for this evidence is often necessarily vague. The vagueness may be of a statistical nature or contain not well defined linguistic terms. This imprecision also applies to the specification of what constitutes a good decision or plan and also to the background knowledge of rules, laws, and facts used in conjunction with the evidence in drawing conclusions. The same conclusion may be drawn using different sources of evidence and background knowledge but with varying supports. How are these supports to be combined? Furthermore, one evidence may point in favour while another against a given decision establishing a form of conflict. How is this conflict to be resolved? Support Logic Programming provides a means to provide answers to these questions provided certain assumptions are satisfied.

KEYWORDS

Evidence Theory; Expert Systems; Fuzzy Sets; Logic Programming.

INTRODUCTION

An expert system is a computer system which can act in a similar way to a human expert in a restricted domain of application from the point of view of solving problems, taking decisions and giving advice. The computer system consists essentially of two parts

(i) a knowledge base consisting of that knowledge used by the expert in his performance

(ii) an inference engine which allows queries to be answered by asking questions of the environment and performing logical deductions using the answers in conjunction with the statements in the knowledge base.

The actual form of knowledge representation is open to debate and various forms have been used in expert systems to date including

a) production rules
b) semantic nets
c) first order logic

Production rules take the form of

IF <conditions> THEN <actions>

so that if the conditions specified are satisfied in a short term memory then the actions indicated are taken which may include certain modifications of short term memory. Semantic nets are a form of graph representation in which the nodes represent concepts and the labelled arcs represent relations between concepts. Of particular importance in this respect is the representation by conceptual graphs as given in (Sowa, 1984). In this paper we will not discuss this further but application of these graphs to knowledge engineering can be found in (Baldwin and Crabtree, 1986) and (Morton and Baldwin, 1986).

In this paper the form of knowledge representation which will be used is that of a Horn clause logic, (Kowalski, 1979), which is a restricted form of first order predicate logic. A query can be viewed as a theorem to be proved and the inference engine is a general theorem prover which will prove the theorem true or false. If the theorem is true then the query will have an answer and this will be obtained during the proof. For our expert system we wish to complicate this so that we can take into account various forms of uncertainty arising in the application. Thus a theorem will not be proved true or false but will be supported to a certain degree. In fact this degree of support will take the form of a support pair in which the first number represents a necessary support and the second number represents a possible support. An easy interpretation of this would be to say that the degree of support lies between the necessary and possible supports.

Thus an expert system is a computer program which attempts to emulate the manner of problem solving and decision taking of a human expert within a restricted context. The knowledge base made up of facts and rules representing the expert's view of the application is separated from the inference mechanism. The latter is part of the expert system shell along with other modules which provide facilities for explaining how decisions are reached and a friendly machine/user interface. This separation is an essential feature of an expert system and provides a new style of computer software. In simple terms, if a new problem area is to be looked at, only a new knowledge base need be constucted. Furthermore errors in diagnosis or decision taking will be a result of an incorrectly specified knowledge base of the application. The shell will have been extensively validated. EMYCIN, for example, was the shell of MYCIN and has been used for other applications. In practice it may not be as simple as this and the shell may have to be changed from one class of application to another. It may not be necessary to include uncertainty inference in all expert systems so that the shell can be of a different nature if no uncertainties are involved. A shell should, perhaps, be constructed from a tool kit of shell parts to meet the needs of a given application.

The diagram in Fig. 1 represents an expert system showing this separation of the knowledge base and the inference engine. The user interface is also shown. The user can ask queries of the system and also demand an explanation of how a given answer was deduced. This explanation facility of expert systems is most important and in fact should allow a general dialogue between user and machine. This dialogue is most unsophisticated at the moment and needs to be improved. Even the elementary form of explanation analysis is not particularly suitable since only one level of explanation is given. In a more intelligent system the detail of the explanation would be determined to meet the requirements of the user during the dialogue between user and machine. Nevertheless the requirement of an explanation facility means that the user does not have to accept blindly what comes out of the computer and further queries can be asked to build up the user's confidence. The diagram also shows a path to the expert and paths to modify both the knowledge base and inference engine. When the system is free of queries from the user it can determine expectations for itself and present these to the expert who will either accept or reject them. If he rejects them he should be able to ask the system for some explanation of the failure. This is a difficult problem since there could be many ways in which the system could be modified to correct the system's expectation to match that of the expert. Normally the knowledge base would be modified and this should be done in dialogue with the expert who can query the system in order to accept any change. This modification may take the form of changing an existing fact, rule or combination, or adding further facts of rules to the knowledge base. The disagreement between the computer and the expert may show up a paradox which requires the inference mechanism to be modified and so we also allow for this in the diagram. It should be stressed that present day expert systems do not allow for these types of on line learning mechanisms.

Knowledge acquisition in general is a most difficult part of building an expert system for a given application. It could be said that it is the job of the knowledge engineer to extract the relevant knowledge in the appropriate format from the expert. How does one do this? There are no cook books providing recipes for such a task and while there are aids such as general interviewing techniques, personal construct theoretic techniques as given by (Gaines and Shaw, 1984), inductive learning from examples (Michalski et al, 1983), these approaches are in their infancy. It might be thought that the most important fundamental study for artificial intellignece is to understand how systems can learn for themselves as children do. Firstly it is important to understand what knowledge is, what it means to know, what it is one has to acquire from the expert. Learning how to acquire this, once one knows what is to be acquired in order to know about a given application, may then be a more straightforward task. Humans do not find the study of logic, probability or statistics particularly easy so it is doubtful if acquiring expertise from an expert should assume a shell with a first order predicate logic knowledge representation and a general theorem prover plus a bag of statistical techniques to aid in dealing with the various uncertainties. Of course, the computer does not have to copy the expert in either the form of knowledge representation or inference techniques. It is quite sensible to use logic, probability theory etc., but it does mean that knowledge will be difficult to acquire if one simply thinks in terms of transferring the expertise of the expert to the computer.

As an example of a difficult application which could benefit from the employment of expert system techniques of decision making, consider the problem of image understanding. A 3D scene is photographed and projected onto a 2D screen and stored in the computer as an array of pixels. The most general problem would be to identify objects and relationships between objects in order to come to some understanding of what the scene depicts. For this purpose some form of world knowledge is required to provide high level inference, make decisions with respect to individual objects and control the low level processes such as image processing techniques and elementary pattern recognition. The world knowledge, array of pixels and image processing methods are used by the system to plan the decision making task of answering queries about the scene. This is illustrated in Fig. 2. It is an area of application which has had only limited success to date and the use of artificial intelligence techniques in conjunction with existing techniques of image processing and pattern recognition could prove valuable. Speech recognition is another area in which local recognition techniques of pattern recognition are not enough by themselves. Context plays an important role in both these applications and judgements must be made with respect to the whole in relation to expectations. These applications also suggest a limitation of using the present style of computer architecture of the Von Neumann machine. The human brain is quick and efficient at recognising both scenes and speech and yet biological components have slow switching times in comparision with the electronic components of the present day computer. The hardware of the brain is used much more efficiently than that of the serial computer whose memory/processor split requires so much inactivity of memory. The brain's parallel operation does not have this very restricting split and fast biological switching times of components are not required in order to achieve overall efficiency.

The use of artificial intelligence methods and in particular expert systems should lead to a better performance of decision making by computers than if we try to do the same tasks with number crunching techniques alone. We must expect that new computer architectures will be required to carry out the vast amount of computation needed when using large knowledge bases and general inference procedures. At the present time we are in danger of developing knowledge engineering techniques assuming a serial form of computation. Viewed in the light of parallel computing methods it may be that entirely new forms of decision making are appropriate which require a less sophisticated application of inference techniques for many of its parts.

UNCERTAINTY AND INCOMPLETENESS OF INFORMATION

In this paper we are assuming that knowledge is represented by means of first order logic statements. In other words the knowledge available about the application area is expressed by means of the language of first order predicate logic. It would seem reasonable to suppose therefore that, where possible, queries should be answered by inference methods based purely on logical argument. Logic is concerned with the form of the argument and not its content. A completely automatic method of checking the validity of a given argument is available in the form of the resolution method as described by (Robinson, 1965) and this can be implemented on a computer although present day versions are not efficient enough for general use in an expert system. The algorithm is only semi-decidable so that if the conclusion follows logically from the premises then the argument will be shown to be correct in a finite time but if the argument is not correct then it is possible that nothing is provable in finite time. This would therefore seem to provide a very powerful tool for decision making with regard to complicated application areas in which it is so easy for humans to lose their way.

It does though make one big assumption, namely, that it is possible to express knowledge in the form of statements that, when any variables are instantiated to constants, are either true or false. The knowledge associated with real applications is often not known with certainty. In fact this is almost always the case and for those problem areas which present the greater challenges to the decision maker it is very true indeed. In practice we rely on the use of heuristics, rules of thumb whose truth cannot be guaranteed, but are used by experts in coming to conclusions. We use concepts which cannot be completely defined in that we are unable to provide necessary and sufficient conditions which can be used to assess the applicability of a given concept to a given situation. It is not possible, for example, to give a definition of "a reliable system" which is generally applicable without exception. The same could be said of such concepts as "a pretty woman", "a well educated man", "a stable system", "a car", "a humane society", "a good decision", "a marketable product", "a tree", "a bush", etc. In fact, one learns to use concepts by example. An object is classified as "a car" if it seems to belong to the class of examples of cars one holds in one's head. It does not necessarily have to share a set of properties with each of the template examples but simply to belong to the same cluster of objects as the example cars. It may look quite different from any of the examples, it may have a different means of control, etc., but we still may call it a car. The examples one holds in memory are not simply examples of the object "car" but are more likely to be situations in which "a car" is present. Shape, size, content, context, functionality are all important to the understanding of the concept of "car".

There are many forms of uncertainty that are applicable to expert systems. Data collected and answers given on request by the expert system may contain statistical uncertainties or simply be incomplete. If we are told that the object in a scene contains at least two wheels, we do not know how many wheels the object has. The reason for this could be that part of the object is occluded by some other object or that part of the picture is missing. We can therefore have incompleteness of data as well as incompleteness of definition.

Incompleteness of information does not necessarily prevent a logical inference being concluded. Consider the following example which we will use to illustrate this point in addition to providing an example of the resolution method.

Example

Three people stand in a line with a male on the left and a female on the right. The sex of the person in the middle is not known except that it must be male or female and cannot be both. We can conclude that two persons stand together such that one on the left is a man and the one on the right is a female. This is easily seen through case analysis but we present below a logic representation of the problem and a proof by refutation using the mechanical method of resolution.

Logic representation:

male(a).
female(c).
left_of(a,b).
left_of(b,c).

$\forall$X male(X) v female(X).
$\forall$X NOT(male(X) $\wedge$ female(X)).

Prove: $\exists$X $\exists$Y left_of(X,Y) $\wedge$ male(X) $\wedge$ female(Y).

The method of refutation is to negate the theorem to prove and show that this is then inconsistent with the premises. With the method of resolution, the premises and negated theorem are first put into clause form giving

Clause form:	left_of(a,b).	(1)
	left_of(b,c).	(2)
	male(a).	(3)
	female(c).	(4)
	male(X) v female(X).	(5)
	NOT male(X) v NOT female(X).	(6)
	NOT left_of(X,Y) v NOT male(X) v NOT female(Y).	(7)

The resolution method is then applied to obtain the nil clause. Any two clauses can be clashed if a substitution of the variables can be given which allows an atom of one clause to match the negated atom of the other clause. The result of the clashing is to give a new clause which is the union of the two clashed clauses with the clashed atoms removed and any substitutions used to provide a matching of atoms included. If the nil clause can be obtained then the conclusion does follow logically from the premises,

Resolution:	NOT male(b) v NOT female(c)	using (2) and (3)	(8)
	NOT male(b)	using (4) and (8)	(9)
	female(b)	using (5) and (9)	(10)
	NOT male(a) v NOT female(b)	using (1) and (7)	(11)
	NOT female(b)	using (3) and (11)	(12)
	NIL	using (10) and (12)	

so that argument is correct. We present this to show the simplicity of the method. It should be realised that at any stage of the proof, in general, there will be a large choice of clauses which can be clashed. If one makes the wrong choice the proof will become much longer. It is not easy to provide an intelligent control of the order of clashing and this can lead to very inefficient proofs by a computer.

The example illustrates well an important point in knowledge engineering, namely, that one cannot live with data-bases alone. Inference is required to be able to answer all questions with possible answers for a knowledge base. A data base can manipulate the data to provide the answer required but in the case of this example it would conclude that it was unsure of the answer because of the missing information concerning the middle person's sex.

So far we have discussed various forms of uncertainty that are present in the knowledge base of an expert system. Both rules and facts used for making inferences are subject to uncertainties and cannot be guaranteed to be true, so that statements inferred from them cannot be logical truths. Conclusions can be drawn and a degree of belief may be able to be associated with them. It is also possible that certain evidence may point strongly in favour of a given conclusion while other evidence may point strongly against it without the cancatination of evidences in any way being incompatible. Acceptance of conclusions are not made in practice because they logically follow from the rules and facts, but because when taking all the available evidence into account they seem reasonable in comparison with their negations. Any individual piece of evidence may only make a small contribution to the acceptability of the conclusion and the final acceptance comes as a result of combining many such pieces of evidence. Can we model this practical reasoning process taking into account the various forms of uncertainty that can arise. The support logic programming system, described briefly below and more fully in (Baldwin 1986a, 1986b, 1986c), is an attempt to do this. It uses a restricted form of first order logic, called Horn clause logic, to represent knowledge and derives support measures for any statement which is logically valid when the uncertainties are ignored. The calculus for this evidence theory is indicated and examples of its use given.

Support logic will not model all forms of approximate reasoning. Reasoning by analogy can be a powerful way of deriving conclusions. At school plotting functions was done by taking sub-ranges of the argument and for each sub-range approximating the function by a more simple function whose graph we could plot. If continuity could be proved then a continuous smooth fit was made at the joins of the sub-regions and this smooth fit was assumed to be simple. A problem can be solved by assuming a solution of an easier problem, one involving a relaxation of some of the constraints, and using this solution to generate improved solutions. We should not lose sight of the variety of techniques that are a part of the expert's tool-kit for making decisions in every day affaires.

SUPPORT LOGIC PROGRAMMING

The motivation for the work described in this paper is to provide a form of knowledge representation and inference suitable for Expert Systems. We will show how the ideas from the theory of fuzzy sets as developed by (Zadeh, 1978, 1979) and a theory of evidence as given by (Shafer, 1976) can be combined to form a suitable framework for a logic programming style of reasoning under uncertainty. A restricted form of logic programming in the style of prolog will be used. We could formulate this theory in terms of the first order language of predicate logic but we choose not to do so for computational efficiency considerations. A theorem prover based on the full resolution method with first order predicate logic cannot be made to work fast enough with present techniques of computer implementation. The restriction to Horn clause form allows for a procedural interpretation which can be efficiently implemented on a computer. In prolog, negation is defined as negation by failure which means that any statement is false unless it can be proved true. Thus any fact which is not in the knowledge base is assumed to be false. This is not a true logic negation and is not used in the support logic programming system. A closed world assumption is therefore not required with support logic programming.

Uncertainty, in various forms, plays an important part in the expert's view of his/her application as we have discussed above. A rule, such as, something is true, or will happen, or must happen if certain conditions are satisfied, may not always apply. Our knowledge of the world consists of many statements which we know are not always true but generally are. For example, hard working, intelligent students usually obtain a good degree and computer science graduates normally have no difficulty in obtaining employment. The uncertainty in the application of the rule can be expressed as a probability but there may still be doubt about the actual value of this probability. It may be more honest to express the probability in this case as a linguistic term, such as "high", "large" or "very probable", rather than attempt to give a point value and thus approximate through forced precision. In this case we have a mixture of uncertainties. The application of the rule is governed by a fuzzy probability since such terms as "high", "large", etc., have no precise definition. A method of defining the membership function of such fuzzy sets in the form of recursive definitions using support logic programming is given in (Baldwin, 1986).

If a fact is known to be true then it will be necessarily supported to degree 1 while if it is known to be false, its negation will be necessarily supported to degree 1. Uncertainty arises when a proposition and its negation are necessarily supported to degrees x and y respectively, where x and y are non negative numbers less than 1 and furthermore $x + y <= 1$. If $x + y < 1$, then x and y are not probabilities and there is an unsureness in the uncertainty equal to $1 - x - y$. Degrees of support will be treated in the Shafer sense so that $1 - x - y$ will represent the support given to the disjunction of the proposition and its negation without any additional commitment to either. Thus an uncertain fact would have zero support for itself and also its negation. We could allow $x + y > 1$ and interpret this case as representing an inconsistency but we will not develop this in this paper. It should be emphasised that a necessary support for a given proposition does not determine the necessary support for its negation. With the restriction for consistency given above, certain limits can be deduced for the support of the negated proposition. If the condition of consistency is dropped even this is not true. This meets with intuition. For example, the observation that the man has a headache gives a little support to the fact that he has flu but no support to the fact that he has not got flu. We introduce later the concept of possible support in addition to the necessary support and these two supports provide a support pair. The support pairs of the proposition and its negation are related as shown later.

In practical affairs, deductive reasoning based on first order predicate logic plays only a minor role since rules and facts cannot, in general, be guaranteed to be true. In mathematics it plays an important part and is important for theorem proving and validation of methods. At a meta level it is also important for real life. Computer programs should be validated using methods based on logic by showing that the specification of the program expressed in first order logic statements is met. The difficulty is writing the specification which often can only be given a fuzzy definition. Methods used in Science and Engineering should also be validated if possible. This does not imply that a scientific theory can ever be validated completely or that an engineering design can ever be shown to be completely what the customer wants. In these circumstances we can only provide a measure of support for the applicability of a scientific theory or the usefulness of a given design. In practice we must be concerned with conflicting evidences and find ways of resolving the conflict. One piece of evidence may point in one direction while another may point in the opposite direction. The pieces of evidence are not inconsistent and if complete information were available the apparent conflict would be resolved. In practice we only have partial information and the conflict arising from different evidences will only reduce the support given to the individual conclusions. Consider a man digging near the site where a dead body is found. Is he digging a grave for his murdered victim? He says he is digging for gold and he is known to have done this in other places before. The evidences conflict so that little support can be given to the statement that he is digging a grave for his victim. Each evidence in turn points strongly in one direction. The truth is that while digging for gold he found the body and put it to one side.

In real life, as for scientific method , induction and abduction play a more central role than deduction. If P entails Q and P is true, then we can deduce that Q is true. This corresponds to deduction. An example might be as follows. If a person has flu he will at the same stage have a high temperature. John has flu. Therefore at some stage John will have a high temperature. It is, of course, more likely that the rule would only be generally true but not necessarily always true. Furthermore how do we arrive at this rule. Do we observe lots of cases and since it holds for each of these decide that it is always true. This would be an example of forming a universal generalisation from supported instances and corresponds to induction. We could replace the universal generalisation with a probabilistic statement and say that it is very likely that anyone who has flu will have a high temperature. The method of induction is used by engineers to form rules of thumb and by the knowledge engineer to form rules representing the expert's knowledge. Rules of thumb are not necessarily universal generalisations but only assumed to be true most of the time. When a rule is not always true, this must be indicated, for its use will involve a risk which may be acceptable on some occasions but not on others. When attempting a diagnosis we must use the rule the other way round. We are told that John has a high temperature. Can we deduce that he has the flu. The answer is obviously not, since a high temperature can be the result of many illnesses. We can say that it is possible that John is suffering from flu but we would prefer to give some measure of support to this statement. How can we determine this measure of support? No easy answer is available but cause and effect considerations would seem to be important. This use of the rule in the backward direction was called abduction by (Peirce, 1933). From P entails Q and Q we abduce a certain support for P. Consider the example

> IF it rains for a long period
> THEN shale tennis courts will become flooded
>
> This tennis court is flooded
>
> THEREFORE large support that it has been raining for a long period.

World knowledge allows for a large support in this case. Other possible causes for the tennis court being flooded such as the groundsman had a heart attack while watering the courts and the hose pipe was not turned off are not likely.

Consider also the following example

> IF X is in the ladies toilet
> THEN X is female
>
> Mary is female
>
> THEREFORE little support for Mary in ladies toilet.

In this case there are many places that Mary could be even given the fact that she is female.

A method for determining the supports for conclusions of abductive reasoning is required. Support logic programming does not provide such a method but could be used to program an approach based on finding cause and effect relationships from which the support pairs could be calculated. This is a most difficult area but very important to the field of expert systems. Thus what is required is a method which will provide a degree of plausibility depending on finding a suitable explanation for the conclusion to be true. This explanation will provide a certain weight of evidence in support of the conclusion. In the practical world one reasons using cues. Certain evidence is supportive to a proposition while other evidence supports its negation. Various evidences must be compared and combined to give a final judgement of whether to accept or reject a given proposition. Not enough information is available to deduce the truth of the proposition using deductive logic. The lack of information means that a certain risk must be taken in commiting oneself to a truth value for the proposition. Lack of support for a proposition does not necessarily support its negation. The lack of evidence which prevents any purely deductive method being used can arise because of hidden information or lack of definition. To decide if a person is tall or not may be difficult, not because the person is hidden from view, but from the fact that no precise definition of "tall" can be given. The mind prefers discrete categories while the real world possesses a continuity so that borderline cases are inevitable.

Once again certain evidence will point in the direction of one category while other evidence may contradict this and point to some other classification. It is being assumed that some form of inductive reasoning is possible, that hypotheses can be seen to be probable if not shown to be true. This is a form of scientific method that not everyone would accept and we must not lose sight of the difficulties that any suggested programme of verification will have. We can of course use the various rules and facts for our expert system knowledge base to make diagnoses, predictions, etc. in the same way that we can use a scientific theory to make predictions. The difficult problem is how do we validate our expert system or even come to the conclusion that any results it gives will probably be true. This is the same problem as verifying a scientific theory and has relevance to the setting up of the expert system in the first place and to the learning that we expect to go on as the expert system is used in practice. We cannot validate our expert system in the sense that we cannot prove by deductive means that it is valid. Nevertheless we can test it by seeing how it performs under the most stringent conditions. This is the process of validation which we must use. We might add that validation of computer programs in general requires the same approach even if the program can be validated as far as the specification is concerned The question remains does this specification do its job properly and this must be tested but cannot in general be validated.

In the theory of support logic programming there is no attempt to distinguish between the various forms of uncertainty that can occur. It is, of course, recognised that there are different forms of uncertainty and different algorithms will be required to determine the support pairs for the various cases. It is assumed that thereafter the only consideration required is the measure of support provided, this being in the form of a support pair. This simplifies the treatment considerably from the case when the various forms of uncertainty are remembered and used to determine the final judgement taking into account the many rules and facts used in deriving a conclusion. This simplification allows for a simple calculus of support pairs to be derived which will allow for computational efficiency.

KNOWLEDGE REPRESENTATION

A support logic program is a set of program clauses. A program clause is of the form

A :- B1,B2,...,Bn : [S1,Su].

where A,B1,...,Bn are atoms. This should be understood as a prolog clause with the addition of the support pair [S1,Su]. It can be given the following procedural interpretation. For each assignment of each variable occuring in the clause, if B1,...,Bn are all true then A is necessarily supported to degree S1 and NOT A is necessarily supported to degree (1 - Su). The support pair [S1,Su] is therefore a conditional support. We shall refer to S1 as the necessary support and Su as the possible support. These supports satisfy the following constraint

S1 + (1 - Su) <= 1.

(Su - S1) measures the unsureness in the support of the rule pair

{A :- B1,B2,...,Bn ; NOT A :- B1,B2,...Bn}

A is known as the rule head and (B1,B2,...,Bn) as the body of the clause. In the case when the support pair is [1,1], the clause is an ordinary prolog clause and is interpreted as follows. In order to prove A, the conjunction (B1,B2,...,Bn) must be proved.

If the body of the clause is empty we have a unit clause, represented as

A : [S1,Su].

This has the following procedural interpretation. For each assignment of each variable, "A" is necessarily supported to degree S1 and "NOT A" is necessarily supported to degree (1 - Su). Again the constraint

S1 + (1 - Su) <= 1

is satisfied and (Su - S1) measures the unsureness associated with the support for the pair

A ;{NOT A}.

In probabilistic terms, if S1 = Su then the support can be interpreted as a probability. Furthermore, if we assume that the probability of a fact lies somewhere in the interval [a,b], then we can put S1 = a and Su = b.

We will also allow statements of the form

A :- B1;B2 : [S1,Su].

where ";" signifies disjunction and B1 and B2 are single atoms or a conjunction of atoms. Thus in this case "A", "NOT A" are necessarily supported to degrees S1, (1 - Su), respectively, if for each assignment of each variable (B1 OR B2) is true.

It should be observed that the sum of the necessary supports for an atom and its negation do not necessarily add up to 1. The necessary support for the negation of an atom is not determined from the necessary support of the atom. Instead we constrain the necessary support of the negation of an atom to be that amount which the possible support of the atom is different from unity. We therefore have the following interpretation for negation.

If P :- Q : [S1,Su].

then nec_sup(P|Q) = S1 ; pos_sup(P|Q) = Su

nec_sup(NOT P|Q) = 1 - Su ; pos_sup(NOT P|Q) = 1 - S1

where Q is a conjunction, disjunction or mixture of atomic formulae and

If P : [S1,Su].

then nec_sup(P) = S1 ; pos_sup(P) = Su

nec_sup(NOT P) = 1 - Su ; pos_sup(NOT P) = 1 - S1

We can further state that

nec_sup(P OR NOT P) = 1 ; nec_sup(P AND NOT P) = 0.

We can consider some examples of the support logic programming form of representation of statements expressed in natural language. The statement "most fair haired people have blue eyes" could be represented as

has_col_eyes(X,blue) :- has_col_hair(X,fair) : [0.7,0.9].

and the statement "few fair haired people have brown eyes" as

has_col_eyes(X,brown):- has_col_hair(X,fair) : [0.1,0.2].

which indicates that there is a strong support of 0.8 for the fact that anyone having fair hair does not have brown eyes. It should be that capital letters stand for variables so that X can be instantiated to any constant.

The clause

friends(X,Y) :- NOT likes(X,Y) ; NOT likes(Y,X): [0,0.1].

gives strong support for X and Y not being friends if at least one of them does not like the other. The use of NOT in the body of the clause should be noted. It cannot be used in the head of the clause.

The statement   is_heavy(X) :- is_light(X)   :   [0,0].

says that anything that is light cannot be heavy, while

is_heavy(X) :- is_very_heavy(X)   :   [1,1].

says that anything that is very heavy is necessarily heavy.

If $h \in H$

and   is_tall(X) :- person(X),height(X,h) : [Sh,Sh].

and we let $\chi_{tall}(h) = 1 - Sh$ and $\chi_{NOT\ tall}(h) = 1 - Sh$

then χ_{tall} is a membership function for the fuzzy set "tall".

Thus the clause   is_tall(X) :- person(X),height(X,h) : [Shl,Shu].

is a generalisation of the concept of the fuzzy set "tall" since we do not require Shl = Shu.

It might be argued that the numbers Sl,Su representing the supports should not be precisely given. It is certainly true that these supports are not easy to determine and in general can only be given in vague, linguistic terms. There is nothing in the theory presented which says that they must be pure numbers and in fact they could be fuzzy numbers. The use of pure numbers simplifies the arithmetic when calculating the support pair for any derived conclusion and for many practical situations will provide adequate representation of the uncertainties involved.

SUPPORT LOGIC CALCULUS

In this section we will summarise the computational rules for determining the support pairs for compound statements, such as conjunctions and disjunctions of atoms. We will also give the computation rules for making inferences and for combining evidences from different sources. The treatment will be by illustration and example only. For a more general development of the theory reference should be made to (Baldwin, 1985) and (Baldwin, 1986) and (Baldwin and Monk, 1985).

In order to motivate the need for these computations we will consider first how queries are answered in the support logic programming system. Consider the program

```
a(X)  :-  b(X),c(Y)  :  [s1,s2].
a(X)  :-  d(X)   :  [s3,s4].
b(i)  :   [s5,s6].
c(j)  :   [s7,s8].
d(i)  :   [s9,s10].
```

We can answer the query

```
?- a(i).
```

and the system will reply

```
YES   :   [s11,s12].
```

and the support pair [s11,s12] will be determined as a function of the support pairs given above. Suppose for the moment that each rule and fact above were true, corresponding to sk = 1 for all k. Then in order to prove a(i) we can use the first rule and infer a(i) providing we can prove that the conjunction b(i),c(Y) is true for some instantiation of the variable Y. We know from the first two facts that b(i),c(j) is true so that a(i) is true. Alternatively we could have used the second rule to prove a(i) by showing that d(i) is true which is a fact in the knowledge base. There are therefore two possible proof paths for providing a(i). For the more general case in which we have any values for the support pairs, we find the support pair associated with a(i) by combining the support pairs associated with all possible proof paths for a(i). The support pair associated with a proof path is determined from the support pairs of its component parts according to the rules of conjunction or disjunction which ever is applicable. In this example the support pair of the first proof path is determined from [s5,s6] and [s7,s8] according to the rule for conjunction. The result will be [s5*s7,s6*s8]. This is then used with [s1,s2] according to the inference rule to form the final support for a(i) using the first proof path.

We could have asked the query

a(X).

and the system would have replied

X = i : [s11,s12]

In this case the instantiation of the variable in the query, required in order to prove a(X), is given as the solution along with the corresponding support pair.

The interpretation here corresponds to the procedural semantic interpretation of prolog.

We now give some motivation for the use of the various rules for the calculus of the support logic defined below. The approach given is not meant to constitute any sort of proof but may give some insight into the use of support pairs.

Inference Rule

Consider the following schemata

P :- Q
Q

Therefore P

This says that if whenever Q is true, P is true and it is known that Q is true so that it logically follows that P is true. Let us suppose that we do not know that Q is true for certain, but we estimate that

$Pr(Q) = x$

can we conclude anything about P? If Q is true then P is true while if Q is false we can conclude nothing about the truth of P.

i.e. IF P :- Q , Q THEN P
IF P :- Q , NOT Q THEN P ∨ NOT P

Thus we can conclude P with probability x and P ∨ NOT P with probability 1 - x. We can represent this as

P : [x,1]

with the following interpretation

IF P : [Sl,Su] THEN

$Sl \le Pr(P) \le Su \quad ; \quad 1 - Su \le Pr(NOT\ P) \le 1 - Sl$

$$\Pr(P \vee \text{NOT } P) = 1 \quad ; \quad \Pr(P \wedge \text{NOT } P) = 0$$

For example, $\Pr(P \vee \text{NOT } P) >= x + (1-x) = 1$.

We thus have the following schemata

$$\frac{\begin{array}{l} P \ :- \ Q \ : \ [1,1] \\ Q \ : \ [x,x] \end{array}}{\text{Therefore } P \ : \ [x,1]}$$

We can generalise this to the case where

$$P \ :- \ Q \ : \ [S1(P|Q), Su(P|Q)]$$

which is to be interpreted as

$$S1(P|Q) \ <= \ \Pr(P|Q) \ <= \ Su(P|Q)$$

$$1 - Su(P|Q) \ <= \ \Pr(\text{NOT } P|Q) \ <= \ 1 - S1(P|Q)$$

For the more general case in which Pr(P|Q) is not necessarily 1 and in fact exact probabilities are not known, we use the following schemata

$$\frac{\begin{array}{l} P \ :- \ Q \ : \ [S1(P|Q), Su(P\ Q)] \\ Q \ : \ [S1(Q), Su(Q)] \end{array}}{\text{Therefore } [S1(P|Q)*S1(Q),\ 1 - (1 - Su(P|Q))*S1(Q)]} \qquad .....(I)$$

The above schemata is a special case of this one. We give no further justification for this in this paper.

If for the above example we want to calculate a definite probability for P we can use the schemata

$$\frac{\begin{array}{l} P \ :- \ Q \ : \ [1,1] \\ P \ :- \ \text{NOT } Q \ : \ [0,0] \\ Q \ : \ [x,x] \end{array}}{\text{Therefore } P \ : \ [x,x]}$$

for this says that P logically follows with probability >= x and NOT P follows logically with probability >= (1 - x). But since $\Pr(P \vee \text{NOT } P) = \Pr(P) + \Pr(\text{NOT } P) = 1$ we must have that PR(P) = x and Pr(NOT P) = 1 - x giving the above conclusion. This is a special case of the use of the probability law

$$\Pr(P) = \Pr(P|Q)*\Pr(Q) + \Pr(P|\text{NOT } Q)*\Pr(\text{NOT } Q)$$

The more general use of this law of probability is the schemata

$$\frac{\begin{array}{l} P \ :- \ Q \ : \ [x,x] \\ P \ :- \ \text{NOT } Q \ : \ [y,y] \\ Q \ : \ [u,u] \end{array}}{\text{Therefore } P \ : \ [x*u + y*(1-u),\ x*u + y*(1-u)]}$$

For the more general case in which exact probabilities are not known, we generalise this to the following schemata

$$\frac{\begin{array}{l} P \ := \ Q \ ; \ [S1(P|Q), Su(P|Q)] \\ P \ :- \ \text{NOT } Q \ ; \ [S1(P|\text{NOT } Q), Su(P|\text{NOT } Q)] \\ Q \ : \ [S1(Q), Su(Q)] \end{array}}{\text{Therefore } P \ : \ [S1(P), Su(P)]}$$

where

$$S1(P) = S1(P|Q)*S1(Q) + S1(P|NOT\ Q)*(1 - S1(P|Q))$$
$$Su(P) = 1 - ((1 - Su(Q))*(1 - Su(P|NOT\ Q)) + (1 - Su(P|Q))*S1(Q))$$

The schemata I given above can be derived from this one using

$S1(P|NOT\ Q) = 0$; $Su(P|NOT\ Q) = 1$

The assignment $[0,1]$ to any statement represents total uncertainty about the truth of the statement, i.e.

r : $[0,1]$

is interpreted as

$0 <= Pr(r) <= 1$; $0 <= Pr(NOT\ r) <= 1$
$Pr(r \vee NOT\ r) = 1$; $Pr(r \wedge NOT\ r) = 0$

Conjunction and Disjunction

Rules can be of the form

P :- Q : $[X,Y]$

where Q is a conjunction, disjunction or mixture of literals. We must therefore be able to determine $[U,V]$ for

Q : $[U,V]$

where Q = Q1,Q2 or Q = Q1;Q2
when Q1 = $[X1,Y1]$ and Q2 = $[X2,Y2]$ are given.

If we consider the special case when the support pairs for Q1 and Q2 are known, i.e. Q1 : X1,X1 and Q2 : X2,X2 then in general

$$Q1,Q2 : [[MAX(X1 + X2 - 1,0),MIN(X1,X2)],[MAX(X1 + X2 - 1,0),MIN(X1,X2)]]$$

This is easily proved but can be illustrated using the following example. Suppose a bag contains objects, some of which are spherical and some of which are red and the proportions with these attributes are known to be X1 and X2 respectively. From these proportions we wish to determine the proportion of objects which are both spherical and red. If we know nothing else then we cannot determine a unique value for this proportion. The minimum proportion of spherical and red objects is obtained in the situation where as many as possible of the objects do not share the two attributes. This number is given by MAX(X1 + X2 - 1,0). The greatest proportion is obtained in the situation where as many as possible of the objects share the two attributes and this will be MIN(X1,X2).

The difficulty here is that we have intervals within intervals and this multiplicity of nesting increases with the length of conjunction chains. In order to retain simplicity we wish to give unique values to U and V so that we only have to consider simple intervals. We could choose $[MAX(X1+X2-1,0),MIN(X1,X2)]$ for the above case for $[U,V]$ but this assumes maximum separability of the two classes of objects, those being spherical and those being red, when calculating U and minimum separability when calculating V. We could list all the possible object patterns that give the required proportions X1 and X2. There is no reason to suppose without further information that any one of these patterns is more reasonable than any other. Each possible pattern will give a value for the proportion of objects with the two attributes. If we take each pattern as equally likely and take the expected value of the proportion U then

$$U = X1*X2$$

and we have

Q1,Q2 : [X1*X2, X1*X2]

This is the same result which would obtain if

Pr(Q1|Q2) = Pr(Q1) and Pr(Q2|Q1) = Pr(Q2)

i.e. that the two events of an object being red and an object being spherical are independent.

This is the assumption that support logic uses in the absence of further information and the user should be aware of this when modelling his application. It is possible to include additional information such as 'the two propositions Q1,Q2 are mutually exclusive' but this case will not be further discussed in this paper. In practice, one would not use a rule whose body contained the conjunction Q1,Q2 of mutually exclusive propositions. Nevertheless, the assumption of complete independence may not always be true. In this case we may use the statement

Q1 :- Q2 : [S1(Q1|Q2),Su(Q1|Q2)]

if this were known to determine U. On the other hand, if this or its dual statement are not provided, we would still argue that the multiplication rule should be used to provide the support for U.

For the more general case first stated above we have the schemata

Q1 : [X1,Y2]

Q2 : [X1,Y2]

Therefore Q1,Q2 : [X1*X2,Y1*Y2]

and by similar arguments, for the disjunctive case we have

Q1 : [X1,Y1]

Q2 : [X2,Y2]

Therefore Q1;Q2 : [X1 + X2 - X1*X2,Y1 + Y2 - Y1*Y2]

<u>Combining Supports from Different Proof Paths</u>

Consider that one proof path gives

P : [X1,X2]

and another proof path gives

P : [Y1,Y2]

for proving the proposition P. How do we combine these two support pairs to give an overall support for P, namely

P : [X,Y]

We can consider this in box form as in the diagram below. The entries in the boxes represent the necessary supports associated with the statement in the box. Each box row sums to the corresponding left hand support and similarly with the columns with respect to the top supports. There is a necessary support of

X1*(1 - Y2) + (1 - X2)*Y1 = S say

for the inconsistent statement P AND NOT P and this must be redistributed amongst the other boxes in some way.

	P Y1	NOT P 1 - Y2	UNCERTAIN Y2 - Y1
P X1	X1*Y1 P	X1*(1 - Y2) P AND NOT P (not allowed)	X1*(Y2 - Y1) P
NOT P 1 - X2	(1 - X2)*Y1 P AND NOT P (not allowed)	(1 - X2)*(1 - Y2) NOT P	(1 - X2)*(Y2 - Y1) NOT P
X2 - X1 UNCERTAIN	(X2 - X1)*Y1 P	(X2 - X1)*(1 - Y2) NOT P	(X2 - X1)*(Y2 - Y1) UNCERTAIN

There are two possibilities

(1) Redistribute the support S amongst the other boxes in proportion to the original supports. This is effectively a normalisation process. The necessary overall supports for P and NOT P are then given by

$$S1(P) = (X1*Y1 + X1*(Y2 - Y1) + (X2 - X1)*Y1)/K = X$$

$$S1(NOT\ P) = ((1 - X2)*(1 - Y2) + (1 - X2)*(Y2 - Y1) + (X2 - X1)*(1 - Y2))/K = 1 - Y$$

where

$$K = 1 - X1*(1 - Y2) - (1 - X2)*Y1$$

This rule of combination is associative in that it does not matter what order the proof paths are combined, two at a time, if there are more than two proofs.

(2) Redistribute the support S to the box labelled UNCERTAIN. In this example assuming only two proof paths then

S1(P) and S1(NOT P) take the same values as above but with K = 1.

This does mean that the original supports are effectively modified. Order of combination of pairs if more than two proof paths are present does matter and all possible ways of determining the final support pair must be considered. An average can then be determined to provide the final solution. Details of this will be discussed in a future paper.

The second rule does provide a combination rule which can reduce the support of what appears to be a true statement when contradictory evidence comes along. The combination rule above does not allow this. Which combination rule should be used depends upon the application. This context dependency does seem necessary and it must be admitted that the choice of combination rule is to some extent ad hoc. Nevertheless, the above two rules can be justified in certain cases. For the remainder of this paper we will assume the first of the two rules.

RULES FOR SUPPORT LOGIC CALCULUS

We can now give the rules for the support logic programming calculus for determining the support pair for a given proof path and also for combining the support pairs of different proof paths to give an overall support. The following is taken from the user manual written by R Monk.

IF

fact1(X) : [f1l,f1u].

fact2(X) : [f2l,f2u].

fact3(X) : [f3la,f3ua].

fact3(X) : [f3lb,f3ub].

rule(X) :- fact1(X) : [rl,ru].

prob_rule(X) :- fact1(X) : [pl,pu].

prob_rule(X) :- NOT fact1(X) : [np$l$,np$u$].

THEN

1. Conjunction

fact1(X),fact 2(X) : [cl,cu]

cl = f1l*f2l ; cu = f1u*f2u

2. Disjunction

fact1(X);fact2(X) : [dl,du]

dl = f1l + f2l - f1l*f2l ; du = f1u + f2u - f1u*f2u

3. Negation

NOT fact1(X) : [nl,nu]

nl = 1 - f1u ; nu = 1 - f1l

4. Conditional

rule(X) : [ic$l$,ic$u$]

ic$l$ = rl*f1l ; ic$u$ = 1 - (1 - ru)*f1l

5. Probability Rule

prob_rule(X) : [pr$l$,pr$u$]

pr$l$ = pl*f1l + (1 - f1u)*np$l$; pr$u$ = 1 - ((1 - f1u)*(1 - np$u$) + (1 - pu)*f1l)

6. Same Conclusion

fact3(X) : [sc$l$,sc$u$]

Conflict = f3la*(1 - f3ub) + f3lb*(1 - f3ua)

sc$l$ = (f3la + f3lb - f3la*f3lb - Conflict)/(1 - Conflict)

sc$u$ = (f3ua*f3ub)/(1 - Conflict)

The rules given here have been justified using probabilistic type arguments. A similar justification for these rules can be made when the uncertainty measures are determined from fuzzy considerations. Further discussion of this point is made in (Baldwin, 1985).

EXAMPLES OF SUPPORT LOGIC PROGRAMMING

The following examples are given to illustrate a simple use of the support logic programming system. In the second example the concept of semantic unification is introduced. If John is known to be a little above average in height then there is some support for the fact that John is tall and this is represented by a support pair whose values are determined from fuzzy set theory using possibility and necessity measures. The head of a clause expressing "has_ht(X,tall)" unifies with the fact has_ht(john,above_av) with a certain support pair. Of course, syntactically there is no unification so we introduce the term semantic unification. The support logic programming system automatically introduces the following clause

```
has_ht(X,tall)  :- has_ht(X,above_av)  :  [sl,su].
```

and the support pair [sl,su] is calculated from the definitions of the two fuzzy sets "tall" and "above_av".

In the examples below, the underlined text gives answers to queries returned by the system.

Example 1

```
design(X,ok)  :- performance(X,good),
                 looks(X,modern)  :  [0.9,1].
design(X,ok)  :- cost(X,expensive)  :  [0,0.05].
design(X,ok)  :- NOT reliability(X,high)  :  [0,0.2].

performance(X,good)  :- engs_report(X,ok),
                        reliability(X,high)  :  [0.9,1].

reliability(des1,high)  :  [0.7,0.8].
reliability(des2,high)  :  [0.8,0.8].

looks(des1,modern)  :  [0.8,1].
looks(des2,modern)  :  [0.9,1].

engs_report(des1,ok)  :  [0.7,1].
engs_report(des2,ok)  :  [0.9,1].

cost(des1,expensive)  :  [0.6,1].
cost(des2,expensive)  :  [0.3,1].

?- design(X,ok).
X = des1  :  [0.143869,0.453103]  ;
X = des2  :  [0.398856,0.759902]  ;
No more solution
```

A trace facility of the system allows the user to see how the supports are found and combined but we will not give details here.

Example 2

We now give an example of the use of semantic unification. The fuzzy sets "tall" and "average", in relation form, are defined in the following tables

tall	height	Sl	Su
	68	0	0
	72	1	1
	75	1	1

average	height	Sl	Su
	69	0	0
	70	1	1
	71	0	0

Linear interpolation is allowed when reading these tables. For example, a height of 70 satisfies "tall" to a detree 0.5

i.e. $Sl(tall(70)) = Su(tall(70)) = 0.5$

If we further have the knowledge base

wears(X, large_shoes) :- height(X,tall) : [0.9,1].

height(john,average) : [1,1].

We can ask the query, corresponding to 'does john wear large shoes',

?- wears(john,large_shoes).

and the system will return the answer

YES : [0.36,1]

This uses the idea of semantic unification, discussed briefly above, to give a certain degree of match between the concepts "tall" and "average". The system uses the rule

height(X,tall) :- height(X,average) : [a,b]

with a,b determined using certain results from fuzzy set theory concerning certainty and possibility measures.

CONCLUSIONS

A support logic programming system has been introduced and the rules of the associated calculus discussed. It can model various forms of uncertainty including fuzzy and probablistic uncertainties. The support is in the form of a support pair and in this paper the interpretation given to this has been discussed from a probabilistic point of view. This is by no means the only view point and its modelling of fuzzy uncertainties is just as powerful. The support programming language provides an easy method to write expert systems which involves uncertainties of various natures. It can be used as a systems programming language to express theories of knowledge, develop expert systems shells and generally experiment with ways of coping with uncertainty within the field of knowledge engineering.

REFERENCES

Baldwin, J.F. (1986)."Support Logic Programming" in Fuzzy Sets Theory and Applications (Ed. A.I. Jones et al), D. Reidel Pub. Co.

Baldwin, J.F., Monk, M.R.M. (1986). "SLOP - a system for support logic programming", ITRC research report, University of Bristol.

Baldwin, J.F. (1986). "An evidential support theory for knowledge engineering" (To appear)

Morton, S., Baldwin, J.F. (1986) "Conceptual graphs and fuzzy qualifiers in natural language interfaces" (To be published in special issue of Fuzzy Sets and Systems)

Baldwin, J.F., Crabtree, B. (1986) "CRIL - a Conceptual Relational Inference Language for knowledge engineering", in Fuzzy Logics in Knowledge Engineering (Ed. Negosta, C.V. and Prade, H.), Verlag TUV Rheinland.

Gaines, B.R., Shaw, M.L.G. (1981) "New directions in the analysis and interactive ilicitation of personal construct systems", in Recent Advances in Personal Construct Technology, (Ed. Shaw, M.L.G.), Academic Press.

Kowalski, R. (1979) "Logic for Problem Solving", North Holland.

Michalski, R.S., et al (1983) "Machine Learning", Tioja Pub. Co.

Peirce, C.S. (1933) Collected Papers, (Ed. Hartshorne and Weiss), Vol.2, Cambridge, Mass.

Robinson, J.A. (1965) "A machine oriented logic based on resolution principle"

Journal of the Association for Computing Machinery, Vol.12, No.1
Shafer, G. (1976) "A mathematical theory of evidence", Princeton Univ. Press.
Sowa, J. (1984) "Conceptual Structures", Addison Wesley.
Zadeh, L.A. (1978) "Fuzzy sets as a basis for a theory of possibility", Fuzzy Sets and Systems, Vol.1.
Zadeh, L.A. (1979) "A theory of approximate reasoning", in Machine Intelligence Vol.9, (Ed. Michie, D and Mikulich, L), John Wiley.

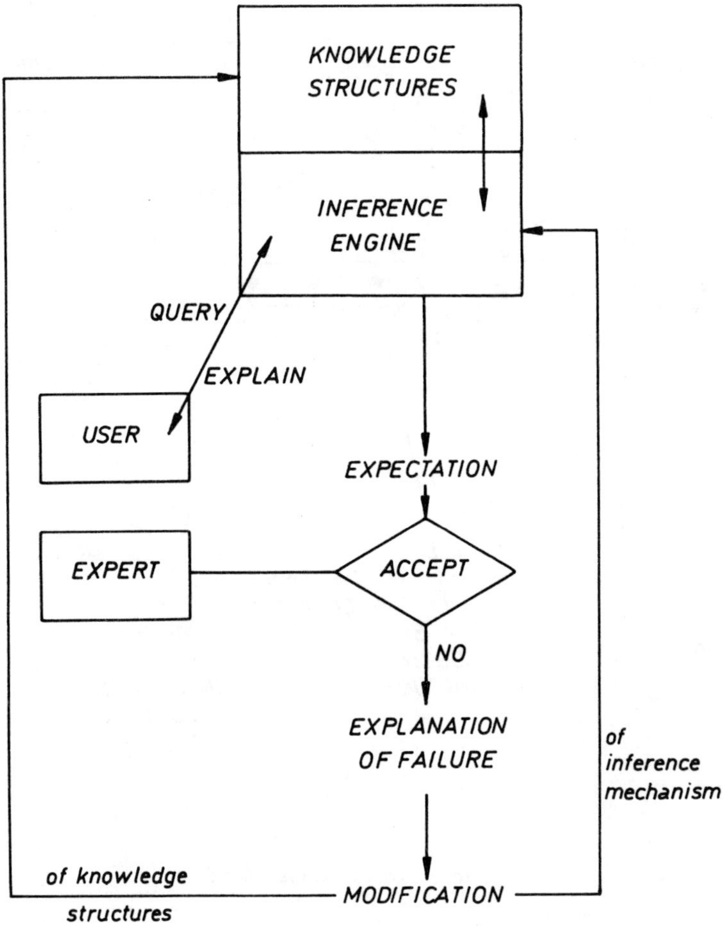

Fig.1 Expert Systems

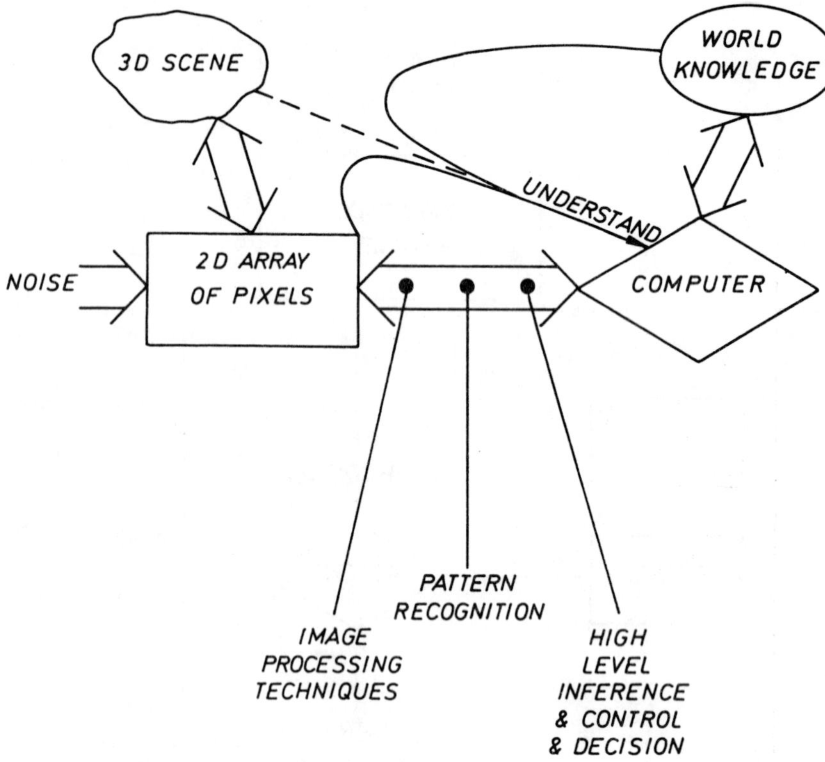

Fig. 2 Image Understanding

Automatic Generation of Verbal Comments on Results of Mathematical Modelling

V. NOVÁK

Mining Institute of the Czechoslovak Academy of Sciences, Hladnovská 7, 710 00 Ostrava 2, Czechoslovakia

ABSTRACT

Given the numerical results of mathematical model of stress in the rock being computed using a finite element method. We may encounter the problem that the results are too extensive to be easily and exhaustively interpreted by the user. This paper presents a method for automatic generation of simple verbal comments which may help the user to get the orientation in the results. The method is based on fuzzy set theory and its application in linguistics.

KEYWORDS

Application of fuzzy sets; linguistic modifiers; interpretation of results; aproximate reasoning; computer linguistics; heuristic methods.

INTRODUCTION

When applying mathematical models in the practice, we must be careful about the interpretation of results. The model should be as exact as possible, and since simplifications are necessary, we usually compute more variants and compare one with another. In this case, however, we may face the situation that the results are very extensive and careful inspection of them is very labours and time consuming. Moreover, we can easily overlook some important details. In fact, we encounter the effect of the principle of incompatibility (Zadeh,1973) where the numerical results represent the detailed information and our interpretation represents the relevant statements we want to obtain about the studied problem .

In this paper we demonstrate that fuzzy sets can be used in a way to model some human reasoning when interpreting the results and, thus to help the user to be able to concentrate himself on important facts. We present a method for generation simple comments in natural language to the results of the model. They serve as an overall information about the results and can help the user to find the desired relevant statements about the problem. It is used for interpretation of the results of the mathematical modelling in mining geomechanics and is based on the fuzzy set theory and its applications in linguistics.

THEORETICAL ASSUMPTIONS

Form of the Results

We can assume for simplicity that the results form a two dimensional field of elements containing some values. This form of results we encounter e.g. in tasks of lin. elasticity in the plane which are solved using the finite element method.

The values are scalar characteristics derived from the stress tensor (for example, compressive stress, shearing stress, energy etc). Of course, we can consider three-dimensional problem, or the results organized in a completely different way. We would have to solve some specific problems but the main idea contained in the following method remain the same.

In general, the field is a set U. Acording to some external criteria, we can define some domains U_c in the field U where c is a subscript ranging trough the domains. We assume each U_c to be a fuzzy subset of U, $U_c \subsetneq U$, i.e.

$$U_c : U \rightarrow L$$

where L is the set of membership degrees. For example, if the field U represents a sectional view of the coal seam with its surroundings then the domains can be defined according to the mining technology and geological situation (hanging wall, foot wall, pillar, caved ground, etc.). Some of them can be defined exactly but most of them will be purely fuzzy in the nature (upper part of the footwall, lower (higher) hanging wall etc.). In the practice, some domains must be defined by the user and the rest can be defined automatically e.g. on the basis of the known geometrical description.

The intersection or union of two domains c,c is represented by the intersection or union of the corresponding fuzzy sets U_c, U_c .

Each element $u \in U$ is adjoined a real number. We will denote it by $Val(u) \in \mathbb{R}$.

Basic Principles

Context. Any relevant statement in natural language must be made in some context. It is a specific feature of the vagueness. Consider, for example, the statement "The values are high". What does it mean in fact? In which respect they are high? Even in such a simple example we ensounter the context which we often accept unconsciously in the communication.

The method presented in this paper must be general and independent of the context. Therefore we use the following simple procedure.

Let $u \in U$ and u^{min}, u^{max} be some chosen numbers such that $u^{min} < u^{max}$. Then we put

$$NVal(u) = \begin{cases} 1 \text{ if } Val(u) \geqq u^{max} \\ \dfrac{Val(u) - u^{min}}{u^{max} - u^{min}} \quad \text{if } u^{min} < Val(u) < u^{max} \\ 0 \text{ if } Val(u) \leqq u^{min} \end{cases}$$

The values NVal(u) are normalized dimensionless numbers which will be used instead of the original values $Val(u), u \in U$. The numbers u^{min}, u^{max} represent the context. We distinguish two kinds of contexts:

(a) Relative context.

$$u^{max} = \sup \{Val(u);\ u \in Supp(U_c)\}$$

$$u^{min} = \inf \{Val(u);\ u \in Supp(U_c)\}$$

i.e.the context is relative with respect to the domain c.

(b) Absolute context.

The numbers u^{min}, u^{max} are derived on the basis of technology, properties of the minerals and many other outer charakterics of the studied system. They are usually given explicitly by the user .

Evaluating terms. In the comments generated by the method presented further we use the so called evaluating terms. By an evaluating term we understand special couples of words of the form

adverb - adjective .

The adverb is one of the following:

- higly,
- very,
- rather

- more or less,
- roughly,

i.e. they are the linguistic modifiers introduced in the fuzzy set theory. We also accept the case when the adverb is missing (in this case, we will sometimes use the term empty modifier).

The adjective is one of the following:

- small,
- average,
- big.

They express the basic rough specification of values in the ordered universe (in our case, it is the interval $\langle 0,1 \rangle$). We will often refer to them as to the atomic terms. The modifiers induce an ordering of evaluating terms. Let $\prec$ denote this ordering and $\mathcal{A}$ be an atomic term. Then we have

$$\text{highly } \mathcal{A} \prec \text{very } \mathcal{A} \prec \text{rather } \mathcal{A} \prec \mathcal{A} \prec$$
$$\prec \text{more or less } \mathcal{A} \prec \text{roughly } \mathcal{A}$$

(in the case of $\mathcal{A}$ = "average" we omit the modifier highly and very is replaced by purely). Let $\mathcal{A}$, $\mathcal{A}'$ be two evaluating terms. If

$$\mathcal{A} \prec \mathcal{A}'$$

then $\mathcal{A}$ is narrower than $\mathcal{A}'$ and $\mathcal{A}'$ is wider than $\mathcal{A}$. The atomic term small is negative, big is positive, and average is zero.

Let $\mathcal{A}$ be an atomic term. Then its meaning $M(\mathcal{A})$ is a fuzzy set $A \subseteq \langle 0,1 \rangle$. The membership functions of positive, negative, and zero atomic term are denoted by A^+, A^-, A^0 respectively. We will assume that A^+ is S^+ curve, A^- is S^- curve, and A^0 is Π curve (cf. e.g. Esragh and Mamdani, 1979).

The meaning of a linguistic modifier m is a pair of functions

$$M(m) = \langle S_{m,\mathcal{A}}, \nu_m \rangle$$

where $S_{m,\mathcal{A}} : \langle 0,1 \rangle \rightarrow \langle 0,1 \rangle$ and $\nu_m : L \rightarrow L$.
The meaning of an evaluating term $m\,\mathcal{A}$ is a composition of functions

$$M(m\mathcal{A}) = \nu_m \circ A \circ S_{m,\mathcal{A}} .$$

For $L = \langle 0,1 \rangle$ we define:

$$\nu_{highly}(\alpha) = \;^{3}$$
$$\nu_{very}(\alpha) = \alpha^2$$
$$\nu_{rather}(\alpha) = (2\alpha^4 \wedge \alpha^2) \vee (-2\alpha^4 + 4\alpha^2 - 1)$$
$$\nu_{more\ or\ less}(\alpha = 2\alpha - \alpha^2$$
$$\nu_{roughly}(\alpha = -\alpha^4 + 4\alpha^3 - 6\alpha^2 + 4\alpha$$

where $\alpha \in \langle 0,1 \rangle$ and $\vee$, $\wedge$ denote supremum (maximum) and infinum (minimum) respectively. In the sequel, we will suppose that $L = \langle 0,1 \rangle$.

The function $S_{m,\mathcal{A}}$ depends on the atomic term $\mathcal{A}$ and was experimentally derived as follows. Let $\| Ker(A) \|$ be the length of the smallest interval containing the kernel

$$Ker(A) = \{ x;\ Ax = 1 \},$$

and let $s_{\mathcal{A}}$ be a center of this interval. Then

$$S_{rather,\mathcal{A}} = id$$

(identical function) and for m ≠ "rather" we put

$$S_{m,\mathcal{A}}(x) = x + (-1)^k . d . \| Ker(A) \| \qquad (1)$$

where k is given in Table 1.

TABLE 1 values of k in the equation (1)

modifier / atomic term	highly very	more or less roughly
$\mathcal{A}^+$	k = 1	k = 2
$\mathcal{A}^-$	k = 2	k = 1
$\mathcal{A}^o$ and $x \leqq S_{\mathcal{A}}$.	k = 1	k = 2
$\mathcal{A}^o$ and $x > S_{\mathcal{A}}$.	k = 2	k = 1

The number d is assesed to fall in the interval $\langle 0.25, 0.4 \rangle$. It seems to be suitable to put d = 0.25 for m = "very" or m = "more or less", and d= 0.4 otherwise . Of course, other values of d, and even other form of (1) might be found on the basis of deeper study of linguistic modifiers. Some more detailed information on this problem can be found in (Novák, in press).

Principles of choice. In our method, we need some heuristic principles of choice. The most often used principle in the fuzzy set theory is the maximizing principle. We will use it in the following form. Let

$$\mathcal{T} = \left\{ \mathcal{A}_i ;\ i \in I \right\}$$

be a finite of evaluating terms with the meanings $A_i \subseteq U$ and let $x \in U$. Then x is evaluated by such a term $\mathcal{A} \in \mathcal{T}$ which fulfils the equation

$$Ax = \sup \left\{ A_i x ;\ i \in I \right\}.$$

In the case there are more such terms we must use some additional external criterion.

Assume x is evaluatedby a term $\mathcal{A}$. Thenthe evaluation is improved (in the sense of the ordering $_T\!\prec$) using the restricted maximizing principle. Let $\alpha^T \in (0,1\rangle$. Then x is evaluated by the narrowest term $m\mathcal{A} \prec \mathcal{A}$ which fulfils the inequality

$$M(m\mathcal{A})x \geqq Ax \wedge \alpha^T.$$

It is suitable to put $\alpha^T = 0.9$.

Let the support Supp(A) of the fuzzy set A be a finite fuzzy set, Card (Supp(A)) = n. Then the relative cardinality of A is the number

$$Rc(A) = \frac{\sum_{x \in Supp(A)} Ax}{n}$$

Standard relative cardinality of a fuzzy set $A \subseteq \langle 0,1\rangle$ with differentiable membership function is

$$\overline{Rc}\,(A) = \int_{\langle 0,1\rangle} dAx$$

Let $\mathcal{A}_1, \mathcal{A}_2$ be two neighbouring evaluating terms $\mathcal{A}_1 \prec \mathcal{A}_2$. Then

$$Dt(\mathcal{A}_2) = \overline{Rc}(M(\mathcal{A}_2)) - \overline{Rc}(M(\mathcal{A}_1))$$

is a difference of the term $\mathcal{A}_2$.

GENERAL FORM OF THE VERBAL COMMENTS

The verbal comments have simple structure which was proposed on the basis of careful analysis of analogous comments of the results of mathematical modelling given by man. We present three basic types of comments which cover the main kinds of overall statements about the results. They are supposed to help the user to obtain a general picture about the situation and to focus only on the most interesting things.

Evaluation of the Maguitude of the Results

This comment gives an overall information about the maguitude of all the values in the given domain. It has the following structure:

> In the domain < name of the domain > there prevails
> < evaluating term > < name of the charakteristics>
> [there is, however, also < evaluating term >
> <charakteristics >]

where the part in the square brackets needs not be present.

Generation of the comment. Given the domain U_c and denote $x = NVal(u)$, $u \in U$. We construct fuzzy sets $C_{m,1}$, $C_{m,2}$, $C_{m,3}$ determined by the membership functions

$$C_{m,1}u = M(m\ small)x \wedge U_c u$$

$$C_{m,2}u = M(m\ average)x \wedge U_c u$$

$$C_{m,3}u = M(m\ big)x \wedge U_c u$$

for each linguistic modifier m and $u \in U$. These fuzzy sets express the judgement of the values of the elements $u \in U$ in the given (fuzzy) domain U_c from the point of view of the respective evaluating terms.

Since we want to generate the comment as exact as possible we look for the narrowest term in the sense of the ordering $\prec$. For each atomic term small, average, big we start with the narrowest modifier and choose a wider modifier only in the case that

$$Rc(C_{m^2,i}) > Rc(C_{m^1,i}) + Dt(m^2\mathcal{A}) \qquad (2)$$

holds true where $i=1,2,3$, $\mathcal{A}$ is the corresponding atomic term and $m^1\mathcal{A} \prec m^2\mathcal{A}$. It means that we choose the last evaluating term $m\mathcal{A}$ for which (2) still holds true.

Let the terms m^1 small, m^2 average, m^3 big have been chosen on the basis of the above mentioned procedure. We construct the fuzzy set

$$D = C_{m^1,1} \cup C_{m^2,2} \cup C_{m^3,3}$$

and the fuzzy sets

$$C'_{m^1,1} = D - C_{m^1,1}$$

$$C'_{m^2,2} = D - C_{m^2,2} \qquad (3)$$

$$C'_{m^3,3} = D - C_{m^3,3} \,.$$

We choose the term $m^j \mathcal{A}$ for which the relative cardinality

$$Rc(C'_{m^j,i}),\ j = 1,2,3\ ,\ i = 1,2,3 \qquad (4)$$

is the smallest one. Then we generate the comment

<u>In the domain c there prevails m $\mathcal{A}$ <name of the charakteristics></u>

The additional part of the comment is generated analogously on the basis of the fuzzy sets $C'_{m^j,i}$.

<u>Example 1.</u>
Given the non-fuzzy domain <u>hanging wall</u> with the charakteristics <u>shearing stress</u> as follows

2.6	3.9	5.7	2.9
3.5	3.1	12.1	7.6
2.7	1.7	5.9	10.2

Let the absolute context be given by $u^{min} = 2$ and $u^{max} = 15$. Using the above described procedure we find the fuzzy sets (3) for the narrowest evaluating terms as follows:

<u>rather small</u>

0	0	.36	.007
0	0	.77	.979
0	0	.155	.68

<u>average</u>

1	.92	.37	.997
.96	.99	.71	0
1	1	0	0

<u>big</u>

1	.92	.58	.997
.96	.99	0	.975
1	1	.28	.975

The cells contain resulting membership degrees. The membership functions of the terms <u>small</u>, <u>average</u>, <u>big</u> have been chosen to be the six-parameters curves presented in (Novák, in press) with the parametrs estimated according to the best intuition.
The relative cardinalities (4) are

$$Rc\ (C'_{rather,1}) = 0.246$$

$Rc\ (C_2') = 0.66$
$Rc\ (C_3') = 0.758.$

Since the smallest relative cardinality is for the term rather small, we generate the comment

In the domain hanging wall there prevails rather small shearing stress

Comments on Distribution of the Values of the Results

We will present the method for generating two comments which characterize the distribution of the values in the given domain U_c.

The first comment has the form

The < name of the charakteristics > is < modifier > monotonously distributed in the domain < name of the domain >

Given the domain U_c, Card $(Supp(U_c)) = u$. Let us partition the interval $< 0,1 >$ into p classes $d_1, \ldots, d_p$ and assume the values $x = NVal(u)$, $u \in Supp(U_c)$ fall into s different classes d_i and in each class there are m_i values x, $i = 1,2,\ldots,s$. We find the longest connected interval of the classes d_{j_k}, $k = 1,\ldots,q$ such that $m_{j_k} \neq 0$ holds for each k and

$$\sum_{k=1}^{q} m_{j_k} \quad \text{is maximal.}$$

Set

$$r = \frac{\sum_{k=1}^{q} m_{j_k}}{n}$$

$$t = \frac{s}{z \cdot q \cdot p}$$

where $z > 1$ is a constant close to 1.

Using the maximizing principle we determine, if r is big or average and using the restricted maximizing principle we find the narrowest modifier suitable to one of these atomic terms.

Analogously we decide whether t is small. Then, on the basis of the following heuristically defined table, we determinne the modifier suitable to the atomic term monotone.

TABLE 2 Choosing a Linguistic Modifier

modifier	r	t
very	very big highly big	very small highly small
rather	rather big	rather small
-	big	small
more or less	more or less big	more or less small
roughly	average	average

The items of the table contain the worst values (in the sense of the ordering $\prec$) acceptable for choosing the correspon- ding modifier.

Example 2.

Let the shearing stress in the domain hanging wall be as follows:

10.8	12.1	9.5	10.9
12.6	13.8	10.3	10.5
10.7	9.8	10.1	11.7

The context is relative. We choose the partition of the interval $\langle 0,1 \rangle$ into 10 subintervals $\langle 0, 0.1 \rangle$, $(0.1, 0.2 \rangle ,\ldots,(0.9, 1 \rangle$. Then we obtain

$$r = 0.66$$

and

$$t = \frac{7}{z.4.10} = 0.16$$

for z = 1.1. According to the above procedure we evaluate r by the term <u>more or less big</u> and t by the term <u>small</u>. Then, on the basis of the Table 2 we generate the comment

<u>The shearing stress is more or less monotonously distributed in the domain hanging wall</u>

The second comment has the form:

There are < number > < locality > of < evaluating term > <name of the charakteristics> in the domain < name of the domain >

This comment helps the user to find the places of concentration of some chosen (usually big) values of the given charakteristics in the domain U_c. It is accompanied by a picture representation of the discovered localities.

Let the evaluating term m $\mathscr{A}$ be given. We put to zero all the elements $x = NVal(u)$, $u \in Supp(U_c)$ for which

$$(mA)x \neq \sup \left\{ A'x;\ A' = M(\mathscr{A}) \text{ for all evaluating terms } \mathscr{A} \right\} \tag{5}$$

holds true. Thus, only those values $x = N\,Val(u)$, $u \in Supp(U_c)$ are non-zero which are distingnished with respect to the evaluation by the term m $\mathscr{A}$.

Now we find all the localities in $Supp(U_c)$ with non-zero values x. Two localities are different if there is no non-zero element common to both of them. Let the number of elements in the locality be m and $n = Card\,(Supp(U_c))$. Then

$$v = \frac{m}{n} \tag{6}$$

is the relative number of elements in the locality.

We use three kinds of names of the localities:

$\mathscr{A}_f$ - focus

$\mathscr{A}_d$ - mean domain

$\mathscr{A}_b$ - big domain

Some of them can be made narrower using the linguistic modifiers. Then we use the following synonyms

highly $\mathscr{A}_f$ = very small focus

very $\mathscr{A}_f$ = small focus

highly $\mathscr{A}_b$ = extensive domain

very $\mathscr{A}_b$ = extensive domain

A suitable name of the locality is found on the basis of v in (6) using the maximiring and restricted maximizing principles.

Example 3.

Let the values in the domain from Example 1 be distributed as follows:

4.2	7.1	5	4.6
3.1	12.5	14.7	10.2
5.7	8.1	7.9	3.5

We want to find the localities of big shearing stress.

After the normalization and using (6) we obtain

0	0	0	0
0	0.81	1	0
0	0	0	0

The discovered locality is marked by the circle. We have m=2, n=12 and on the basis of the above procedure we generate the comment.

There is 1 focus the big shearing stress in the domain hanging wall

RESULTS OF EXPERIMENTS AND FUTURE DEVELOPMENTS

The procedures described above have been implemented on HP 9845. The comments concern the results of mathematical modelling of stress situation in the surroundings of the caved coal seam. The task is solved using the theory of linear elasticity in two dimensions and the numerical results are obtained using the finite element method. The system is capable to solve effectively about 6 000 linear equations. The user can choose from 9 various scalar charakteristics decribing the stress situation. When realizing that we always compute more variants of the model, we see that the user must do much labour to interpret the results as exhaustively as possible.

The systemfor generation of verbal comments to the results of mathematical modelling seems to be very promissing, expecially when combined with graphical representation. The experiences show that the comments are quite in accordance with intuition. Of course, in details may the oppinions of man and computer differ. The computer represents an average man. The content of the comments depend on the parameters of the used membership functions and other heuristically determined finenesses of the above described procedures (cf. eg. Table 2.). On the other side, the methods appear to be very robust with respect to slight changes of the parametrs and the results on input. This is, in our oppinion, an important property of the vagueness of natural language. It can also be considered as experimental proof that fuzzy sets can be effectively used for this purpose.

There is, however, still much work to be done . The repertoire of the comments is fairly poor and it should be extended to grasp more finenesses of the real situation and to meet the user's language more properly. However. this will lead to more detailed linguistic analysis. We also prepare the comments which express the mutual comparison of two variants. From the point of the user, comments of this kind will be even more useful but the problem is more complicated.

Such a system is the first step to the sofisticated system of artificial intelligence which will imitate human reasoning when interpreting the complex model covering both mathematical model and practical experience, and which will be capable to process also the data which are non-numerical in nature (for example,"the mineral is covered by small fissure creeks", "the wall is crumbling"etc.). We are convinced that fuzzy sets are quite suitable tool for this purpose.

REFERENCES

Dostál, Z. and others (1985). The Research of Numerical Methods and Mathematical Modelling for Solution of Stress States in a Rock Massive. Mining Institute of the Czechoslovak Academy of Sciences, Ostrava (in Czech).

Esragh, F. and Mamdami, E. H. (1979). A General Approach to Linguistic Approximation. Int. J. Man-Mach. Stud.,11, 501 - 519.

Novák, V. (in press). Fuzzy Sets and Their Applications . Adam Hilger, Bristol.

Novák, V. (1984). A note on linguistic hedges and the hedge "very". BUSEFAL 19, Univ. Paul Sabatier, Toulouse.

Zadeh, L. A. (1973). Outline of a new approach to the analysis of complex systems and decision processes. IEEE Trans. Syst. Man. & Cybern. 1, 28 - 44.

Portfolio Analysis Using Possibility Distributions

J. J. BUCKLEY

Mathematics Department, University of Alabama at Birmingham, Birmingham, AL 35294, USA

ABSTRACT

This paper considers the important problem in finance of ranking investment proposals, characterized by uncertain future cash flows, project duration and interest rates, from best to worst. Uncertainty is modeled by possibility distributions defined by fuzzy numbers or discrete fuzzy sets. Using the concepts of conditional, joint and marginal possibility distributions we compute one possibility distribution, representing average net present value, for each project. The proposals are then ranked producing a set of undominated projects all considered equally best.

KEYWORDS

Finance, Possibility Distribution, Net Present Value, Fuzzy Numbers.

INTRODUCTION

The purpose of this paper is to show how possibility distributions may be used to solve an important problem in finance. Quite often in finance future cash amounts and interest rates must be estimated. One usually employs educated guesses, based on expected values or other statistical techniques, to obtain future cash flows resulting from some investment, and future interest rates. Statements like "approximately between $22,000 and $26,000" must be translated into an exact amount, such as $24,000, before input into a financial formula. That is, financial calculations use real numbers and not fuzzy numbers. Possibility distributions, modeled as fuzzy numbers, can be used to capture the vagueness of "approximately between $22,000 and $26,000". This paper develops an alternative to having to use exact amounts for interest rates, cash amounts and time periods in financial calculations.

We will be using compound interest and not simple interest. Interest rates are usually quoted as some percent per year and then converted to the correct decimal rate per interest period. For example, 12% per year compounded quarterly becomes 12/(4)(100) = 0.03 per quarter. We will always assume that r is the interest rate, as a decimal, per interest period.

Throughout this paper we will place a bar over a symbol if it represents a fuzzy set. Therefore, $\bar{A}$, $\bar{S}$, $\bar{r}$, $\bar{n}$, etc. are all fuzzy sets. The membership functions for these fuzzy sets will be denoted by $\mu(x|\bar{A})$, $\mu(x|\bar{S})$, $\mu(x|\bar{r})$, $\mu(x|\bar{n})$, etc. A fuzzy number $\bar{M}$ is a special fuzzy subset of the real numbers. Its membership function is defined by

$$\mu(x|\bar{M}) = \left(m_1, f_1(y|\bar{M})/m_2, m_3/f_2(y|\bar{M}), m_4\right), \tag{1}$$

where: (1) $m_1 < m_2 \le m_3 < m_4$; (2) $x = f_1(y|\bar{M})$ is a continuous monotone increasing function of y for $0 \le y \le 1$ with $f_1(0|\bar{M}) = m_1$ and $f_1(1|\bar{M}) = m_2$; and (3) $x = f_2(y|\bar{M})$ is a continuous monotone decreasing function of y for $0 \le y \le 1$ with $f_2(0|\bar{M}) = m_4$ and $f_2(1|\bar{M}) = m_3$. In order to discuss the graph of $y = \mu(x|\bar{M})$ let us assume that the x-axis is horizontal and the y-axis is vertical. Then the graph of $y = \mu(x|\bar{M})$ is: (1) zero for $x \le m_1$; (2) $x = f_1(y|\bar{M})$ for $0 \le y \le 1$; (3) one for $m_2 \le x \le m_3$; (4) $x = f_2(y|\bar{M})$ for $0 \le y \le 1$; and (5) zero for $x \ge m_4$. It is convenient in fuzzy number arithmetic to have x a function of y on $[m_1, m_2]$ and $[m_3, m_4]$. We will say that $\bar{M}$ is positive if $m_1 \ge 0$ and $\bar{M}$ is negative whenever $m_4 \le 0$. We may employ straight line segments for $y = \mu(x|\bar{M})$ on $[m_1, m_2]$ and $[m_3, m_4]$ and then

$$\begin{aligned} x &= f_1(y|\bar{M}) = (m_2 - m_1)y + m_1, \\ x &= f_2(y|\bar{M}) = (m_3 - m_4)y + m_4, \end{aligned} \tag{2}$$

for $0 \le y \le 1$. In this case we denote $\mu(x|\bar{M})$ simply as $(m_1/m_2, m_3/m_4)$. These fuzzy numbers are easy to use and their interpretations are also easily explained to people not knowledgeable in fuzzy set theory. For example, "around \$12,000" could be represented by (10,000/12,000, 12,000/14,000), a triangular fuzzy number and "approximately between \$22,000 and \$26,000" might be expressed as (20,000/22,000, 26,000/28,000), a trapezoidal fuzzy number. We will use the standard arithmetic of fuzzy numbers (Dubois and Prade, 1980, chapter 2). Addition and multiplication of fuzzy numbers will be written as $\oplus$ and $\odot$, respectively. We will also employ the technique presented in Buckley (1985a, 1985b) to rank fuzzy sets. We will always assume future cash amounts and interest rates are fuzzy, however crisp data is also acceptable. A real number M is a special fuzzy number where $\mu(x|M) = 1$ if and only if $x = M$ and it is zero otherwise. Therefore, real numbers $M, N, \cdots$ will be written as (special) fuzzy numbers $\bar{M}, \bar{N}, \cdots$.

A cash amount in the present is denoted by A, the interest rate per period is r, the number of interest periods is n, and the equivalent cash amount after n periods is S. Their fuzzy analogues are $\bar{A}$, $\bar{r}$, $\bar{n}$, and $\bar{S}$. $\bar{A}$, $\bar{r}$, and $\bar{S}$ are possibility distributions defined by fuzzy numbers but $\bar{n}$ is a discrete possibility distribution. The membership function $\mu(x|\bar{n})$ is defined by a collection of positive integers n_i, $1 \le i \le K$, where $\mu(n_i|\bar{n}) = \lambda_i$, $0 < \lambda_i \le 1$, for $1 \le i \le K$, and $\mu(x|\bar{n}) = 0$ otherwise. The value λ_i is then the possibility that the number of interest periods is n_i. Also, $\mu(x|\bar{r})$ gives the possibility that the interest rate is x. The algebra of possibility distributions follows from the extension principle. If Π_i, $1 \leq i \leq n$, are possibility distributions and $F: R^n \to R$, then the possibility distribution $\Pi = F(\Pi_1, \cdots, \Pi_n)$ is defined from the extension principle. The algebra of possibility distributions is therefore much easier than the algebra of probability distributions. All our possibility distributions will be normalized and hence may be used to define possibility measures (Banon, 1981; Dubois and Prade, 1983).

The fuzzification of the elementary mathematics of finance has been initiated in Buckley (1986), and in the next section we will briefly review the results needed in the remainder of the paper. The financial problem to be studied is presented in the third section followed by our solution in the fourth section. The last section contains a brief summary and our conclusions.

BACKGROUND

What is needed in the next two sections is the fuzzification of the present value $PV(S)$ of a cash amount S, n periods in the future, if the interest rate per period is r. $PV(S)$ is that amount, if invested today at rate r, that will accumulate to S in n periods. Therefore

$$PV(S)(1 + r)^n = S, \quad (3)$$

or equivalently (in non-fuzzy mathematics)

$$PV(S) = S(1 + r)^{-n}. \quad (4)$$

We will define $PV(\bar{S},n)$ as the present value of a fuzzy amount $\bar{S}$, n (crisp) periods in the future, if the fuzzy interest rate is $\bar{r}$, a positive fuzzy number, per period. We will require two definitions of $PV(\bar{S},n)$: one for positive $\bar{S}$; and one for negative $\bar{S}$.

<u>Definition 1</u>

$PV_1(\bar{S},n) = \bar{A}$ if and only if $\bar{A} \odot (1 \oplus \bar{r})^n = \bar{S}$.

<u>Definition 2</u>

$PV_2(\bar{S},n) = \bar{A}$ if and only if $\bar{A} = \bar{S} \odot (1 \oplus \bar{r})^{-n}$.

The membership function for $PV_1(\bar{S},n)$ is defined by

$$f_i(y|\bar{A}) = f_i(y|\bar{S})[1 + f_i(y|\bar{r})]^{-n}, \quad (5)$$

for $i = 1,2$ and $a_1 = f_1(0|\bar{A})$, $a_2 = f_1(1|\bar{A})$, $a_3 = f_2(1|\bar{A})$, $a_4 = f_2(0|\bar{A})$. The membership function for $PV_2(\bar{S},n)$ is determined from

$$f_i(y|\bar{A}) = f_i(y|\bar{S})[1 + f_{3-i}(y|\bar{r})]^{-n}, \quad (6)$$

for $i = 1,2$ and $a_1 = f_1(0|\bar{A})$, $a_2 = f_1(1|\bar{A})$, $a_3 = f_2(1|\bar{A})$, $a_4 = f_2(0|\bar{A})$. The possibility distributions $PV_i(\bar{S},n)$ will not exist if it turns out from equations (5) or (6) that $a_3 < a_2$, or $f_1(y|\bar{A})$ is not increasing, or $f_2(y|\bar{A})$ is not decreasing.

Theorem 1 (Buckley, 1986)

1. If $\bar{S}$ is negative, then $PV_1(\bar{S},n)$ exists as a negative fuzzy number. Otherwise, $PV_1(\bar{S},n)$ may not exist.
2. If $\bar{S}$ is positive, then $PV_2(\bar{S},n)$ exists as a positive fuzzy number. Otherwise, $PV_2(\bar{S},n)$ may not exist.

For the rest of this paper we will use $PV_1(\bar{S},n)$ if $\bar{S}$ is negative and $PV_2(\bar{S},n)$ when $\bar{S}$ is positive.

Suppose E is a non-fuzzy (crisp) subset of the real numbers and let $\mu(x|\bar{S},n)$ be the membership function for $PV_1(\bar{S},n)$ or $PV_2(\bar{S},n)$. Then (Zadeh, 1978, 1981)

$$\text{Poss}[E] = \sup\{\mu(x|\bar{S},n) \mid x \in E\} \tag{7}$$

is the possibility of E. Poss[E] is the possibility of event E when the possibility of the elementary events is given by $\mu(x|\bar{S},n)$. For example, if $E = [1000, +\infty)$, then Poss[E] would be the possibility that the present value of $\bar{S}$ is at least $1,000. In this way the possibility distributions $PV_i(\bar{S},n)$ can be used to define possibility measures.

THE PROBLEM

The financial problem is to rank investment alternatives, defined by uncertain cash flows, durations and interest rates, from "best" to "worst". A commonly used method of comparing mutually exclusive investment alternatives is net present value (NPV). Let $A = A_0, \cdots, A_n$ be a given, or estimated, net cash flow of a proposed investment project over n periods. If an $A_i < 0$, then $-A_i$ is the net investment (total investment minus total return) made in the project at the end of the ith period. If $A_i > 0$, then A_i is the net return (total return minus total investment) from the project at the end of the ith period. We assume that $A_0 < 0$ because this is an investment project that always starts off with an initial investment.

In the NPV method one finds the present value of all future net returns discounted at the appropriate cost of capital to the firm (r), minus any initial cash outlays. Therefore, the NPV of the cash flow A is

$$NPV(A,n) = A_0 + \sum_{i=1}^{n} A_i(1 + r)^{-i}. \tag{8}$$

If we have a number of investment proposals under consideration with cash flows $A, B, \cdots$, then one ranks those proposals with $NPV > 0$ from highest NPV to lowest NPV and selects investments in that order until the investment capital of the firm is exhausted. At first glance this procedure appears sound, but do not forget that all future cash flows have to be estimated and the interest rate r to be used may also be estimated.

Therefore, we now consider a fuzzy net cash flow $\bar{A} = \bar{A}_0, \cdots, \bar{A}_n$ with $\bar{r}$ the fuzzy interest rate representing the cost of capital to the firm. We have assumed that the duration n of the project is known with certainty and later we will allow n to be fuzzy. $\bar{A}_0$ is a negative fuzzy number, the other $\bar{A}_i$ can be positive or negative fuzzy numbers and $\bar{r}$ is a positive fuzzy number. The fuzzy net present value of $\bar{A}$ is

$$NPV(\bar{A},n) = \bar{A}_0 \oplus \sum_{i=1}^{n} PV_{k(i)}(\bar{A}_i, i), \tag{9}$$

where $\sum$ is fuzzy addition and $k(i) = 1$ when $\bar{A}_i$ is negative, $k(i) = 2$ if $\bar{A}_i$ is positive.

It is shown in Buckley (1986) that the possibility distribution $NPV(\bar{A},n)$ is actually easy to compute using equations (5) and (6). If the termination date for a project is not known precisely, then we need another approach to find its net present value.

Let $\bar{n}$ denote the duration for the project $\bar{A}$. We assume that $\bar{n}$ is normalized (some $\lambda_i = 1$). If $NPV(\bar{A})$ is this project's net present value, then its membership function is given by

$$\mu(x|\bar{A}) = \max_{1 \leq i \leq K} \left(\min\left(\mu(x|\bar{A},n_i), \lambda_i\right)\right), \tag{10}$$

where $\mu(x|\bar{A},n_i)$ is the membership function for $NPV(\bar{A},n_i)$.

In Buckley (1986) the extension principle was used to derive $\mu(x|\bar{A})$ when $\bar{n}$ is fuzzy, and there it was shown that equation (10) is true if all $\bar{A}_i$, $i \geq 1$, are positive. We will now define the possibility distribution $NPV(\bar{A})$ by equation (10) even when some $\bar{A}_i$ are negative. Our reasoning for doing this is based on the fact that $NPV(\bar{A},n_i)$ and $\bar{n}$ are possibility distributions. $NPV(\bar{A},n_i)$ is a conditional possibility distribution given $n = n_i$. Since $\bar{n}$ is a possibility distribution, if we first determine the joint possibility distribution of $NPV(\bar{A})$ and $\bar{n}$, and then project onto $NPV(\bar{A})$ to obtain the marginal possibility distribution, we obtain the expression in equation (10) (Zadeh, 1978, 1981). Notice that $NPV(\bar{A})$ may not be a fuzzy number because $y = \mu(x|\bar{A})$ may be increasing, or decreasing, on a number of disjoint intervals. The possibility distributions $NPV(\bar{A},n)$ and $NPV(\bar{A})$ may be used to define possibility measures on subsets of the real numbers.

The firm is not sure what the future holds in terms of interest rates so they wish to consider a number of possibilities $\bar{r}_\ell$, $1 \le \ell \le L$. The firm also obtains, through expert opinion or otherwise, a possibility distribution for the fuzzy interest rates given by $\mu(\bar{r}_\ell) = \alpha_\ell$, $0 < \alpha_\ell \le 1$, for $1 \le \ell \le L$ and $\mu(\bar{r})$ is zero otherwise. We also assume that this possibility distribution is normalized so that some α_ℓ equals one.

This financial problem may be summarized as follows: given proposals $\bar{A},\bar{B},\cdots$, some with uncertain termination dates, and given possible interest rates $\bar{r}_\ell$, determine the best projects using the net present value concept.

SOLUTION

This financial problem is a classical decision problem which may be described by a decision matrix. Let the rows be labeled by the proposals $\bar{A},\bar{B},\cdots$ and the columns by the interest rates $\bar{r}_\ell$. The entree in the $(\bar{B},\bar{r}_\ell)$ cell is $NPV_\ell(\bar{B},n_b)$ if the duration is known to be n_b, or $NPV_\ell(\bar{B})$ if the termination date is uncertain. We also have possibilities associated with the columns. The firm must choose some projects without knowing the correct state of nature (the $\bar{r}_\ell$).

Using the possibilities α_ℓ we can "average" across the states $\bar{r}_\ell$ to obtain one possibility distribution for each proposal. For proposal $\bar{A}$, the average net present value will be denoted by $\overline{NPV}(\bar{A},n_a)$ if the duration is known to be n_a periods and by $\overline{NPV}(\bar{A})$ if it has uncertain duration. Let $\mu_\ell(x|\bar{A},n_a)$ and $\mu_\ell(x|\bar{A})$ be the membership functions for $NPV_\ell(\bar{A},n_a)$ and $NPV_\ell(\bar{A})$, respectively. In $NPV_\ell(\bar{A},n_a)$, or $NPV_\ell(\bar{A})$, it is assumed that $\bar{r} = \bar{r}_\ell$. The average net present value is specified by the membership functions

$$\theta(x|\bar{A},n_a) = \max_{1\le\ell\le L} \left(\min\left(\mu_\ell(x|\bar{A},n_a),\alpha_\ell\right)\right),$$

or (11)

$$\theta(x|\bar{A}) = \max_{1\le\ell\le L} \left(\min\left(\mu_\ell(x|\bar{A}),\alpha_\ell\right)\right).$$

Similarly, we compute the average net present value for all projects. The possibility distribution $\overline{NPV}(\bar{A},n_a)$, or $\overline{NPV}(\bar{A})$, defines a possibility measure on the subsets of the real numbers. For example, let $E = (0, +\infty)$. The possibility that the net present value, averaged across all uncertain interest rates, of project $\bar{A}$ with uncertain duration, is positive is

$$\text{Poss}[E] = \sup\{\theta(x|\bar{A}) \mid x > 0\}. \quad (12)$$

The reasoning in employing equation (11) in defining average net present value is the same as that used in employing equation (10) for net present value. $NPV_\ell(\bar{A},n_a)$, or $NPV_\ell(\bar{A})$, is a conditional possibility distribution given $\bar{r} = \bar{r}_\ell$. If we first find the joint possibility distribution and then project onto $\overline{NPV}(\bar{A},n_a)$, or $\overline{NPV}(\bar{A})$, we obtain equation (11).

We next must discard any project whose average net present value is not greater than zero. Let $\bar{G}$ be some fuzzy set considered by the firm to represent "greater than zero". The firm might accept $\mu(x|\bar{G}) = (1000/5000, +\infty/+\infty)$, where it equals one for all $x \geq 5000$, as a suitable statement of "greater than zero". Project $\bar{A}$ is discarded unless

$$\mathrm{Poss}[\bar{G}] = 1, \tag{13}$$

where (Zadeh, 1978, 1981)

$$\mathrm{Poss}[\bar{G}] = \sup_x \left(\min\left(\mu(x|\bar{G}),\theta(x|\bar{A},n_a)\right)\right). \tag{14}$$

We would use $\theta(x|\bar{A})$ for $\theta(x|\bar{A},n_a)$ if the duration of the project is uncertain.

After the test described by equation (13) is performed, suppose the remaining proposals are $\bar{A},\bar{B},\cdots$. We now rank the fuzzy sets $\overline{NPV}(A,n_a)$ $\left(\text{or } \overline{NPV}(\bar{A})\right)$, $\overline{NPV}(\bar{B},n_b)$ $\left(\text{or } \overline{NPV}(\bar{B})\right),\cdots$ as described in Buckley (1985a, 1985b) obtaining a partition of the remaining projects into sets $H_1,H_2,\cdots$. The set H_1 contains all the undominated projects and they are all ranked highest, or equally best. The next set H_2 contains all the undominated proposals after those in H_1 have been deleted.

The solution procedure might look very complicated but the whole method can be handled on a personal computer. Color graphics can be used to display the possibility distributions associated with the highest ranked proposals in H_1 for visual comparison.

SUMMARY AND CONCLUSIONS

In this paper we developed a new procedure for ranking investment proposals, characterized by uncertain cash flows, durations and interest rates, based on the net present value concept. The uncertainty in future cash flows and interest rates was modeled by possibility distributions defined by fuzzy numbers. The uncertainty in the termination date of a project was modeled by a discrete possibility distribution. Using these possibility distributions, we defined a possibility distribution for the net present value of a project. We also considered multiple states of nature given by different uncertain interest rates and a possibility distribution over these states of nature. Using the possibility distribution over the states of nature, we determined the average net present value possibility distribution for each proposal. The projects are then ranked, after those whose average net present value does not exceed zero are discarded, to obtain a collection of undominated proposals all considered equally best.

The whole solution method may be handled on a personal computer using color graphics to display the possibility distributions associated with the highest ranked projects. Other financial problems which employ probability distributions and random variables may also be modeled using possibility distributions. It is impossible to judge which model is best without studying the exact problem and the type of data that goes into the problem. However, the mathematical manipulations necessary to obtain a final solution might be easier using possibility than using probability.

REFERENCES

Banon, G. (1981). Distinction between Several Subsets of Fuzzy Measures. *Fuzzy Sets and Systems*, 5, 291-305.

Buckley, J. J. (1985a). Ranking Alternatives Using Fuzzy Numbers. *Fuzzy Sets and Systems*, 15, 21-31.

Buckley, J. J. (1985b). Fuzzy Hierarchical Analysis. *Fuzzy Sets and Systems*, 17, 233-247.

Buckley, J. J. (to appear). The Fuzzy Mathematics of Finance. *Fuzzy Sets and Systems.*

Dubois, D., and H. Prade (1980). *Fuzzy Sets and Systems.* Academic Press, New York.

Dubois, D., and H. Prade (1983). Ranking Fuzzy Numbers in the Setting of Possibility Theory. *Information Sciences*, 30, 183-244.

Zadeh, L. A. (1978). Fuzzy Sets as a Basis for a Theory of Possibility. *Fuzzy Sets and Systems*, 1, 3-28.

Zadeh, L. A. (1981). In L. Cobb and R. M. Thrall (Eds.), *Mathematical Frontiers of the Social and Policy Sciences.* Westview Press, Boulder, Colorado. pp. 69-129.

A Fuzzy Decision Support System for Strategic Planning

N. GREEN HALL

School of Business and Economics, Mercer University, 3001 Mercer University Dr., Atlanta, GA 30341, USA

ABSTRACT

Decision scientists seeking to devise decision aids for strategic managers have been hampered by problems associated with the non-quantitative nature of some decision variables and the impossibility of precisely measuring future events. STRATASSIST is a recent application of fuzzy math technology to decision support which has been tested with good results. This prototype fuzzy DSS assembles a data base of natural language values for input to a fuzzy expert system which generates possible strategies for the strategic planned to consider. Subjects using STRATASSIST developed strategic plans which were judged to be superior to those produced in the control groups. This supports implementation and further development of the DSS.

KEYWORDS

Decision support system; fuzzy expert system; strategic planning; natural language values; qualitative variables.

INTRODUCTION

Planning is widely recognized as one of the basic functions of managers. Designing the long range activities of a firm, or strategic planning, is an important responsibility of senior managers. Business firms today face many challenges. As Ansoff (1979, p.35) observes, "..a major escalation of environmental turbulence....has meant a change from a familiar world of marketing and production to an unfamiliar world of strange technologies, strange competitors, new consumer attitudes, new dimensions of social control..." Managers must defend the profitability of their firms by developing new products, exploring new markets, and turning problems into opportunities in order to ensure the long run survival of their organization. Furthermore, "...the birth and death of key ideas, that is of good strategies, must be expected to occur with much greater frequency than it has in the past under these new, dynamic, and interdependent environmental conditions." (Schendel and Hofer, 1979, p.7) Thus, planning managers are forced to solve an increasingly complex and ill-defined problem which recurs at an ever increasing rate. Strategic decision makers need assistance with this important job.

Challenge of Strategic Planning to DSS

Decision science develops methods to improve the quality of decisions made by people at all levels of organizations. Traditionally, applications of decision theory and developments in analytical techniques have been heavily quantitative in orientation. Particularly in the area of computerized assistance for decision making, we have focused on matters which involve measurable variables. Techniques such as linear programming and regression analysis have contributed to the decision process in organizations, especially at the operations level. In this part of the organization the problems one faces tend to be fairly well-structured and generally involve variables which can be counted, weighed, or otherwise quantified.

At the strategic apex of an organization, the situation is complicated by pressures from the environment. Not only are more variables outside the control of the manager, but the nature of their relationships may be unknown or more complex. In addition, many of the variables that a strategic manager must examine are difficult to quantify. It is possible to measure market share and express it as percent of the whole market in industries where the product or service is well standardized, but how can one use a number to characterize the overall competitive position of a firm? In addition to market share, this feature includes such aspects as the firm's reputation and the nature of its distribution channels. One may qualify them with words such as "strong" or "weak" without compromising accuracy, but to assign a quantitative value would be both arbitrary and artificial.

Even in those instances in which a number is available, such as net profit for the year, a qualifier such as "high" may actually convey better information than the dollar amount, unless two firms to be compared are the same size and in the same industry. A difference in size can be surmounted by expressing net profit as a percent of sales but the comparison may be without merit still because financial ratios are highly context dependent. A ratio that reflects good performance in one industry or market may reflect only mediocre performance in another. Why not step up another level of abstraction to descriptors such as "high" or "low" which can characterize the number in its total context and give us an accurate, if somewhat vague, summary of its meaning? The human mind has long been accustomed to processing this type of information and using it to make decisions.

The complexity of the strategic environment and the non-quantitative nature of some strategic information have impeded progress in designing and building aids to the strategic decision process. Managers must still rely heavily on informed judgement and intuition for the selection of strategies for their firms. Unfortunately, experience at the operations level and in middle management does not necessarily prepare a manager to do strategic planning. Since many senior managers have had no formal training in the strategic aspects of planning, either, this is an area in which a fuzzy expert system may be of use. The production rules of such a system could embody the knowledge of experts in this area and thus fill the role of a pseudo-consultant which examines the firm and its competitive environment, as described by the manager, and offers some opinions or suggestions (Whalen, 1986). Negoita (1983) argued forcefully for the use of fuzzy DSS in this situation. He emphasized that fuzzy sets technology accomodates professional expertise and judgements and is thus ideally suited to a DSS in an unstructured situation. He identified computer based planning systems as a particularly appropriate area for fuzzy decision support for three reasons: 1) the necessity to deal with values from an uncertain future; 2) the need to incorporate nonfinancial (and thus largely non-quantifiable) aspects of the organization; and 3) the requirement of an interactive relationship between decision maker and computer which would explicitly encompass "...the irreplaceable commodity called 'professional expertise and judgement.' The development of new planning systems able to work with fuzzy parameters offers their users a superb bargain in terms of human effectiveness." (Negoita, 1983,p.32).

Potential for Fuzzy Math Technology in DSS

Recent developments in fuzzy sets theory suggest considerable potential for a DSS which incorporates fuzzy math technology in the use of natural language values for decision variables and a fuzzy expert system which processes these values and outputs some suggested decision alternatives for the strategic planner to consider.

This approach follows from Zadeh, who reasons that, because they are generally less precise than numbers, words are appropriate means to characterize approximately phenomenaa which are too complex or too ill-defined to be amenable to description in conventional quantitative terms (1975). Since these inexact expressions cannot be used by precise algorithms, he suggests ways to model mankind's "fuzzy thinking" which are now called "approximate reasoning" (1972). In classical logic, given the statement that "If $\underline{X}$ is $\underline{A}$, then $\underline{Y}$ is B", when we find that X is indeed A, we can state with confidence that $\overline{Y}$ is B. Unfortunately, if X is not exactly A we can make no statements about Y at all. In approximate reason ing, however, if we find that X is "sort of A", then we can state that Y is "sort of B." The strength of the assertion depends upon the degree to which "sort of A" resembles A and the type of implication relation one uses.

A fuzzy expert system consists of a number of IF...THEN... statements which encapsulate some type of expertise. Such a system can process user-supplied "X is A" descriptions and produce "Y is B" responses which reflect the amount of compatibility between the user description and the expert characterization in the production rule. It is this ability of the fuzzy expert system to reason approximately from imprecise values that makes it peculiarly appropriate to a DSS for strategic planning. As Negoita observes, "Vagueness is not to be eliminated in the process of using a model if we can use a mechanism to model it." (1983,p.31) He further observes that all too often we omit "...admittedly highly significant subjective evaluations..." because of our preoccupation with precise quantification. This view is shared by Channon (1979, p.125) who noted the need to "...take into account less quantifiable socio-political variables which are taking on increasing strategic importance." Is it possible for a fuzzy DSS to use the information available to strategic planners and provide practical assistance leading to better strategic plans for business firms?

A FUZZY DECISION SUPPORT SYSTEM

STRATASSIST is a prototype fuzzy DSS which shows promise of overcoming some of the problems inherent in the strategic planning decision. STRATASSIST is designed for use by small to medium sized firms with predominantly a single product/market. It is programmed for use on an IBM PC or compatible computer. The managers using STRATASSIST may be seasoned planners, but they may also be relatively inexperienced. Many young entrepreneurs are starting their own businesses with a bright idea and a shoestring budget. Since this is where much of our innovation and job creation occurs, these naive managers need all the help they can get to create successful strategies for their firms.

When fully developed, STRATASSIST will consist of an interactive data-acquisition module followed by several data processing modules, including a fuzzy expert system and a color graphics module. Prototypes of the data-acquisition and fuzzy expert system modules are being tested during the initial phase of experimentation. The theoretical framework for both modules is based on Competitive Strategy by Michael Porter (1980).

Description of Prototype

Data-acquisition module. The questions inthe data-acquisition module are organized around the five areas which Porter thinks a firm should consider in connection with its own strengths and weaknesses: threat of new entries, threat of substitutes, buyer group power, supplier group power, and rivalry within the industry. The questions are specific, e.g. "How do you rate the importance of personal service in the distribution of your product?". The decision maker's attention is drawn in a coherent, sequential fashion to potentially important attributes of his firm and its industry.

This aspect of the survey module has a value quite apart from its function in assembling a data base for further processing. Klein (1973) addresses the importance of using a prescriptive method to direct a planing manager's attention to a broad sweep of interactions with the environment as they relate to his firm's products and resources. The danger of selective perception is ever present and may prevent early warning of change if it comes from an unexpected direction.

The system keeps track of the user's responses so that this burden is removed from the manager. Furthermore, the decision maker answers the questions in natural language rather than in precise numbers or ratios. This has the ad= vantages mentioned above plus another, suggested by Whalen (1982), that it may be easier and better in the long run to get a fuzzy set of values from the user and use these values in the analysis rather than first forcing a reluctant user to choose some particular number and later assessing the consequences if that number is inappropriate. As Gaines puts it, "Natural language is not precise in itself but it does 'exactly'express out thoughts." (1976, p.662). There is also a benefit in time and ease of use since most senior managers of a small or medium sized firm can respond quickly and confidently in qualitative terms to questions about the performance of the firm and its competitors, while it might require time and effort to get a more precise value, given that one could be obtained and that it would be meaningful.

The information the survey module of the DSS gathers is stored in the form of a tuple: X, A. The X portion consists of a string such as "importance of personal service in the distribution of your product" from the sample question given above. The A portion is a ten cell vector which contains the Wenstop (1980) translation of the user's response, such as "upper medium" or "very low." Each cell of the vector contains a value from 0 to 1 and the pattern of these values is unique for a specific word or phrase from the list of acceptable responses shown to the user.

Fuzzy expert system module. The data base of tuples assembled by the survey module is processed by the fuzzy expert system module to provide some suggested strategies and strategic actions for the manager to consider. The tested prototype contains 52 production rules which were based on opinions Michael Porter expressed in his book, Competitive Strategy, (1980). Roughly a dozen rules each pertain directly to the three generic strategies in his theory: cost leadership, differentiation, and focus. The remaining rules concern strategic actions which could be used to implement one or another of the broad strategies.

From the user's point of view, the more production rules relating to any one strategy, the better, so that "...multiple weak and individually-fallible chains of reasoning...converge into an accurate solution." (Whalen and Schott, 1983,p.128). This allows the user to weave a strong cord out of many strands. Should one strand prove to be weak or even broken, the integrity of the cord is not greatly impaired. On the other hand, one would require truly compelling evidence to accept that the future of a firm should be directed by the output of a single production rule. The concepts of necessary and sufficient apply here. With a problem as complex as the strategic plan, it would be very unusual that a single attribute of the firm or its competitive environment would be sufficient to completely determine the choice of a strategy to pursue. On the other hand, there are a number of attributes which would be necessary to some degree for the success of a strategy. Even in situations when the firm's characteristics do not match exactly the values Porter uses in his opinions, multiple "near misses" may carry as much weight for the user as a single "direct hit." (Whalen, 1982).

The fuzzy expert system prototype in STRATASSIST functions as follows. Each production rule consists of an "If...then..." statement in the form of "If X is A then Strategy (or Strategic action) should be B." For example, "If the importance of personal service in the distribution of your product is at least more or less high, then strategic action should be distribute firm's product or service through small, flexible, local units." The A value, in this case "more or less high", is stored in the same type of ten cell matrix following Wenstop (1980) that has been described earlier. A production rule is processed by comparing the X string from the left-hand proposition with the X string from each data base item. If the Xs match, the production rule is fired and the two A values are compared by max-min composition of relations.

The scalar resulting from this calculation is a measure of the degree of similarity between the two A values. A 1 represents a match, such as "high" with "high", while a 0 represents no match, "low" with "high", for example. Decimal fractions between 0 and 1 reflect varying degrees of compatibility between the two values. This scalar is reported to the user as a representation of the possibility that the associated strategy or strategic action in the right-hand portion of the production rule is appropriate for the manager's firm.

The fuzzy expert system module prints out the results from processing all its rules with the items arranged in descending order of the possibility ratings. Each rating is accompanied by the associated strategy or strategic action and the firm/environment characteristic which has triggered the rule. The user must then exercise his own judgement to determine how to interpret this information and how to use it in designing a strategy with appropriate strategic actions for his firm.

TESTING THE PROTOTYPE

The STRATASSIST prototype was tested for effectiveness as an aid to decision making during the Spring quarter of 1985 at Georgia State University (Green-Hall, 1985).

Experimental Design and Administration

Experimental subjects. Ninety-nine Georgia State University MBA students participated in the initial trial of the two prototype DSS modules for strategic planning. The students were enrolled in the capstone policy course of the degree program. There were two distinct experience levels in the group. Forty-three were members of the Executive MBA program of Georgia State and fifty-six were members of the regular MBA program. The admission requirements for the two programs, while basically similar, differ in one important respect: a prerequisite for admission to the Executive MBA program is a minimum of ten years' work experience as a manager. Because of this difference, it seemed likely that the Executive MBA group as a whole would have more work experience, especially at management level. If age is an adequate surrogate for work experience, this assumption can be supported because the mean ages of the two groups differ by ten years. This difference in age/experience might have been an important dimension of the experimental problem.

Experimental task. In the place of an actual firm or firms, the researcher selected a policy case Michael Porter had written for use in the policy classes at Harvard University, "Sierra Log Homes." The subjects were given the case a week before they performed their research task with instructions to read it carefully. The task they were subsequently required to perform consisted of playing the role of the strategic planner for the firm in the case and writing a five to seven page statement of what the subject perceived to be the appropriate strategy and associated strategic actions for the firm in the case to pursue. The experiment was conducted during regular class time for both groups and was assigned as part of the course work.

Treatments administered. The subjects were divided into three treatment groups, each of which received a handout of materials which they were to use to assist them in their task. Treatment level A was designed to be a non-treatment or control group and consisted of summaries of Porter's theories which the subjects had studied earlier in the course. Treatment level B contained the prototype of the interactive survey module. This was a series of fifty-two questions designed to acquire descriptions of the specific firm or environment characteristics which appear in the left-hand proposition of the fifty-two production rules in the fuzzy expert system prototype. Each question was answered in accordance with the information contained in the case the subjects were using. Treatment level C included the survey-questionnaire and answers from treatment B and the ordered list of possibility ratings, suggested strategies/strategic actions, and firm/environment cues produced when the fuzzy expert system module processed the information provided by the data-acquisition prototype. The three treatment levels can be viewed as a non-treatment, a partial treatment, and a full treatment, since group C received both prototype modules of STRATASSIST. The treatments were administered double-blind and were spread randomly and equally across the two MBA groups.

Evaluation. The subjects' strategy statements were typed and submitted anonymously in batches of 25 (26) to twelve judges. Each judge's packet contained representative proportions of treatment level and experience level combinations. The twelve assortments were varied as much as possible within this constraint. An individual strategy statement was evaluated by three judges to produce a total of 297 ratings for each of two criteria. The judges used a Likert-type scale of 1 (lowest rating) to 7 (highest rating). Two thirds of the judges circled integers and one third used an accompanying number line, which indicated deciles, in order to rate 4.8 or 5.5, for example. The judges were selected from academia and industry and consisted of professors of business policy from two universities (four judges), managers from the strategic apex of their respective organizations (four judges), planning specialists (three judges), and one management consultant specializing in mergers and acquisitions.

The judges were asked to focus on two criteria, assigning a rating for each. the "FIT" criterion reflected the theoretical concern that a firm should seek the proper fit between its own strengths and weaknesses and the challenges and opportunities of its competitive environment. The judges' instructions on this criterion asked them to consider the following questions. How well does the over-all strategy fit the Sierra Log Home case? Does it address the issues that should be addressed by the CEO? Does it use Sierra's strengths while trying to protect its weaknesses? Does it confront appropriately the challenges and opportunities in Sierra's competitive environment? The "GOOD" criterion asked for a more practical focus on such things as completeness and implementing actions. The instructions for this criterion posed several more questions. How good is the strategy as a whole? Is it complete (not missing any major pieces you expected to see)? Is it internally consistent? How well has the subject fleshed out the broad strategy with appropriate strategic actions?

Research hypothesis. The research hypothesis was that the use of the prototype DSS modules would help the subjects to produce a strategy which the judges would perceive to be better than those strategies the control groups would develop unassisted. A secondary hypothesis was that the Executive MBA subjects as a group would perform better than the regular MBA subjects.

Analysis of Results

The evaluation procedure produced a total of 297 ratings on each of two criteria, distributed across three treatment levels and two experience levels. The experience levels will be referenced as "X" for Executive MBA and "R" for regular MBA. The three treatment levels will be represented by letter as "A", "B", and "C". An experience level/treatment level combination is thus XA for Executive MBA group, treatment level A, for example.

The two sets of 297 ratings were analyzed using SPSS packages (Nie and others, 1975). Results of the ANOVA are given in Tables 1 and 2. The significance of the main effects on both criteria produces a p-value of .03. This is sufficient to indicate that there is something happening to cause the subjects' performance to vary in a systematic fashion, but one must examine the results on the two experimental factors separately in order to determine which is responsible. For the treatment effects the p-value is less than .02 for either criterion, while the experience effect does not achieve statistical significance. Thus, the treatments administered did produce different outcomes for both experience levels that were statistically significant and differences in experience do not appear to influence the subjects' performance in and of themselves.

Interpretation of results. An examination of the cell means in Table 3 and

TABLE 1 Analysis of Variance of Fit Rates

Fitrate by Treatment/Experience

Source Var'tn	Sum of Squares	DF	Mean Square	F	p-Value
M. Eff.	12.508	3	4.169	3.028	.030
Treat.	11.955	2	5.978	4.341	.014
Exper.	.629	1	.629	.457	.500
Int'actn	15.149	2	7.574	5.501	.005
Expl.	27.657	5	5.531	4.017	.002
Resid.	400.678	291	1.377		
Total	428.335	296	1.447		

TABLE 2 Analysis of Variance of Good Rates

Goodrate by Treatment/Experience

Source Var'tn	Sum of Squares	DF	Mean Square	F	p-Value
M. Eff.	13.814	3	4.605	3.011	.030
Treat.	12.442	2	6.221	4.068	.018
Exper.	1.270	1	1.270	.830	.363
Int'actn	15.685	2	7.842	5.128	.006
Expl.	29.499	5	5.900	3.858	.002
Resid.	445.023	291	1.529		
Total	474.522	296	1.603		

Table 4 show that the differences occurred in the predicted direction; that is, that the subjects receiving assistance from the prototype DSS modules (groups B and C) performed better than those not receiving such help. The strong interactions between the treatments and the two experience levels warrant further study. Nevertheless, it does appear that experience alone is not sufficient to prepare managers for the task of strategic planning, and thus their decision making will produce better results when assisted by a DSS.

As pointed out above, the "FIT" criterion was designed to focus the judges' attention on specific, theoretically determined aspects of strategic planning. In this regard, the orientation of the "FIT" criterion was congruent with the thoretical concerns and opinions contained in the fuzzy expert system. One would expect a subject who was influenced by the output of the fuzzy expert system to have addressed the theoretical questions which it

TABLE 3 Cell Means from ANOVA of Fit Rates

Total Population

4.68
(n=297)

Treatment			Experience	
A	B	C	RegMBA	ExMBA
4.40 (n=99)	4.82 (n=99)	4.83 (n=99)	4.72 (n=168)	4.63 (n=129)

		Experience	
		RegMBA	ExMBA
Treatment	A	4.66 (n=57)	4.05 (n=42)
	B	4.60 (n=54)	5.09 (n=45)
	C	4.90 (n=57)	4.73 (n=42)

TABLE 4 Cell Means from ANOVA of Good Rates

Total Population

4.55
(n=297)

Treatment			Experience	
A	B	C	RegMBA	ExMBA
4.26 (n=99)	4.68 (n=99)	4.71 (n=99)	4.40 (n=168)	4.63 (n=129)

		Experience	
		RegMBA	ExMBA
Treatment	A	4.37 (n=57	4.11 (n=42)
	B	4.32 (n=54)	5.10 (n=45)
	C	4.77 (n=57)	4.63 (n-42)

embodied. Thus the judges would have perceived the strategies developed under this influence to have achieved better "FIT". The mean rating of the RC group, 4.90, is clearly higher than those of the RB and RA groups, which suggests that they were influenced by the possibility ratings from the expert system and its underlying foundation in Porter's theory. Just as rocks on a shoreline which are under the surface of the water reveal their presence in the action of the water washing over them, so the theoretical underpinnings of the fuzzy expert system reveal themselves in the strategies created by the RC subjects.

At the same time, one would expect that those subjects having more practical experience would have reflected a more pragmatic orientation in the strategy statements they wrote. When the "GOOD" criterion focused the judges' attention on practical considerations, one would expect that they would have rated these strategies higher than those of the less experienced subjects, who might not have realized the importance of internal consistency in a plan, nor have had a repertoire of activities to use as building blocks. Interestingly, the experienced subjects appear not to have used the putput from the fuzzy expert system, as the lower mean rating for the XC group on "FIT" than on "Good" demonstrates. This group's responses on a follow-up questionnaire reflect a perception that the C treatment was not clear. This negative reaction to the fuzzy expert system output may have interfered with their performance as compared to the XB group which received only the survey-questionnaire prototype.

The RC group performed much better than either the RA or RB groups on the "GOOD" criterion although they were unable to match the performance of the Executive MBA subjects who received the data-acquisition prototype. Nevertheless, the intervention of the fuzzy expert system prototype does appear to have had a systematic positive effect. The higher mean rating for the RC group on "FIT" than on "GOOD" can be ascribed to the theoretical principles expressed in the fuzzy expert system in the former case, and to the lack of practical management experience in the latter.

Interaction effects. The strong interaction effects between the experience levels and the treatment levels warrant further investigation as the prototype is implemented and field tested. One scenario which may explain the outcomes of the various treatment level/experience level combinations is the following.

Treatment A,the non-treatment, consisted of a summary of Porter's theory which all subjects had studied earlier in the policy course. Perhaps the younger group (mean age 29) was closer to their undergraduate days and thus more resigned to plowing through theoretical expositions and trying to make some use of them. Their school to work (theory to practice) ratio was higher than that of the XA subjects and they may have been able to use the treatment materials to better advantage than the other group. By contrast, the older group (mean age 39) may have been impatient with an abstract, theoretical treatise and thus derived no assistance from the treatment. The A treatment had been designed as a placebo, but it may be that only with the XA group do we see the expected (non-)effect.

The unexpectedly good performance of the XB group may arise from the succinct, structured, information rich nature of the survey questionnaire, which was used as a prototype of the future interactive data-acquisition module. The 52 questions were grouped in logical categories with responses appropriate to the case they were using. Furthermore, this handout was very similar in nature and content to the management reports which managers are accustomed to receiving from subordinates and which they routinely use to make decisions. The more naive subjects, on the other hand, were probably more accustomed to theoretical essays than to the stripped-down, facts oriented survey. The very similar performance of the RA and RB groups on the two criteria plainly demonstrates that RB received about the same benefit from their treatment as the RA group. The higher mean rating on "FIT" which the RB subjects achieved substantiates the influence that the underlying theoretical structure of the survey exercised on their performance.

Finally, the weaker performance of the XC group than their peers in XB, may be explained by resistance on the part of these seasoned managers to what they perceived to be an attempt to direct their decision making rather than to aid it. The fuzzy expert system output seems to be useful to those who are willing to be influenced by it, as shown by the fact that the RC group achieved a higher mean rating than the XC group on both criteria. The difference in means is not statistically significant at the .05 level, but it does suggest that the fuzzy expert system prototype can improve the performance of those who are willing to be influenced by it. If the experienced managers' negative reaction to the fuzzy expert system module of the DSS is substantiated in further testing, the fuzzy expert system processing of the data base could be optional.

FUTURE DEVELOPMENTS

The research described in this paper supports the feasibility of further development of a fuzzy DSS for strategic planning.

A Color Graphics Module

A third module of the planned DSS which will be tested in the near future may provide an effective bridge between the needs of users with varying experience levels (Green, 1984). This module will use the natural language values the system obtains during the interactive survey portion and will organize them around Porter's theoretical framework, but it will make no attempt to lead the decision maker as the fuzzy expert system may appear to do. Instead, the information will be presented with color graphics and will invite the user to discover for himself what relationships are significant for his firm.

Rationale. This visual approach is based on the following rationale. Webster's New International Unabridged Dictionary (1979), defines "strategy" as "1) the science of planning and directing large-scale military operations, specifically, of maneuvering forces into the most advantageous position prior to actual engagement with the enemy; 2) a plan or action based on this." This definition of strategy contains elements which are appropriate to the business world. It includes the idea of an adversary relationship which is basic for any market/industry consisting of more than one firm. More importantly, this definition clearly expresses the primacy of the disposition of opposing forces in a problem space which is tangible (i.e. actual hills and rivers) and which can be represented on maps or charts by topographical symbols.

In the business world, the problem space is not so readily identifiable as a physical battlefield, but theorists such as Michael Porter are exploring the underlying structure within which a strategist for a firm will wish to deploy his forces. Graphical representation of the information in the data base reveals the "topography" of the competitive battlefield in order that the strategist may study the "lay of the land" and position his firm to best advantage. This visual approach to alternative strategy generation relies on spatial relationships rather than semantics, complementing the verbal/logical approach of the fuzzy expert system and following the advice of Sage (1981) that an appropriate planning and decision support process should provide for nonverbal support, as well as the more common verbal and quantitative aspects. Klein (1979, p,149) also urges "...visual display of environmental /organizational interactions...to allow for wholistic inspection of formalized environmental paradigms..."

Procedure. The information contained in the database will be presented to the decision maker in graphical form as follows. All data will be organized around Porter's five sources of competitive pressure plus a sixth group of strengths/weaknesses of the firm. A different color will be associated with each of these six categories and all related information will be displayed using the identifying color. One graph per category will present the relevant data, plotted using fuzzy coordinates chosen by the decision maker. For example, one source of competitive pressure for a firm is the bargaining power of the buyer group as a whole. The degree of concentration of a firm's buyer group relates directly to the amount of pressure the group can exert on the firm. The decision maker would assess how significant concentration is as a source of pressure relative to other contributing characteristics of the buyer group. He would also evaluate the degree of concentration of his firm's buyer group in terms of relative advantage/disadvantage to his firm. These assessments illustrate the two coordinates which are used to position graphically all information collected regarding the firm and its buyer group.

The decision maker will study the graph to see whether he can identify any patterns. Rumelt characterizes strategy formulation as problem solving of the most unstructured sort. "The creative phases of this process draw heavily on perceptual skills and imagination. Here, pattern recognition and the ability to perceive new meanings amidst complexity play key roles." (1979, p.196) When the user recognizes a pattern, it may be that he can then suggest strategies or strategic actions which will capitalize on an advantage or defend a weakness of the firm. Any two or more graphs may be superimposed at the decision maker's request. When this is done, the distinctive color associated with each basic category will permit the viewer to distinguish between the two or more groups of "datapoints".

Bonini (1980) observes that identifying relationships is the hardest and most time consuming part of analysis. In addition to the relationships which Porter believes exist, which are built into the framework of this visual processing of the data base, it may be possible for the decision maker to perceive others. Careful study of the individual graphs will encourage perception of within-category relationships, while study of composite graphs will facilitate identification of between-category relationships. Any of these insights could inspire the formulation of a possible strategy or strategic action for the firm. This visual approach seeks to stimulate the user's pattern-recognition skills and perhaps incite the intuitive leap to pattern creation. The goal is to get the decision maker truly involved in the alternative generation phase of the strategic decision process.

User Modification of STRATASSIST

In order for an individual user to tailor STRATASSIST to his firm's particular situation, another goal in the development of the DSS is to provide for user modification of the system. A strategic manager may wish to delete inappropriate questions from the survey. He may want to add other questions which he thinks are important for his firm. He may need to modify survey items to reflect more familiar terminology. A user may wish to write new production rules which would incorporate his own experience of strategy into the expert system. He may also want to delete non-germane rules to save processing time and conserve memory space. All of these modifications are possible with existing technology and would enhance the full scale DSS. A decision maker is more likely to view a DSS as a friendly assistant when he is able to modify it to suit himself and his firm. This would enhance the usefulness of STRATASSIST to strategic managers.

CONCLUSION

STRATASSIST has demonstrated empirically that it can aid decision makers in strategic planning. Both the survey questionnaire module and the fuzzy expert system module had a positive influence on performance. A DSS such as STRATASSIST can cope with the challenges of measurement, complexity, and ill-structuredness which have plagued strategic planning managers. Using fuzzy math technology, a DSS can elicit from the planner, store, and process more chunks of information than is possible for human memory, while imposing minimal restrictions and distortions on the way the knowledge is represented (Whalen and Schott, 1983). STRATASSIST works with information in the natural language form used by the decision maker. It augments his information processing capability by using a fuzzy expert system to comb the data base for possible strategy/strategic action cues. The DSS leaves to the user the task of evaluating all the alternatives suggested. The ability to exercise critical judgement is still a uniquely human characteristic and one that is vital to strategic planning. STRATASSIST combines the strengths of the computer with those of the human mind to help strategic planners do a better job.

REFERENCES

Ansoff, H. I. (1979). The changing shape of the strategic problem. In D. E. Schendel and C. W. Hofer (Eds.), Strategic Management. Little, Brown, Boston. Section 1, pp. 30-43.

Bonini, C. (1980). Computer Models for Decision Analysis. The Scientific Press, Palo Alto.

Channon, D. F. (1979). Commentary. In D. E. Schendel and C. W. Hofer (Eds.), Strategic Management. Little, Brown, Boston. Section 3, pp. 122-133.

Gaines, B. R. (1976). Foundations of fuzzy reasoning. Int. J. Man-Mach. Stud. (GB), 8, 623-668.

Green, N. L. (1984). Interfacing interactive graphics with fuzzy production rules in a DSS. Proc. IEEE Int. Conf. Syst., Man & Cybern., IEEE Catalog No.: 84CH2063-6, 226.228.

Green-Hall, N. L. (1985). Using a fuzzy expert system for decision support of the strategic planning process. Doc. Dissert., Georgia State University.

Klein, H. E. (1973). Incorporating environmental examination into the corporate strategic planning process. Doc. dissert., Columbia University.

Klein, H. E. (1979). Commentary. In D. E. Schendel and C. W. Hofer (Eds.), Strategic Management. Little, Brown, Boston. Section 3, pp. 144-151.

Negoita, C. V. (1983). Fuzzy sets in decision support systems. Human Systems Management, 4, 27-33.

Nie, N. H., C. H. Hull, J. G. Jenkins, K. Steinbrenner and D. H. Bent, (1975). SPSS, 2nd ed. McGraw-Hill, New York.

Porter, M. E. (1980). Competitive Strategy. Little, Brown, Boston.

Rumelt, R. P. (1979). Evaluation of strategy: Theory and models. In D. E. Schendel and C. W. Hofer (Eds.), Strategic Management. Little, Brown, Boston. Section 4, pp. 196-211.

Sage, A. P. (1981). Behavioral and organizational considerations in the design of information systems and processes for planning and decision support. IEEE Trans. Syst., Man & Cybern. (USA), SMC-11, No. 9, 640-673.

Schendel, D. E., and C. W. Hofer, Eds., (1979). Strategic Management. Little, Brown, Boston.

Wenstop, F. (1980). Quantitative analysis with linguistic values. Fuzzy Sets & Syst., 4, 99-115.

Whalen, T. (1982). What can fuzzy mathematics offer decision support systems? Unpublished manuscript, Georgia State University, Atlanta.

Whalen, T. (1986). A linguistic inference system with mixed-initiative dialog. Paper accepted for presentation for NAFIPS 1986, New Orleans.

Whalen, T., and B. Schott, (1983). Representing and manipulating fuzzy knowledge about forecasting problems and techniques. Proc. Int. Conf. Syst., Man & Cybern., Bombay, 127-131.

Zadeh, L. A. (1972). Fuzzy languages and their relation to human intelligence. Proc. Int. Conf. on Man and Computer, Bordeaux, 130-165.

Zadeh, L. A. (1975). The concept of a linguistic variable and its application to approximate reasoning, part II. Inf. Sci., 8, 301-357.

A Clinical Alarm System Using Techniques from Artificial Intelligence and Fuzzy Set Theory

S. J. HENKIND*,**, R. R. YAGER***, A. M. BENIS* and M. C. HARRISON**

*Mount Sinai School of Medicine, Department of Cardiothoracic Surgery, One Gustave L. Levy Place, New York, NY 10029, USA
**New York University, Courant Institute of Mathematical Sciences, Department of Computer Science, 251 Mercer Street, New York, NY 10012, USA
***Machine Intelligence Institute, Hagan School of Business, Iona College, New Rochelle, NY 10801, USA

ABSTRACT

Computerized alarm systems have been well accepted in clinical medicine but suffer from several major limitations. In particular, they are generally not able to handle patient/disease specificity, temporal changes, multivariable combinations, and dynamic patterns. In addition, the crisp nature of the alarm limits is counterintuitive. In this paper, we describe these limitations in detail. We also present an approach for building alarm systems that do not suffer from these limitations. This approach uses techniques from artificial intelligence and from fuzzy set theory. In particular, a production system is used to initialize the alarm system, and fuzzy techniques are used to interpret the incoming data. A prototype system for the cardiac surgical intensive care unit is currently under development.

KEYWORDS

Alarm system; artificial intelligence; cardiac surgery; cardiac tamponade; computerized monitoring; fuzzy set theory; intensive care unit.

INTRODUCTION

Over the past several decades, the computer has been applied to many areas in the practice of medicine. Computers can now be found in hospital laboratories, medical record departments, and at the bedside. One potential application that has received a great deal of attention is computer-assisted diagnosis. Early attempts focused on various statistical, pattern recognition, and related approaches (Rogers, 1979). More recently, artificial intelligence techniques have been explored (Clancey, 1984). There has also been significant work on applying fuzzy set theory to diagnostic problems (Adlassnig, 1982; Sanchez, 1979). Although computer-assisted diagnosis systems have shown great promise, they are still largely research efforts, and with only a few exceptions, e.g., the PUFF system (Aikins, 1983), they have not yet become a standard part of clinical practice.

For certain medical applications, however, computers are widely accepted and are, indeed, indispensable. For example, CAT scanners and other sophisticated image processing devices would not be possible without powerful processing units.

Computers are also widely used in automated alarm systems. In a typical system, several physiologic transducers are attached to a patient. The analog signals from these transducers are then converted to digital values and fed to a processor. Using certain predefined criteria, the processor then analyzes the values, and determines if an alarm should be triggered (e.g., a flashing light, buzzer, etc.). Although such alarm systems have existed for many years and are in widespread use, they are, in some respects, quite rudimentary.

We have identified several major limitations in conventional computer-based alarm systems. In this paper, we describe an approach using techniques from artificial intelligence and fuzzy set theory that seeks to overcome these limitations. A prototype system is currently under development and should be operational shortly. This system is intended to be used in the cardiac surgical intensive care unit (CSICU).

THE CARDIAC SURGICAL INTENSIVE CARE UNIT

The typical surgical patient in a hospital is sent to a recovery room during the first few postoperative hours, and is then discharged to a normal ward. However, patients who have undergone cardiac surgery, may be quite unstable in the initial postoperative period, and require highly specialized management. Therefore, these patients generally spend one or more days in a cardiac surgical intensive care unit after surgery.

The cardiac surgical intensive care unit is staffed by highly trained nurses and physicians. Each nurse is assigned to care for only one or two patients (in a less intensive setting a nurse may be responsible for ten or more patients), while the physicians circulate throughout the unit. Much of the patient management is fairly routine, e.g., the changing of dressings, the administration of drugs, etc. The goal of this routine management is to stabilize the patient so that he or she may be discharged from the unit.

The most specialized expertise of the unit personnel lies in their ability to handle the nonroutine: in particular, their ability to recognize and treat emergencies. Crises in the unit can occur suddenly, are often life-threatening, and must be promptly recognized and treated if the patient is to survive.

In order to provide information on which to base patient management decisions, a tremendous amount of data is gathered in the unit. Vital signs, e.g., body temperature are taken frequently, and the urine output, chest tube drainage (bleeding from the surgical incision), and other variables are measured periodically. The values are recorded in written form, or may be entered into a computer system which incorporates them into an automated chart.

Patients will generally have multiple transducers in place: for example, intracardiac and arterial catheters. Readings from these transducers are also recorded periodically. In some intensive care units computers are used to collect data directly from the transducers. Typically, the transducer signal is averaged or sampled over a preset time interval, and the data saved on tape or disk. The information may be recalled as desired, and hard-copy summaries are produced for use by the staff. Since the recording of data in the chart by hand is quite time consuming, automated data acquisition can lead to significant savings in time for the nursing staff (Sheppard, 1979), hence increasing the time available for routine patient management.

CONVENTIONAL COMPUTER-BASED ALARM SYSTEMS

Computers are also used to assist in aspects of nonroutine patient care. In particular, many systems use decision tables or other simple techniques to trigger alarms. These alarms are intended to alert the staff to emergencies in the patient's condition. The basic paradigm that is used is the following (Fig. 1.) : Each physiologic variable is viewed as running along a numeric scale. On this scale are two distinguished points -- "Low" and "High." These limits are either preset in the alarm program, or input by the physician. If the measured value of the variable falls out of the range between Low and High, then the value is considered pathologic, and an alarm signal is activated. If the value falls between the limits, then it is considered "normal" and no action is taken. Sometimes this paradigm may be extended or modified: for example, a value may have to be out of limits for a certain minimum amount of time before an alarm is triggered, or there may be only one alarm limit.

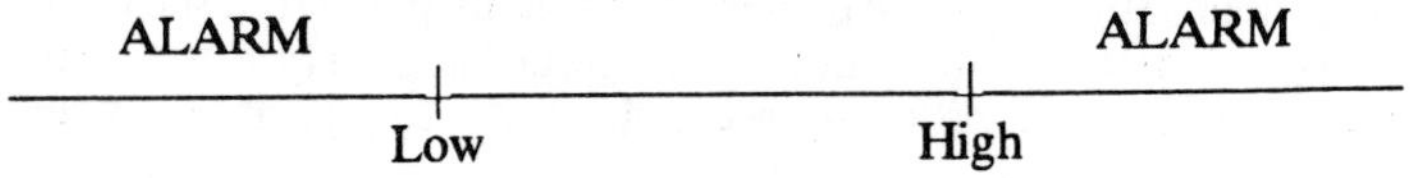

Fig. 1. Conventional alarm paradigm.

Many systems have been built using this paradigm, and it seems to be well accepted. Nevertheless, there are several limitations inherent with this approach.

Patient/disease specificity:

An alarm system may behave appropriately for some patients, but not for others. This limitation stems from the fact that expected physiologic values are highly dependent on the particular nature of the patient and his or her disease. For example, a patient with ventricular hypertrophy is expected to have significantly higher intracardiac pressures than a patient without hypertrophy. If alarm limits are preset to a certain range, or set by hand to inappropriate values, then a system may generate false alarms or miss pathologic values (Type I or Type II error).

Temporal changes:

For a given patient, an alarm system may behave appropriately at one point in time, yet behave inappropriately at another point. This is due to the fact that the expected values of some of the physiologic variables change over time. For example, chest tube drainage is expected to be quite high immediately after surgery, but low several hours later. In a conventional alarm system the alarm limits (whether preset or set by hand) are fixed over time, hence errors can result.

Multivariable combinations:

Conventional alarm systems generally do not take account of multivariable combinations. For example, suppose that the cardiac index and atrial pressures are both "within normal limits," but the cardiac index is low and the atrial pressures high. An experienced clinician would know that the patient may be in trouble, yet a typical alarm system would not issue an alert because each variable is viewed in isolation from the others.

Dynamic patterns:

Conventional alarm systems generally do not take account of the relative ordering of events. Such orderings can be extremely significant. For example, if the arterial pressure decreases and then atrial pressures increase the patient is probably in no danger; but if the atrial pressures increase and then the arterial pressure decreases, the patient may be deteriorating rapidly.

In actual practice the good clinician (nurse or doctor) is aware of the limitations of conventional alarm systems. By adjusting alarm ranges as appropriate, integrating information from multiple sources, and so forth, he or she is able to circumvent those limitations. Unfortunately, however, the personnel in the unit are not always fully experienced. Moreover, even the most highly trained individuals sometimes forget or make mistakes. Therefore, an alarm system that is not subject to the aforementioned limitations would seem to be a valuable supplement for patient care.

There has been only a limited amount of previous work in this direction. Benis (1980) describes a system that bases its alarm criteria on the values of two physiologic variables. The VM system (Fagan, 1984) uses a frame based approach to monitor patients being mechanically ventilated. Work is also underway on a system that incorporates information from multiple sources to assist in the monitoring and management of patients with cardiac arrhythmias (Long, 1983).

PRAGMATIC CONSIDERATIONS

There are several properties that any computer system must have if it is to be accepted for clinical use in an intensive care unit. Certainly, it must do its assigned task well, but by itself this is not enough. One major consideration is that in order for a system to be accepted and used, it must be carefully integrated into the unit (Sheppard, 1979). In particular, a system -- no matter how promising -- that requires drastic changes in the daily routine of the clinical staff is unlikely to be accepted. Alarm systems are already well integrated into many CSICUs, so integrating a more sophisticated system (assuming that it works well) should pose few problems.

Since the CSICU is so busy, a computer system can make only limited demands on the time of the staff. In particular, the nurses and physicians have little time to answer questions posed by the computer. Note, however, that a tremendous amount of data is available directly to the computer in those systems which incorporate automated charts and on-line data collection.

In any alarm system, there is an inevitable tradeoff between sensitivity and specificity: as the system begins to pick up more true alarms (increased sensitivity) it also begins to exhibit more false alarms (decreased specificity). Conversely, as the false alarm rate is lowered (increased specificity), more true alarms are missed (decreased sensitivity). The choice of whether to emphasize sensitivity, specificity, or strike a balance is based upon pragmatic considerations.

Physicians and nurses working in the CSICU at the Mount Sinai Hospital have indicated that although they are concerned with both sensitivity and specificity, the latter needs to be emphasized. Their rationale is the following: It is crucial to keep the false alarm rate as low as possible because any system with an excessive false alarm rate will be quickly turned off by annoyed staff members. Moreover, due to the high level of staffing in the unit, an alarm system is viewed as being a *supplement* to the clinician (i.e., a fail-safe that looks for things that the clinical staff is also watching for, but might miss due to fatigue, oversight or error), and therefore it is acceptable that it miss a few true alarms.

Parenthetically, in a different clinical environment, it might be advisable to emphasize sensitivity. For example, in a unit that is less heavily staffed than the CSICU, an alarm system might be viewed as a *replacement* for the clinician, and hence missing true alarms would not be acceptable. This is, in fact, the choice that is made in coronary care units: alarm systems relieve nurses of the burden of continually following EKG tracings, but such systems have notoriously high false alarm rates (Long, 1983). Also note that should the CSICU staff begin to rely on an alarm system to such an extent that it becomes more than a supplement, then it might be necessary to readjust the sensitivity and specificity.

BASIC APPROACH

In this section we present an approach for building alarm systems that are not subject to the conventional limitations. This approach is a modification of an architecture that we suggested two years ago (Henkind, 1984). We are currently building such a system that tracks chest tube drainage, urine output, cardiac index, right atrial pressure, left atrial pressure, and mean arterial pressure. It is emphasized that the system has not been completed yet. Note that in the following discussion, the "user" is the nurse or physician who is currently interacting with the system.

Handling patient/disease specificity:

One difficulty in conventional alarm systems is that appropriate low and high limits differ from individual to individual (patient/disease specificity). In actual clinical practice this limitation can be overcome because the good clinician knows that there are certain expected limits (i.e., default values) for the "typical patient," but that these limits must be modified depending on the particular pathology. Fortunately, the number of pathologic conditions that can change the expected limits is fairly small. For example, in the typical patient normal left atrial pressure runs in the range of 8 to 12 mm Hg. However, if the patient has (had) ventricular hypertrophy, and/or ventricular dilitation, and/or mitral valve surgery, and/or aortic valve surgery, then the expected range is 14 to 18 mm Hg. This sort of information can be modeled by production rules of the form

> IF pathology present
> THEN set pathologic limits
> ELSE set normal limits.

A collection of such rules constitutes a rule base. By incorporating such a rule base into a production system, it should be possible to determine the appropriate alarm limits for a given patient.

We have implemented such a production system in LISP. For the sake of modularity, it has been divided into two parts. The first part (the questioning module) gathers the needed background information on the patient. The second part (the deductive module) then draws the appropriate inferences, and sets the alarm limits. Both the questioning module, and the deductive module have exhibited good performance in preliminary tests.

The questioning module poses approximately 50 questions about the patient to the user. This demand on the user's time is acceptable since the questions may be posed before the patient is actually brought into the unit. Since not all questions are necessary or appropriate for a given individual, the module varies the questions from patient to patient. In addition, blatantly erroneous responses are screened out.

After the questioning module has finished acquiring initialization information, the deductive module then executes. Based on the information that has been gathered, it sets the alarm limits and performs other necessary initialization tasks. In order to increase user acceptance, physicians are able to override the computer's limits if they so desire. There are currently on the order of 100 rules in the deductive module.

Handling temporal changes:

Another limitation in conventional alarm systems is that some of the physiologic variables change over time. Fortunately, however, it is possible to describe expected temporal curves for these variables. For example, in most cases, the chest tube drainage is initially quite high, and then drops off over the next few hours. See figure 2. Note that these sorts of curves really represent expected ranges rather than expected values.

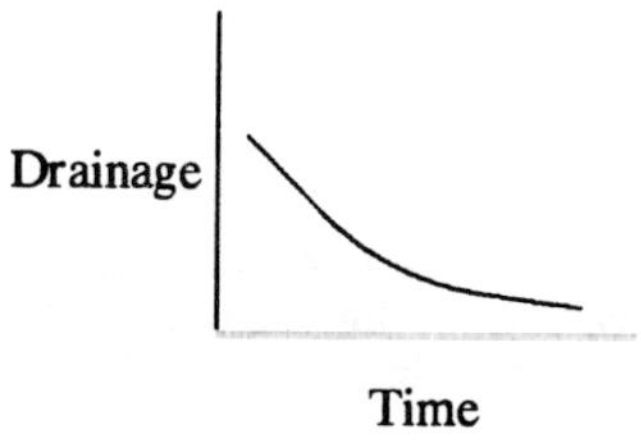

Fig. 2. Expected chest tube drainage.

While all patients do not follow such curves, most patients who are being properly managed and who are on the road to recovery do; thus deviation from a curve can be viewed as pathologic and therefore a stimulus for alarming.

By incorporating some representation of the curves into the system, it is possible to change the alarm limits over time. Currently our system has an internal representation of these curves -- they are approximated by piecewise linear segments, and the midpoints stored in arrays. Note that in some cases, it may be necessary to shift the expected curves; this could be done by the initialization production system.

Handling multivariable combinations:

An important limitation of most conventional alarm systems is that they do not take account of multivariable combinations. A major difficulty in overcoming this limitation is that the number of combinations is exponential: given n variables, there are 2^n combinations.

It might seem desirable that the alarm system examine all multivariable combinations. Unfortunately, due to the exponential nature of 2^n, a system that attempts to do so is doomed to be extremely unwieldy for even small values of n. In order that the system be computationally tractable, it is necessary to select a susbset of the combinations with which to work.

Fortunately, some combinations are of much greater significance than others. The reason for this is the following: Although a given patient may develop virtually any complication after surgery, there are only a limited number of complications that occur frequently in the postoperative period, e.g., myocardial failure, cardiac tamponade, etc. Associated with each of these complications are certain multivariable derangements. For example, in cardiac tamponade one generally will note a low cardiac index, low urine output, high cumulative chest tube drainage, and elevated left and right atrial pressures. Thus, it is important to examine the combination of the above physiologic variables. Other combinations of variables are not associated with typical post-surgical complications, and thus are of less importance: for example, the combination of right atrial pressure and chest tube drainage seems to be of little significance.

By choosing to examine only the most clinically significant combinations, the system is made computationally tractable. In addition, this should come at only a slight cost in terms of missing some true alarms. (Remember that since the system is a supplement, it is acceptable to occasionally miss true alarms.) For our prototype system we are currently concentrating on the multivariable derangements associated with cardiac tamponade.

An important issue that arises in the construction of multivariable alarms is how to combine the individual pieces of information from each variable into an aggregate score (e.g., if four out of five variables are out of range should an alarm be triggered?, and so forth). We discuss our methodology for this in a subsequent section.

Handling dynamic patterns:
The order in which physiologic changes occur can be quite significant, yet few, if any, alarm systems use this information. The idea that we are developing is the following: For many complications there are typical scenarios which occur. For example, if there is a sudden cessation in bleeding, followed by an increase in the atrial pressures, which is in turn followed by a decrease in cardiac index, then the patient almost certainly has cardiac tamponade, and an alarm should be triggered. We are attempting to build a model of these sorts of patterns. The model bears many similarities to the recognition of regular languages by finite automata. To date, this is the most speculative part of our research and the implementation details have not been worked out yet.

FUZZIFYING THE ALARM SYSTEM

We have now presented four limitations in conventional alarm systems, and an approach to handle these limitations. There are, however, some additional difficulties which need to be discussed. Recall that most alarm systems are based on the low-high paradigm. This paradigm can be viewed as the following two-step process:

Step 1) Determine whether or not a given value is pathologic.

Step 2) If the value is pathologic then trigger its alarm.

This process can be expressed in a set theoretic framework. Given that the alarm system monitors n physiologic variables $X_1, X_2, \ldots, X_n$ and has n alarms $A_1, A_2, \ldots, A_n$ where A_1 is the alarm for the first variable, A_2 is the alarm for the second variable, and so forth. (Recall that conventional alarm systems do not handle multivariable combinations). Each of the variables X_i has a corresponding set of values V_i that it can assume (V_1 is the set of possible values for variable X_1, and so forth). Each of these value sets V_i in turn has a subset of values E_i that are considered to be pathologic. The membership of each E_i in V_i can be viewed as a characteristic function $\mu_{E_i}(v_i)$ from V_i to $\{0,1\}$ such that

$$\mu_{E_i}(v_i) = \begin{cases} 0 & \text{iff } l_i \leq v_i \leq h_i \\ 1 & \text{otherwise} \end{cases}$$

where $\mu_{E_i}(v_i)=1$ means that the value v_i belongs to the pathologic subset, $\mu_{E_i}(v_i)=0$ means that the value does not, l_i is the low limit and h_i is the high limit.

EXAMPLE. Given that X_1 is the left atrial pressure. Then $V_1 = [0,30]$ (in mm Hg). Assuming no abnormal pathology then $l_1 = 8$, $h_1 = 12$, and the characteristic function is

$$\mu_{E_1}(v_1) = \begin{cases} 0 & \text{iff } 8 \leq v_1 \leq 12 \\ 1 & \text{otherwise.} \end{cases}$$

Thus, $\mu_{E_1}(10) = 0$, but $\mu_{E_1}(13) = 1$. In other words, a left atrial pressure of 10 is considered normal, but a left atrial pressure of 13 is considered pathologic. More generally, any values between 8 and 12 are considered normal, while all other values are considered pathologic.

Viewed from the set theoretic framework the first step of the paradigm is the computation of the characteristic function. Accordingly, the second step is

$$\text{Trigger alarm } A_i \text{ if } \mu_{E_i}(V_i)=1.$$

Unfortunately, the characteristic functions μ_{E_i} are counterintuitive because they do not capture the idea that some values are more pathologic than others: e.g., a left atrial pressure of 13 and a left atrial pressure of 29 are considered equally bad. Moreover, these functions have disturbing behavior at the set boundaries: for example, a pressure of 8 would be considered normal, while a pressure of 7.99 would be considered abnormal. These difficulties are a result of the fact that the values l_i and h_i are crisp cutoff points. Also note that in order to adjust the sensitivity and specificity of the alarms the clinician must revise the criteria for what is considered pathologic (i.e., l_i and h_i must be reset).

A straightforward solution for these problems is to model the characteristic functions as continuous, rather than two valued functions.

EXAMPLE. Given that X_1 is the left ventricular pressure, and given the same values for l_1 and h_1 as before. Redefine $\mu_{E_1}(v_1)$ as the following function:

$$\mu_{E_1}(v_1) = \begin{cases} 1 & \text{if } v_1<(l_1-2) \\ 1-.5(v_1-(l_1-2)) & \text{if } (l_1-2)\leq v_1<l_1 \\ 0 & \text{if } l_1\leq v_1\leq h_1 \\ 1-.5((h_1+2)-v_1) & \text{if } h_1<v_1\leq(h_1+2) \\ 1 & \text{if } v_1>(h_1+2) \end{cases}$$

Thus $\mu_{E_1}(10) = 0$ (normal), $\mu_{E_1}(13) = .5$ (somewhat abnormal), $\mu_{E_1}(2) = 1$ (abnormal), and so forth. Note how l_1 and h_1 are still incorporated into the characteristic function, but no longer give rise to discontinuous behavior (e.g., $\mu_{E_1}(7.99) = .005$ is very close to $\mu_{E_1}(8)$).

By making the characteristic functions continuous (i.e., converting the pathologic values E_i from classical to fuzzy sets (Zadeh, 1965)), the first step of the paradigm becomes

Step 1) Compute the degree of pathology ($\mu_{E_i}(v_i)$) of the value.

The second step must now also be modified. This can be done by defining threshold parameters c_i:

Step 2) If $\mu_{E_i}(v_i) > c_i$ then trigger alarm A_i.

In other words, if a value v_i is more pathologic than its threshold parameter c_i, then trigger alarm A_i.

It is apparent that each c_i defines a cutoff just as l_i and h_i did. What we have done by our reformulation of the paradigm is to defer the choice of cutoffs from step 1 to step 2. By doing this it is possible to alter the sensitivity and specificity of the system (by adjusting each c_i) without requiring the clinician to provide new criteria for what is considered pathologic (i.e., it is not necessary to alter l_i and h_i).

It should be noted that the need for cutoffs arises because continuous variables are being used to make binary choices (since a given alarm signal is either on or off). There are only two possible ways to eliminate the need for cutoffs in an alarm system. The first way is to make the system nondeterministic. This is clearly not acceptable. The second way is to fuzzify the alarm signals themselves. For example, rather than having a buzzer being either on or off, it could range along a spectrum from inaudible to loud. Although this might be viable in certain environments, clinicians in the CSICU have rejected this approach (although they have suggested that three valued alarms, e.g., *low, medium,* and *high* might be useful).

COMBINING EVIDENCE IN MULTIVARIABLE ALARMS

As was noted previously, it is not feasible to construct an alarm system to monitor all possible combinations of variables. Accordingly, it is necessary to select the most important combinations with which to work. This can be done by choosing those combinations which are associated with typical postoperative complications. For example, an alarm geared for cardiac tamponade would watch for low cardiac index, low urine output, high chest tube drainage, and elevated left and right atrial pressures.

There are several considerations that must be taken into account. First of all, it is clear that each of the individual variables should be interpreted in a fuzzy manner (e.g., "high" atrial pressure is really a continuum, and so forth). This can be done using the techniques described in the previous section, although some modifications may be necessary (e.g., the tamponade alarm is concerned with high left atrial pressure, while the single variable left atrial pressure alarm is concerned with either low or high values).

Given that the alarm system monitors n variables $X_1,X_2, \ldots ,X_n$ and has a multivariable alarm M that observes p of the variables ($p \leq n$). For convenience, we rename the variables that M monitors as $Y_1, \ldots ,Y_p$ (note that the ordering is unimportant). $V_1, \ldots ,V_p$ are the respective value sets. For each of the values sets V_i then, there is a characteristic function $\mu_{E_i}(v_i)$ that determines how "high" (or low, etc.) a given value is.

In the previous section, single variable alarms were modeled as a two step process. In the multivariable case, however, additional computation is necessary since the individual criteria (e.g., low cardiac index, high bleeding, etc.) need to be aggregated in some fashion. Accordingly, we model multivariable alarms by the following three step process:

Step 1) Compute each of the $\mu_{E_i}(v_i)$.

Step 2) Combine the above to give an aggregate score M.

Step 3) If $M > C_M$ then trigger alarm M.

C_M is a cutoff that must be chosen judiciously to regulate the sensitivity and specificity.

Some difficult issues arise in connection with the second step of this process. In particular, appropriate operators need to be selected in order that the alarm give reasonable performance. In the case of tamponade, for example, an intersection operator is needed since the criteria are low cardiac index, *and* low urine output, *and* high chest tube drainage, etc. Various definitions have been proposed for intersection including min, product, and the C_p operator (Yager, 1980). The choice of operators will have a pronounced effect on the performance of the system.

EXAMPLE. Suppose that the multivariable alarm N is to be triggered if x, y and z are high. If x is .5 high, and y is .5 high and z is .5 high then

min[x,y,z] = .5

prod[x,y,z] = .125.

The effects of the choice of connectives have been explored more formally in (Kacprzyk, 1985). We are currently examining various connectives to determine which ones give reasonable performance in our prototype system.

SUMMARY

Computer-based clinical alarm systems are generally based on a simple low-high paradigm. Although such systems have proven to be useful, they also suffer from some major limitations. Several of these limitations stem from the fact that conventional systems do not utilize "high level" information about the patient. We have presented a method of utilizing such information by using techniques from artificial intelligence.

Other limitations stem from the fact that the conventional paradigm views the low and high limits as being crisp cutoff points. We have shown how techniques from fuzzy set theory may be of some help in this regard, although it is not possible to completely eliminate the need for cutoffs. We have designed a prototype system for the cardiac surgical intensive care unit. This system is currently being implemented.

REFERENCES

Adlassnig, K. (1982). A survey on medical diagnosis and fuzzy subsets. In M. M. Gupta and E. Sanchez (Eds.), *Approximate Reasoning in Decision Analysis,* North Holland, New York, pp. 203-217.

Aikins, J. S., J. C. Kunz, E. H. Shortliffe, and R. J. Fallat (1983). PUFF: An expert system for interpretation of pulmonary function data. *Comput. & Biomed. Res., 16,* 199-208.

Benis, A. M., H. L. Fitzkee, R. A. Jurado, and R. S. Litwak (1980). Improved detection of adverse cardiovascular trends with the use of a two-variable computer alarm. *Crit. Care Med., 8,* 341-344.

Clancey, W. J., and E. H. Shortliffe (Eds.) (1984). *Readings in Medical Artificial Intelligence.* Addison-Wesley, Reading Mass.

Fagan, L. M., E. H. Shortliffe, and B. G. Buchanan (1984). Computer-based medical decision making: from MYCIN to VM. In W. W. Clancey, and E. H. Shortliffe (Eds.), *Readings in Medical Artificial Intelligence,* Addison-Wesley, Reading Mass., 241-255.

Henkind, S., L. Teichholz, and M. Harrison (1984). Intensive care unit monitoring using a real-time expert system. *IEEE Computer in Cardiology, 11,* 7-12.

Kacprzyk, J., and R. R. Yager (1985). Emergency-oriented expert systems: a fuzzy approach. *Information Sciences, 37,* 143-155.

Long, W. J., T. A. Russ, and W. B. Locke (1983). Reasoning from multiple sources in arrhythmia management. *Proc. IEEE Frontiers of Engineering and Computing in Health Care.*

Rogers, W., B. Ryack, and G. Moeller (1979). Computer-aided medical diagnosis: literature review. *Int. J. Bio-Medical Computing, 10,* 267-289.

Sanchez, E. (1979). Medical diagnosis and composite fuzzy relations. In M. M. Gupta, R. V. Ragade, and R. R. Yager (Eds.), *Advances in Fuzzy Set Theory and Applications,* North Holland, New York, 437-444.

Sheppard, L. C. (1979). The Computer in the care of critically ill patients. *Proc. IEEE, 67,* 1300-1306.

Yager, R. R. (1980). On a general class of fuzzy connectives. *Fuzzy Sets and Systems, 4,* 235-242.

Zadeh, L. A. (1965). Fuzzy sets. *Information and Control, 8,* 338-353.

Learning from Examples in Presence of Uncertainty

F. BERGADANO, A. GIORDANA and L. SAITTA

Dipartimento di Informatica, Universita di Torino, Via Valperga Caluso 37, 10125 Torino, Italy

ABSTRACT

In this paper a general framework, designed for acquiring knowledge in expert systems especially oriented to pattern analysis, is described.
A knowledge base, structured into clusters of production rules, is acquired in an automated mode by exploiting a large body of general knowledge and of powerful heuristics. The learning methodology explicitly addresses the problem of the presence of errors and noise in the data and utilizes an approximate and non-monotonic reasoning scheme, based on fuzzy sets.
An example of application is presented as well.

KEYWORDS

Approximate Reasoning, Expert Systems, Machine Learning, Pattern Recognition.

1. INTRODUCTION

Discriminating among the instantiations of different concepts, intended in a broad sense, is a recognizedly major component of human thinking, involved, more or less directly, in several activities. Representative, but not exhaustive, examples of such activities can be found in the domain of pattern analysis: for instance, recognition and understanding of images and speech, interpretation of time-varying biomedical signals and of multisensor data, diagnostic problems in natural and man-made systems, multiclass discrimination. All these activities consist of choosing, among a set of alternatives, a subset of them according to prefixed goals.

Traditional approaches for handling this general problem have relied upon procedural methods, using, for the numerical aspects, well established statistical or pattern matching techniques, and, for the structural ones, formal languages. This is especially true for the low-level analysis of signals as, for instance, segmentation and primitive extraction. Exception in the field have been geological prospection and medical consultation, which served very early as test cases for knowledge based methodologies.

Recently, the usefulness, and even the necessity, of extending these methodologies to complex pattern recognition problems has been underlined (Nandhakumar and Aggarwal, 1985) and several attempts to apply them in vision, speech processing and waveform analysis have appeared in the literature (see, just to mention some, Brooks 1983; Nazif and Levine 1984; Mckeown, Harvey, Mcdermott 1985; Mostow and Hayes-Roth 1978; Nii and Feigenbaum 1978; De Mori and co-workers 1984; Lee and Thankor 1984; Birman 1973).

Unfortunately, a major difficulty the knowledge engineer must face in many cases is the dearth or human experts, able to transfer their expertise in a form suitable to be used by an artificial system: for instance, even if understanding speech and interpreting scenes seem to us the easiest and most natural things to do, the mechanisms underlying the human perceptual processes are still largely under investigation.

On the other hand, even when human experts exist, as, for instance, physicians in medical applications, their knowledge is often incomplete and episodic rather than systematic. As a consequence, the possibility of automatically acquiring knowledge directly from some kind of data would greatly enhance both the acceptability and the applicability of knowledge based systems and would raise the hope of building systems with performances continuously increasing over time.

On the other side, machine learning has received a steadily increasing attention, as it is proved, for instance, by the extensive bibliography in Michalski, Carbonell, Mitchell (1983). However, despite the interesting results obtained and the impressive performances of some working systems, automated knowledge acquisition yet remains a long term goal in AI. In particular, the inherent conceptual and computational complexity of the task, suggested to first consider, with few exceptions, cases in which no errors or noise are present, or to direct the efforts towards fields, such as mathematics, in which clear criteria exist to monitor the system behavior and to validate its results.

On the contrary, the task of automatically building up the knowledge base of an expert system, bound to work in one of the domains mentioned at the beginning, poses stringent requirements both on the kind of knowledge to be acquired and on the methodology to be used to obtain the goal. Even if several existing approaches to automated learning are sources of useful and interesting ideas, it is quite safe to say that no learning system yet exists, which could work in a truly real-world environment with acceptable time and space complexity and which be, at the same time, sufficiently general to be used across different applications with minor or no modifications, with the same level of performances.

We hope that the learning system presented in this paper will help to enlighten this relevant and not yet well understood aspect of learning.

The system consists of a learning module, devoted to the acquisition of the knowledge base of a performance system oriented to complex pattern analysis problems. Its main characteristics (domain-independency, low computational complexity, robustness toward noise and uncertainty) derive from a fruitful interaction of ideas from pattern recognition and from conceptual induction.

In particular, the high descriptive power of production rules and logical languages has been coupled with the efficiency (both in the learning and the performance system) of a subproblem reduction process, resulting in an automatically performed partition of the acquired knowledge into separate bodies, organized into a graph structure, which is an extension to decision trees (Shepherd 1983, Arbab and Michie 1985, Quinlan 1983).

The robustness towards errors and noise has been obtained by automatically affecting each piece of knowledge by a measure of uncertainty, assigned on statistical basis, and by introducing fuzzy sets and a continuous-valued semantics in the logical framework.

Finally, the reduction in computational resources requirement is obtained by strongly focalizing the system search in the immense space of possible rules, by supplying the learning module of a separate body of heuristic knowledge; the novelty of this aspect of the system design consists in the fact that this heuristic knowledge is only problem-dependent and not domain-dependent. In fact the used heuristic aims to model the conscious behavior of a human being, trying to discover, by himself, regularities in the descriptions of some set of known examples, by looking at and comparing them, irrespectively of their very own nature.

We stress that this model in no way intends to describe perceptual mechanisms, existing in humans. For instance, interpreting uttered words is seen as the process of visually analyzing some graphs, describing the time evolution of chosen features, in as much the same way one looks at an image.

The used heuristic proved itself a powerful tool to achieve strong focalization, preserving independency from specific applications within the field of conceptual discrimination.

Finally, we point out that the learning module is also provided with mechanisms able to exploit domain-dependent heuristics, when available, to further constrain the search and to validate the acquired knowledge.

2. SYSTEM PHILOSOPHY AND OVERVIEW

The system accepts in input a set of known instantiations (examples) of a given set of concepts and generates in output a network of production rules, allowing to discriminate among the concepts.

Instantiations of real-world phenomena can often be considered as "patterns", intended in a broad sense, describable in terms of a large number of features, possibly analyzed at several levels of detail. Unless a model of the phenomenon is available, or deep expertise has been gained in the field, it is impossible, in most cases, to say what the relevant features and the right level of detail are. Moreover, the relevance of the features may depend on the aim they are used for. This aspect of the analysis is further complicated by the intrinsic variability, which contributes to mask those aspects that truly distinguish semantically different patterns.

Two consequences derive from these facts. One is related to the problem of knowledge validation: it is difficult to decide to what extent discrimination should go on; in fact, it may not be known, a-priori, if a complete discrimination is possible, on the basis of the chosen features, and there is always the danger of overfitting the training samples, by considering irrelevant details, or even noise, as valid cues. In this case the error rate, per se, is not very significant.

The mentioned peculiarities of the task have influenced three main choices: the representation language, the knowledge organization and the search strategy.

As in other similar works (Carbonell, Michalski, Mitchell 1983; Michalski 1983; Hayes-Roth and McDermott 1978; Vere 1980; Mitchell 1982), a First Order Predicate Logic based language has been chosen, and has been "augmented" with some new constructs, especially oriented to handle uncertainty and increase readability by a human user. In particular, fuzzy predicates have been introduced in order to handle the "fuzzyness" with which cues often appear in the patterns. Moreover, fuzzy sets are good tools for mapping (through the definition of linguistic variables) numerical cues into symbolic ones, more suitable for categorical reasoning. At the same time, the possible heterogeneity of the original features (binary, continuous or discrete valued and so on) is encompassed.

A continuous-valued semantics has, then, to be defined for the logical description language. In order to enhance readability and to obtain more compact knowledge, some non-standard connectives and quantifiers (Yager 1985; Zadeh 1983; Lesmo, Saitta, Torasso 1985) have been introduced; in this way complex aspects of patterns can be synthetically described, avoiding to use long and, hence, less expressive formulae.

The acquired knowledge takes the form of production rules, organized into separate clusters, connected to form a graph structure, reflecting existing context-dependencies. Each rule establishes a link between a pattern description (a logical formula in the left hand side) and the most restricted conceptual classification (in the right hand side) which can be hypothesized for the pattern, on the basis of that description. In this way, the process of classifying a pattern consists of the generation of a sequence of more and more specific hypotheses, until the correct one is possibly obtained. The graph organization of the rules reflects this process, and is automatically generated through a recursive subproblem reduction process.

The subproblem reduction has a twofold advantage: on one hand, the search inside each subproblem is reduced, because only a subset of the training examples and a subset of the given concepts are of interest; on the other hand, the subproblem structure helps to exploit context dependencies.

For what concerns the learning strategy, the search for relevant rules is performed through a process of specialization (Buchanan and Mitchell 1978), rather than inductive generalization. In fact, besides requiring a complete description of the input patterns (often unfeasible in a real world domain) a generalization process would necessarily perform, at least during its initial phase, a lot of work for removing from these descriptions redundant or too specific details.

The global scheme of the system is reported in Fig.1. Three main modules are organized around a Relational Data Base (RDB). In fact, the rules generated by the Learning Module (LM) are described by means of "relations", each containing an associated set of examples. In this way, operations on rules can be transformed into a construction of new relations, by means of union and intersection operations. The learning module is not just an induction algorithm, but is itself an expert system, provided with its own knowledge and inference engine. The very nature of the used knowledge will become apparent in the following of the paper.

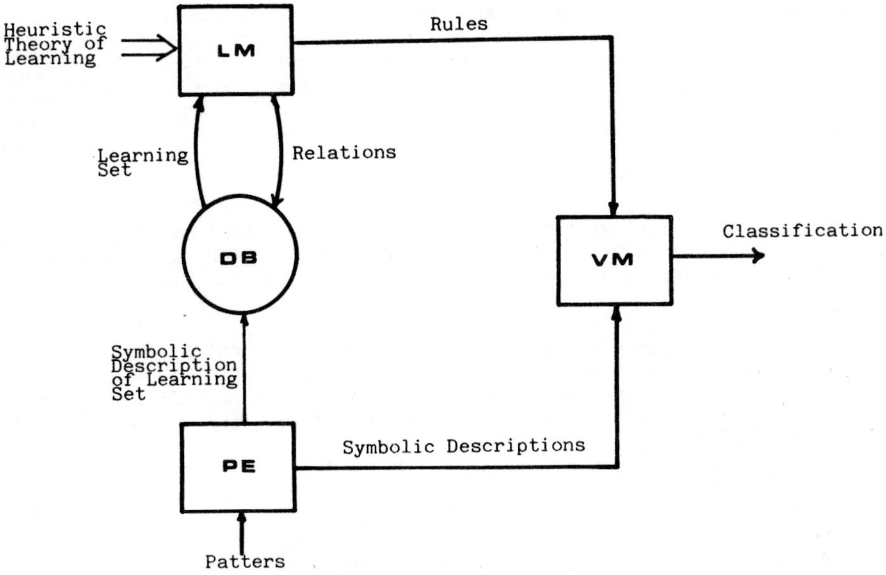

Fig. 1 Global system's architecture.

The Primitive Extractor (PE) is simply a pre-processor, which associates to the input patterns a symbolic description, suitable to be handled by the learning module.

Finally, the Validation Module (VM) provides the tools for monitoring the system behavior and for validating the acquired knowledge, in order to suggest modifications and refinements.

3. KERNEL ACQUISITION

In this section the used terminology and the methodology for acquiring the knowledge of the kernel will be illustrated. However, in order to enhance understandability, informal descriptions are given, whenever possible.

3.1 - Key Notions and Definitions

The process starts by considering a set of patterns and some information given by a teacher. In particular the teacher supplies a set of (not necessarily exhaustive nor mutually exclusive) "concepts" $\Theta^{(0)} = \{\theta_j | j \in [1,J]\}$. The learning problem consists in inferring the knowledge allowing to assign the correct conceptual description to unknown instantiations. Let moreover $\mathbf{R}$ be the (finite or infinite) set of all the possible instantiations of the phenomenon. As in real world problems the set $\mathbf{R}$ is often infinite, we have to consider a finite subset $F^{(0)} = \{f_n | n \in [1,N]\}$ of $\mathbf{R}$, containing instantiations (samples), whose correct conceptual description is supplied by the teacher. The set $F^{(0)}$ is the <u>learning set.</u>

For the sake of simplicity the case of mutually exclusive and exhaustive concepts will be considered in this paper. Each pattern can be described in terms of objects, properties of these objects and relationships among them. In order to handle in a uniform way different types of object's attributes (two valued, ordinal, continuous-valued, etc), a set Λ of linguistic qualifications λ is associated to each attribute A. Every term λ corresponds to a possibility distribution over some base variable ξ. Given an object x occurring in a pattern, the following predicate is defined:

$$\lambda(x) = \text{' } A \text{ is } \lambda \text{ in } x \text{ '}. \tag{1}$$

The evaluation of $\lambda(x)$ will be set equal to $\mu(\xi)$, where ξ is the base variable's value in x. Relationships among objects can be linguistically qualified in an analogous way: the associated predicates will have arity greater than 1.

The language used for describing the samples of the learning set consists of logical formulae in conjunctive form, containing predicates associated to objects properties. The knowledge belonging to the kernel takes the form of <u>production rules</u> organized in a structure described later. These rules fall into two categories:

a) <u>Triggering rules,</u> with the following structure:

$$\phi \xrightarrow{w(s)} \Theta \tag{2}$$

b) <u>Verification rules,</u> with the following structure:

$$\theta_j \xrightarrow{v(s)} \phi \tag{3}$$

In (2) and (3) ϕ represents a logical formula in conjunctive form, but it can also contain quantified subformulae of the following type:

$$q\ m\ [\psi(x_1,\dots,x_k)] \qquad \text{with} \quad \begin{cases} q \in \{ATL, ATM, EX\} \\ m \geq 1 \\ \psi \neq q'\ n\ [\psi'] \end{cases} \tag{4}$$

The meaning of the fuzzy quantifiers is the following: ATL = At Least, ATM = At Most, EX = Exactly. Given q, for instance ATL, the meaning of (4) is that, in a given sample, there are at least m tuples $\langle a_1,..,a_k \rangle$ of objects satisfying ψ.
The right-hand side Θ in (2) is a subset of $\Theta^{(0)}$.

The weights w(s) and v(s) of rules (2) and (3) respectively, require some more explanation, because of the use of a continuous-valued logic. Let $\phi = B_1 B_2 \dots B_k$, where B_j ($1 \leq j \leq k$) is a predicate or a quantified sub-formula (a conjunct in ϕ). Let $\mu(B_j) \in [0,1]$ be the evaluation of B_j; we need to give a meaning to the assertion "ϕ is verified in sample f" (or ϕ "covers" f). To this aim, a criterion δ, belonging to a set Δ of criteria, has to be chosen and the preceding assertion will be transformed into: "ϕ covers f iff δ is met".
The set Δ of criteria is given by the teacher and it currently contains two criteria $\delta_1(s)$ and $\delta_2(s)$, where:

$$\delta_1(s) : \mu(B_j) \geq s, \quad \forall B_j \in \phi \tag{5}$$

$$\delta_2(s) : \mu(\phi) \geq s \tag{6}$$

The value of s in (5) and (6) is called the <u>sieve</u> and belongs to the

interval [0,1]. Criterion (5) does not depend upon the specific semantics of the logical connectives, whereas criterion (6) does.
If formula ϕ in (2) covers a sample f, we will say that rule (2) covers f, too. As mentioned before, a rule like (2) has a scope limited within a subproblem σ' such that $\Theta' \subset \Theta$; let F' be the set of samples contained in σ'. If m samples in F' do not belong to Θ and among those n are covered by ϕ, then n/m is the proportion of counterexamples for rule (2), and w(s) = 1 - n/m. In an analogous way if m' samples in F' belong to θ_j and among them n' are covered by ϕ, then n'/m' is the proportion of examples for rule (3) and v(s) = n'/m'. During the generation of the kernel s is set to 1 and only rules with w=1 or v=1 are accepted.

3.2 - Kernel Generation

Rules in the kernel are not all at the same level: as the overall problem of mapping samples into their correct conceptual description is performed through a sequence of reductions to subproblems, the learned rules are grouped into clusters, each corresponding to a subproblem, and their scope is bounded inside the subproblem itself. The problem of reduction to subproblems is automatically performed by the system. Before introducing the algorithms used, an informal description of the high level process will be given.
In order to solve the initial problem $\sigma_0 = \langle \Theta^{(0)}, F^{(0)} \rangle$, in which all the samples belonging to $F^{(0)}$ are to be mapped into elements of $\Theta^{(0)}$, the system tries to generate a set of reduced problems $\sigma = \langle \Theta, F \rangle$, in which subsets F of $F^{(0)}$ are to be mapped into concepts belonging to a proper subset Θ of $\Theta^{(0)}$. The proposed subproblems are kept in a list (LISTSP), from which some of them are selected and processed one at a time, until at least one of the halt conditions is satisfied.

The subproblem is defined as a complex data type; all the subproblems selected and expanded are linked together into a directed graph G. A subset SOLVED of the nodes in G contains nodes corresponding to terminal subproblems, in which Θ coincides with a single concept θ_j; in this case the corresponding subproblem needs not to be expanded further. In the following, the subproblem generation process, just described, is presented as a high level language procedure:

```
Reduceproblem

LISTSP:={σ0}
SOLVED:= Ø
While   LISTSP ≠ Ø   do
        Select σ from LISTSP using K1;
        Expand σ;
        Update LISTSP and SOLVED.
```

The keyword using in the above procedure has a particular meaning: it indicates that the selection of σ from LISTSP is not made according to a predefined algorithm, but, on the contrary, by performing an approximate reasoning on the basis of heuristic knowledge specified in the knowledge base K1. Rules in K1 allow to evaluate the relevance of a subproblem σ according to several criteria, by mainly taking into account the cardinality of the associated set Θ and considering whether or not the samples to be entered in σ are covered in subproblems precedingly expanded. The outcome of "Expand σ" is a set of new subproblems, some of which have to be inserted in LISTSP and some in SOLVED. Examples of heuristic knowledge are given in Appendix A.

The step in which the selected subproblem σ is expanded is the core of the process. Starting with a set Φ of formulae entering σ, the system tries to split the subproblem σ into new reduced ones. To achieve its goal, the system builds up a tree T such as the one represented in Fig. 2. The nodes of T are formulae, the root is a dummy node "Root", whose sons are the formulae belonging to Φ. The sons of a node correspond to formulae obtained from the father through a process of specialization.

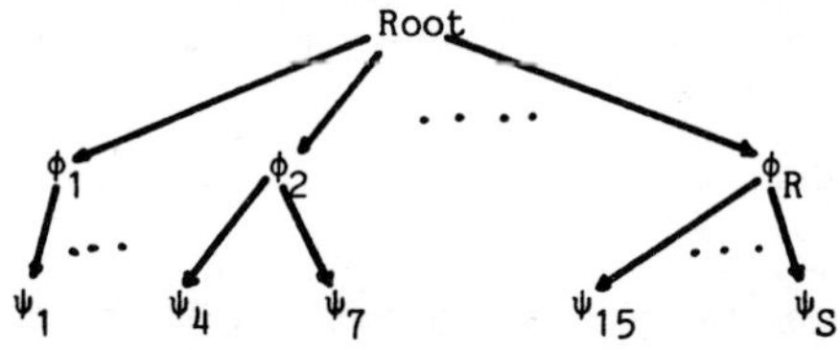

Fig. 2 Structure of the specialization graph inside a subproblem.

While expanding T, the system tries to add new nodes, which are formulae more specialized than their ancestors, and the proposed nodes are evaluated for deciding whether they are worth expanding further or not. If not, they are kept in a set of failures. The nodes which are worth expanding are added to T, the corresponding relation is created in the DB and, eventually, they are added to a list OPEN.

The specialization process consists in applying, to a given set of formulae $\{\phi_1,\dots,\phi_k\}$, one operator selected among a set Ω of specializing operators. One operator ω is said to be a specializing one iff:

$$\mu(\omega(\phi_1,\dots,\phi_k)) \leq \min_{1\leq i\leq k} \mu(\phi_i), \quad \forall\phi_i \in \{\phi_1,\dots,\phi_k\} \tag{7}$$

The currently used set Ω is reported in Table I, where the meaning of each operator is briefly explained.

Table I
Set Ω of specializing operators

Operator	Arguments	Results	Comments	Meaning
$\omega_A(\phi,x\|\Lambda,\lambda_k)$	ϕ,x	$\phi\wedge\lambda_k(x)$	x occurs in ϕ	A value of attribute A in object x is added.
$\omega_\Pi(\phi,x,y\|P)$	ϕ,x,y	$\phi\wedge P(x,y)$	x,y occur in ϕ ; P is the name of a relationship	A relationship between two objects is specified.
$\omega_U(\phi,x,y)$	ϕ,x,y	$\phi\wedge EQ(x,y)$	x,y occur in ϕ	Two objects are recognized as identical.
$\omega_C(\phi,\psi\|AND)$	ϕ, ψ	$\phi\wedge\psi$		The conjunction of two formulae is obtained.
$\omega_E(\phi,OBJ(x))$	ϕ	$\phi\wedge OBJ(x)$	x does not occur in ϕ ; OBJ(x)="There exists an object x"	A new object x is added to a description.
$\omega_Q(\phi\|q,m)$	ϕ	q m [ϕ]	q {ATL,ATM,EX} m>=1	A formula is quantified.

Given a node ϕ in the graph T, heuristic knowledge is used in order to suggest what operators are the most promising ones, if applied to ϕ; nevertheless, the number of these operators can remain quite large. For each one of them an access to the DB has to be performed, in order to decide if the resulting new formula has to be accepted or not. As accesses to the DB are time consuming operations, a kind of "look-ahead" step is inserted, before trying to apply the operators. In particular, a set Γ of "queries" is defined, each query Υ corresponding to one operator in Ω. The queries are defined in such a way that each one requires just one access to the DB, but its answer contains the results of the potential application of a group of operators.

In order to clarify this process, let us consider, for example, a formula $\phi(x_1,..,x_k)$; if the heuristics suggested to try the application of $\omega(\phi,x_1,x_j|P)$, for each x_j occurring in ϕ and such that $x_j\neq x_1$, then (k-1) accesses to the DB have to be performed. On the contrary, the following question could be asked to the DB:

"Which variables y occurring in ϕ, satisfy P(x,y)?"

and all the desired answers can be obtained at the same time. The queries belonging to Γ are listed in Table II.

Table II

Set Γ of look-ahead queries

Query	Result	Meaning
$\gamma_A(\phi,x\|\Lambda)$	$\{\phi \wedge \lambda_k(x) \| \forall\lambda_k \in \Lambda\}$	All the values of the attribute A in object x are tried.
$\gamma_\Pi(\phi,x\|P)$	$\{\phi \wedge P(x,y) \| \forall y \neq x$ occurring in $\phi\}$	The relationship P is tried for x, with respect to all the other existing objects.
$\gamma_U(\phi,x)$	$\{\phi \wedge EQ(x,y) \| \forall y \neq x$ occurring in $\phi\}$	All the objects coinciding with x are searched for.
$\gamma_Q(\phi)$	$\{q\ m\ [\phi] \| \forall q, \forall m\ [(q \in \{ATL, ATM, EX\})\ (m \in [m_1, m_2])]\}$	All the information about the the number of tuples verifying is obtained.

We point out that the described use of the queries acts as a powerful data-driven mechanism of "focus-of-attention" for the search in the solution space.

We are now able to introduce the high level language procedure performing the specialization process, inside a subproblem σ:

```
Expand σ

Initialize σ;
While OPEN ≠ Ø  and COVER ≠ F do
       Take φ  from OPEN;
       Generate Verification rules using K8;
       If φ  Σ_R using K2
          Then Select subset of queries using K3;
               Apply queries;
               Select operators using K4;
               Apply operators obtaining new formulae ψ;
               Decide if ψ  ∈  PROPSP using K5;
               Update T;
               If ψ ∈ PROPSP
                  Then Evaluate ψ using K6;
                       Update OPEN;
Select subset NEWSP from PROPSP using K7.
```

The first operation performed by Expand σ, is the initialization of the variables local to σ.
In particular, the tree T is initialized with the dummy root-node Root and the formulae $\phi_i \in \Phi$, $(1 \leq i \leq R)$.
Furthermore, to each ϕ_i, a measure of its worthiness to be expanded further is assigned, on the basis of the heuristic rules obtained in the knowledge base K6. The set OPEN contains the formulae to be expanded, whereas COVER and PROPSP are sets, whose definition is introduced later. The second step in Expand σ consists in taking a formula ϕ from OPEN and deciding whether ϕ belongs to a set $\sum_R$; $\sum_R$ contains formulae which would be worth expanding, but cover samples which are all contained in COVER. These formulae are added to T and kept for possible later use, but are not expanded immediately.

If $\phi \in \sum_R$, it has to undergo the specialization process; in order to do this, a set of queries is selected and the queries are applied to ϕ. The answers are evaluated, in order to decide whether or not they are worth to be transformed into the corresponding operators; eventually, the selected operators are applied and a set Ψ of new formulae ψ is generated.
If a formula $\psi \in \Psi$ is such that:

$$\psi \xrightarrow{1(1)} \Theta', \qquad \text{with } \Theta' \subset \Theta \tag{8}$$

and, moreover, some other conditions are satisfied, then ψ "proposes" a new subproblem $\sigma' = \langle \Theta', F' \rangle$, where F' is the subset of F containing the samples covered by ψ. Then, ψ is added to PROPSP and the elements of F' are added to COVER.
If ψ does not propose a new subproblem, it is evaluated and added to OPEN.
Not all the subproblems proposed by formulae in PROPSP are really considered and the last step of Expand σ consists in selecting, from PROPSP, a subset NEWSP containing the real candidates for expansion; these candidates are added to LISTSP.

4. APPROXIMATE REASONING SCHEME

In BIMBO approximate reasoning (Prade 1985) is performed at two levels: during the recognition phase, when the network of (object) rules is used to solve a new, unknown case, and during the learning phase, when a decision is taken on the basis of some body of heuristic knowledge; this last consists of a set of rules which obey to the same syntax and semantics as the object rules.

In the following we will refer to a formula ϕ as to the left-hand side of a rule like (2) or to the right-hand side of a rule like (3).

4.1 - Logical Connectives and Quantifiers

In Section 2 we mentioned the fact that a-priori possibility distributions are defined (over some base variable) for each linguistic value assumed by the elementary predicates and, therefore, it is possible to assign to each one of them an 'evaluation' μ.

In this section we will extend the domain of μ in order to include all the formulae ϕ which can occur in the rules. The function $\mu(\phi)$ can be considered as a function assigning to each ϕ a judgement, made by an observer, about the truth of ϕ, on the basis of the gathered information.
A value $\mu(\phi)=1$ ($\mu(\phi)=0$) means that the observer believes with no doubt that ϕ is true (false); a value $\mu=1/2$ means that the pieces of information

gathered by the observer are contradictory, so that he is completely uncertain about the truth of μ. Moreover, the function $\mu(\phi)$ is allowed to assume a special symbol ∞ (unknown) as value. If $\mu(\phi) = \infty$ then ϕ has not yet been evaluated, so that the observer does not know anything about ϕ.
When ϕ is not an elementary predicate, it is built up by means of a set of connectives and quantifiers, whose semantics is defined in the following.

Logical connectives AND, OR and NOT

For the negation (denoted by a bar over a formula), the usual complement to 1 is assumed:

$$\text{If } \phi=\overline{\psi} \quad \text{then} \quad \mu(\phi)=1-\mu(\psi) \tag{9}$$

Let ϕ_1 and ϕ_2 be formulae and let, by definition:

$$\begin{aligned} \mu(\phi_1 \wedge \phi_2) &= \alpha(u,v) \\ \mu(\phi_1 \vee \phi_2) &= \beta(u,v) \end{aligned} \tag{10}$$

In (10) we assume that $u = \mu(\phi_1)$ and $v = \mu(\phi_2)$.
In the present paper, the functions $\alpha(u,v)$ and $\beta(u,v)$ are assumed to be a pair of corresponding t-norm and t-conorm (Weber 1983), verifying the De Morgan's laws with respect to the negation (9). The chosen t-norm is built up from Dombi's generator $f(z)=[\frac{(1-z)}{z}]^a$, with $a > 0$:

$$\alpha(u,v) = \frac{1}{1+[(\frac{1-u}{u})^a + (\frac{1-v}{v})^a]^{1/a}} \tag{11}$$

The value of a is allowed to be locally changed from rule to rule during the learning process, in order to account for emerging contextual information; nevertheless, a default value a=1 is assumed at the beginning. The chosen functions α and β satisfy the following relationship:

$$\begin{aligned} u\cdot v &\leq \alpha(u,v) \leq \min(u,v) & \forall u,v \in [0,1] \\ \mathrm{Max}(u,v) &\leq \beta(u,v) \leq u + v - u.v & \forall u,v \in [0,1] \end{aligned} \tag{12}$$

Fuzzy Quantifiers

Let us consider the quantified formula

$$\phi = \mathrm{ATL}\ m\ [\psi] \tag{13}$$

Given a sample f, let $b_1 \ldots b_r$ be the bindings between the variables in ψ and the objects in f such that ψ covers f. Let $\mu_j(\psi)$ be the evaluation of ψ for the binding b_j $(1=j\leq r)$; let us order the μ_j's in decreasing order:

$$\mu_{(1)} \geq \mu_{(2)} \geq \ldots . \geq \mu_{(r)} \tag{14}$$

The semantic value associated to (13) is computed as follows:

$$\mu(\phi) \begin{cases} \beta(\alpha(\mu_{(1)},\ldots,\mu_{(m)}),\mu_{(m+1)},\ldots,\mu_r) & \text{if } m\leq r \\ 0 & \text{otherwise} \end{cases} \tag{15}$$

Formula (15) states that m best tuples satisfying ψ are AND-ed and the remaining ones ae OR-ed with the result. The following relationships hold:

$$\begin{aligned} \mathrm{ATM}\ m\ [\psi] &= \neg\, \mathrm{ATL}\ (m+1)\ [\psi] \\ \mathrm{EX}\ m\ [\psi] &= (\mathrm{ATL}\ m\ [\psi]) \wedge (\mathrm{ATM}\ m\ [\psi]) \end{aligned} \tag{16}$$

4.2 - Weak Implication

Let us consider a rule like (2):

$$\phi \xrightarrow{w(s)} \Theta \qquad (17)$$

and a sample $f \in \mathbf{R}$, in which ϕ has the value $\mu(\phi)$. We assume that rule (17) conveys some evidence in support of the hypothesis: "The conceptual description Θ applies to f". For this reason we introduce another function:

$$e: \quad 2^{\Theta} \longrightarrow [0,1] \qquad (18)$$

which measures the evidence support gathered in favor of Θ in a given situation. It is assumed that:

$$(\phi \longrightarrow \Theta \text{ does not imply } (\overline{\phi} \longrightarrow \overline{\Theta} \equiv \Theta^{(0)} - \Theta) \qquad (19)$$

If both rules are significant, they have both to appear explicitly. Then, every value $e \in [0,1]$ denotes positive evidence in favor of Θ.
Let us now define how $e(\Theta)$ is computed, on the basis of the $\mu(\phi)$ and w values. By considering rule (17) and a sample $f \in \mathbf{R}$, we define:

$$e(\Theta) = \begin{cases} \text{undefined} & \text{if } \phi \text{ does not cover } f \\ \mu(\phi) \cdot f(w) & \text{otherwise} \end{cases} \qquad (20)$$

Formula (20) needs some explanation. In using the weak implication, it appears that, given a value $\mu(\phi)$, the conclusion $e(\Theta)$ may depend on semantic and contextual information. To take into account this fact, one approach is that of embedding this information in w, letting it be an empirical weight to be estimated case by case or to be given subjectively by a human expert. In the case of automated learning (especially in view of the possibility of automatically verify and optimize the knowledge base), we have chosen to give w a precise meaning, allowing to objectively compute its value. The contextual and semantic effects have been embedded in the function f(w). For f(w) we currently use the following expression:

$$f(w) = e^{-b\frac{1-w}{w}} \qquad (b \geq 0) \qquad (21)$$

The parameter b is allowed to be different from rule to rule, but a default value b = 1/8 is assumed. From (21) we notice that f(w) [0,1] and:

$$\lim_{w \to 0^+} f(w) = 0 \qquad \lim_{w \to 1^-} f(w) = 1 \qquad (22)$$

Let us now consider all the rules which have the same right-hand side Θ and let $e_1(\Theta),\ldots,e_r(\Theta)$ be the evidences in support of Θ obtained from them. Let moreover $e_1(\overline{\Theta}),\ldots,e_p(\overline{\Theta})$ be the evidences against Θ. Rules sharing the right-hand side will be OR-ed. Then we obtain the global evidence in support of Θ:

$$e(\Theta) = \beta(e_1(\Theta),\ldots,e_r(\Theta)) \qquad (23)$$

The same is done for evidence against Θ:

$$e(\overline{\Theta}) = \beta(e_1(\overline{\Theta}),\ldots,e_p(\overline{\Theta})) \qquad (24)$$

Finally, we combine (23) and (24) to obtain:

$$\mu(\Theta) = \Psi(e(\Theta),\ e(\overline{\Theta})) \tag{25}$$

The function Ψ in (25) must satisfy the condition:

$$\Psi(e(\Theta),e(\overline{\Theta})) + \Psi(e(\overline{\Theta}),e(\Theta)) = 1 \tag{26}$$

We currently use the following definition of Ψ:

$$\Psi(e(\Theta),e(\overline{\Theta})) = \frac{1 + e(\Theta) - e(\overline{\Theta})}{2} \tag{27}$$

The various choices made in this section are grounded on motivations, whose discussion is behind the scope of the present paper. Nevertheless, we underline that the knowledge in the kernel is acquired in a way independent of the particular semantics used. This has several advantages and, among others, the one of supplying a body of knowledge on which several different evidential schemes can be compared and tested, "ceteris paribus". For this reason, the presented scheme is to be considered as a tentative one and, hence, subject to possible modifications.

5. AN EXAMPLE OF RULE ACQUISITION

Some details will be given here about the kernel generation process in the following task: learning the knowledge allowing to discriminate among the ten Italian digits uttered as isolated words, on the basis of a symbolic description of the time evolution of the total energy and the zero-crossing. The symbolic descriptions are generated by the Primitive Extractor, which segments the total energy and the zero-crossing graphs into intervals, each labeled with a symbol belonging to the alphabet of Table III.

Table III

Symbolic Description Generated by the Primitive Extractor

Shape	Symbol	Attributes	Comments
	C1	ti te w a h	ti = initial time te = end time
	C2	ti te w a h	h = maximum value of the function in the interval
	C3	ti te w a h	a = integral of the function over the interval
	C4	ti te w a h	w = length of the interval

The basic predicates occurring in the rules are the following:

(eobj x) = x is a total energy object
(zobj x) = x is a zero-crossing object
(ecn x) = x is a total energy object with a Cn shape ($n \in \{1,2,3,4\}$)
(zcn x) = x is a zero-crossing object with a Cn shape ($n \in \{1,2,3,4\}$)
(ts x) = attribute t of x is s, $t \in \{w,a,h\}$ and $s \in \{l,m,s\}$
(l,m,s stand for large,medium,small)
(adj x y) = x and y are adjacent
(follow x y) = y follows x
(over x y) = x and y overlap

In this task an "object" is a time interval. A formula ϕ can be quantified as q m [ϕ], where $q \in \{ATL, ATM, EX\}$. Each rule can only be applied within the context of the subproblem in which it was generated. Thus the learned knowledge is partitioned and forms an acyclic directed graph, the subproblems being the nodes and the rule antecedents labeling the edges. A rule R generated in subproblem σ_i and whose consequent is the set of concepts associated to subproblem σ_j labels the edge from σ_i to σ_j.

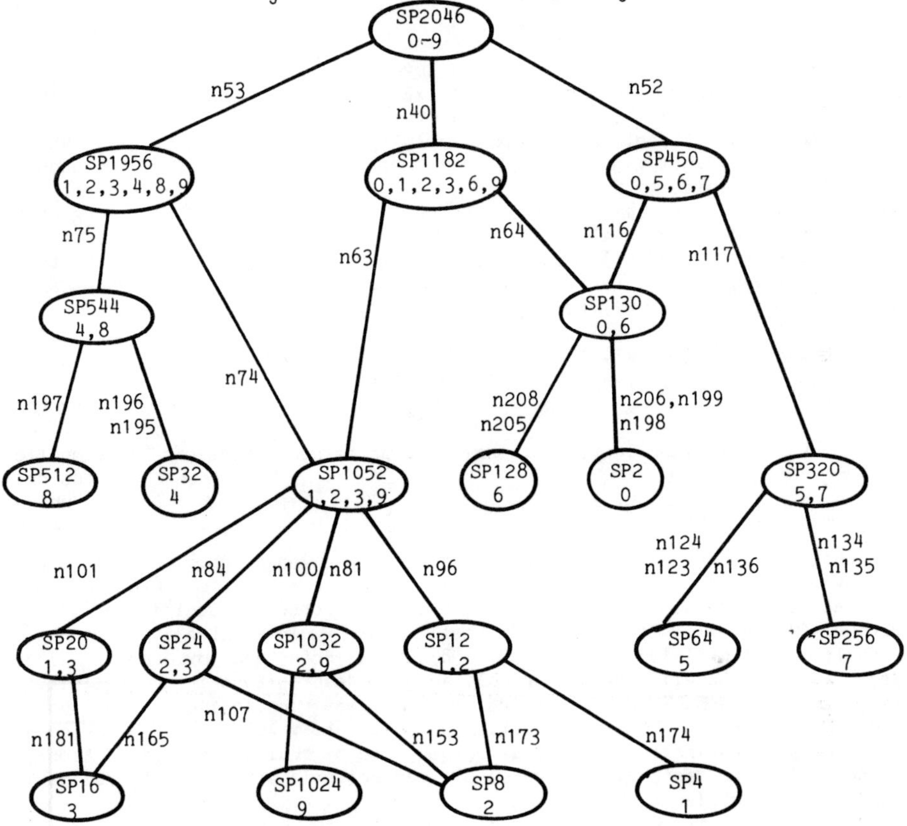

Fig. 3 - The subproblem graph for discriminating among the ten Italian digits. For the sake of compactness, rules labeling edges linking the same pair of subproblems are attached to the same edge.

The learned graph is shown in Fig. 3 whereas Fig. 4 contains the symbolic form of some of the formulae that label the edges.

The experimentation made up to now had the purpose of debugging completely the system. The learned knowledge has been judged reasonable by the human experts, and many hints have been taken in order to improve the system performance by enriching its declarative knowledge base.

```
n40   (exactly 0 ((ec2 x1) (hs x1) (central x1)))
n52   (zc1 y1) (hl y1) (al y1)
n53   (exactly 0 ((zc1 y1) (hl y1) (al y1)))
n63   (exactly 0 ((zc1 y1) (hl y1) (al y1)))
n64   (zc1 y1) (hl y1) (al y1)
n74   (exactly 0 ((ec2 x1) (hs x1) (central x1)))
n75   (ec2 x1) (wm x1) (central x1)
n117  (ec2 x1) (wm x1) (central x1)
n123  (ec1 x2) (exactly 2 nec1))))
n124  (zc1 y1) (hl y1) (al y1) (ec1 x2) (over x2 y1)
n134  (ec2 x1) (wm x1) (central x1) (ec1 x2) (adj x1 x2) (hl x2)
n135   (zc1 y1) (hl y1) (al y1) (ec2 x1) (wm x1)
       (central x1) (ec1 x2) (adj x2 x1) (wl y1)
n196  (ec1 x2) (exactly 3 nec1)
n197  (ec1 x2) (exactly 2 nec1)
n199  (exactly 0 ((ec2 x1) (hs x1) (central x1)))
       (zc1 y1) (hl y1) (al y1) (zc1 y2) (hl y2) (wm y2)
n205  (exactly 0 ((ec2 x1) (hs x1) (central x1)))
       (zc1 y1) (hl y1) (al y1) (ec1 x1) (wl y1)
n206  (exactly 0 ((ec2 x1) (hs x1) (central x1)))
       (zc1 y1) (hl y1) (al y1) (ec1 x1) (wm y1)
n208  (exactly 0 ((ec2 x1) (hs x1) (central x1)))
       (zc1 y1) (hl y1) (al y1) (ec1 x1) (al x1)
```

Fig. 7 - Symbolic form of some rule antecedents mentioned in Fig. 6.

6. CONCLUSIONS

The proposed learning methodology, yet leaving large room for further improvements, constitutes an advance, in several respects, over the current literature in the same field. In fact, existing concept acquisition algorithms (Michalski, Carbonell, Mitchell 1983; Quinlan 1983; Carbonell, Michalski, Mitchell 1983; Michalscki 1983; Hayes-Roth and Mkdermott 1978; Vere 1980; Mitchell 1982) can only acquire descriptions in quite limited languages, no mechanisms are defined to handle weak implication, noisy data and errors in the training set, only discrete-valued features are considered, and the large amount of data, required by real-world applications, cannot often be managed. Moreover, no clear criteria are stated to validate the acquired knowledge.

The present paper is, for some respect, an extension of the work (Michalski 1983) to the case of continued-valued logics and weak implication, with added much more sophisticated mechanisms to focalize the search for specialization.

More resemblant is the well-known Meta-Dendral (Buchanan and Mitchell 1978); in fact, both systems work in real-world domains, use specialization instead of generalization and perform learning in two phases: rule generation and rule refinement. However, Meta-Dendral is basically domain-dependent and the used heuristics have been deeply embedded in procedures. The system proposed here is, on the contrary, domain independent even if task-oriented and uses a separate body of knowledge to reduce the search, integrating, in a very natural way, data-driven and model-driven information.

From the point of view of knowledge organization, this work is also a generalization of (Quinlan 1983), which can only handle two class discrimination, no noisy data and discrete-valued features. The results obtained so far have, on one hand, substantially confirmed the suitability of the proposed learning methodology to real-world problems and, on the other, have suggested improvements and possible future developments. In particular, it seems useful to introduce a step of generalization, when a new subproblem is added to SPGRAPH, in order to determine what the samples have truly in common; this would help in setting precise goals to the planning activity, performed during specialization. On the other side, the development of techniques for learning from experience appear to be the most natural extension to the present approach.

APPENDIX A

In this appendix some examples of the a-priori heuristic knowledge, used to guide the extraction of the kernel, are reported. This knowledge has been given by the teacher and will be modified and enlarged during the life of the system.

Knowledge base K6

This knowledge base is used when new formulae are generated, inside a subproblem, during the specialization process and are to be evaluated in order to see if they are worth to be expanded further. K6 currently contains four rules.

$R_{6,1}$: IF ζ is low
THEN ϕ is good

The parameter ζ in $R_{6,1}$ is a measure of the degree of specialization of ϕ , i.e. the ratio between the number of predicates present in ϕ and the number of predicates potentially present in ϕ if ϕ should give a minimal complete description of the sample. $R_{6,1}$ states that more general (i.e. simpler) formulae are to be preferred to less general ones. The linguistic value low is defined by means of the fuzzy set reported in Fig. 3 (a).

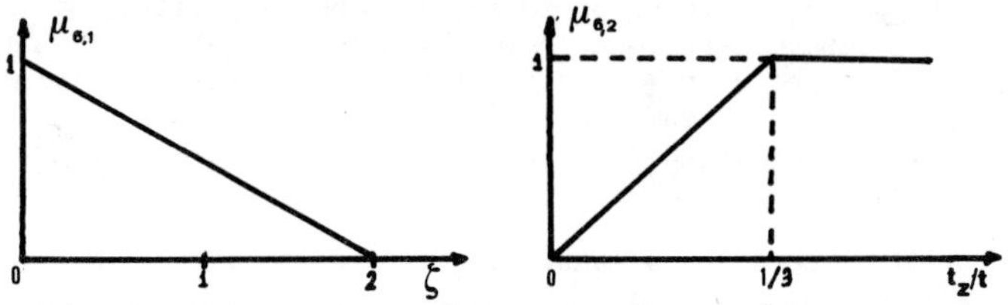

Fig. 3 - Fuzzy sets used in rules $R_{6,1}$ and $R_{6,2}$.

$R_{6,2}$: IF t_z/t is high
THEN ϕ is good

Given the set of concepts Θ, handled in the current subproblem, it is possible that no sample belonging to a set $\Theta_z \subset \Theta$ is covered by ϕ; then $t_z = |\Theta_z|$ and $t = |\Theta|$. Rule $R_{6,2}$ states that formulae more strongly reducing the set of allowed hypotheses are preferable. The term high is defined in Fig 3 (b).

$R_{6,3}$: IF v is high
THEN ϕ is good

The parameter v is the ratio between the number of samples covered by ϕ and the total number of samples handled in the current subproblem. Rule $R_{6,3}$ states that formulae covering more samples are preferable. The term high, referred to v, is defined in Fig 4 (a).

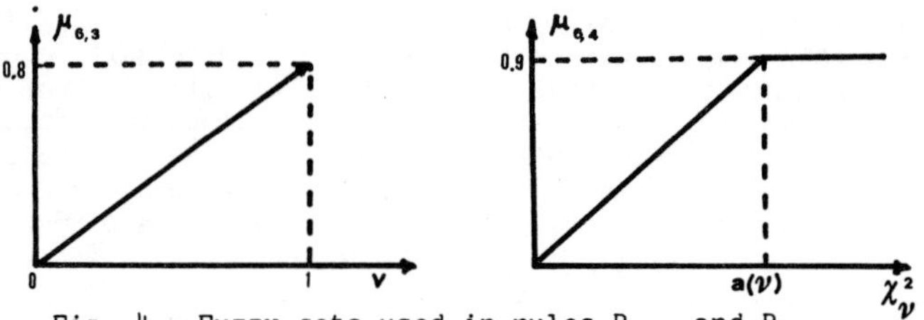

Fig. 4 - Fuzzy sets used in rules $R_{6,3}$ and $R_{6,4}$.

$R_{6,4}$: IF χ_ν^2 is high
THEN ϕ is good

Let us consider the set $\Theta_1 \subseteq \Theta$ of concepts for which there are samples in σ covered by ϕ. If the number of covered samples is distributed in a non-uniform way over the concepts belonging to Θ_1, then ϕ tends to evidentiate some concepts with respect to others and is preferable. The test for uniform distribution is performed by means of a χ_ν^2, with $\nu=|\Theta_1|-1$ and $a(\nu)$ equal to the significance threshold at $p=0.01$. The fuzzy set used for high is reported in Fig. 4 (b). When a formula ϕ has to be evaluated, the parameters ζ, t_z/t, v and χ_ν^2 are computed, and the rules $R_{6,j}$ $(1\leq j\leq 4)$ are applied and OR-ed. For example let $\zeta=0.6$, $t_z/t=0.2$, $v=0.30$ and $\chi_\nu^2=10.3$ ($\nu = 4$ and $a(\nu)= 13.3$). Applying the four rules, and using the approximate reasoning scheme given in Section 3, we obtain:

$$\mu(\phi \text{ is good}) = \beta(e_1,e_2,e_3,e_4) = \beta(0.49,0.60,0.30,0.70) = 0.84 \quad (A.1)$$

In (A.1) a value a=1 in the function β is assumed.

Knowledge base K3

This knowledge base is used when the subset of queries to be applied to a given formula ϕ has to be selected and ranked. K3 is much more complex than K6 and consists of three blocks of rules, each one addressing a particular aspect of the task. Let ϕ be a formula and let VAR(ϕ) be the set of variables (objects) occurring in ϕ. The first subtask is that of eliminating a subset of possible queries, on the basis of an analysis of the syntactic structure of ϕ. Some examples of rules for executing this task are the following:

$R'_{3,1}$: IF ϕ contains a quantified subformula
THEN Not Apply $\gamma_Q(\phi)$

$R'_{3,2}$: IF ϕ contains $P(\bar{x},y)$
THEN Not Apply $\gamma_\pi(\phi,x|P)$

$R'_{3,3}$: IF $\phi\neq\omega_C(\phi_1,\phi_2)$
THEN $\forall x \in$ VAR(ϕ) [Not Apply $\gamma_U(\phi,x)$]

Rules $R'_{3,1}$ and $R'_{3,2}$ are self-explaining, whereas rule $R'_{3,3}$ states that the unification is tried only after the generation of a conjunction.
The knowledge base K3' contains currently 11 rules.

The second subtask consists in eliminating other possible queries on the basis of information about the history of the specialization. An example is given in the following:

$R_{3,1}$: IF [(ϕ' is a subformula of ϕ) AND ($\gamma_A(\phi',x|\Lambda)$) failed]
THEN Not Apply $\gamma_A(\phi,x|\Lambda)$

The knowledge base K3'' has currently 6 rules.

The last subtask is that of ranking the survived queries. This is done according to the knowledge contained in K3''' :

$R_{3,1}$: IF $m^*/m \gtrsim 1$
THEN $\langle \gamma_Q(\phi), \mu_{3,1} \rangle$

The parameters m^* and m represent the numbers of tuples satisfying ϕ and of samples containing tuples satisfying ϕ, respectively. If m^* is much greater than m, it makes sense to ask how many tuples there are in one sample. The fuzzy set for " $\gtrsim 1$" is reported in Fig. 5 (a). The notation $\langle \gamma_Q(\phi), \mu_{3,1} \rangle$ means that the support $e(\gamma_Q)$ is set equal to $\mu_{3,1}(m^*/m)$.

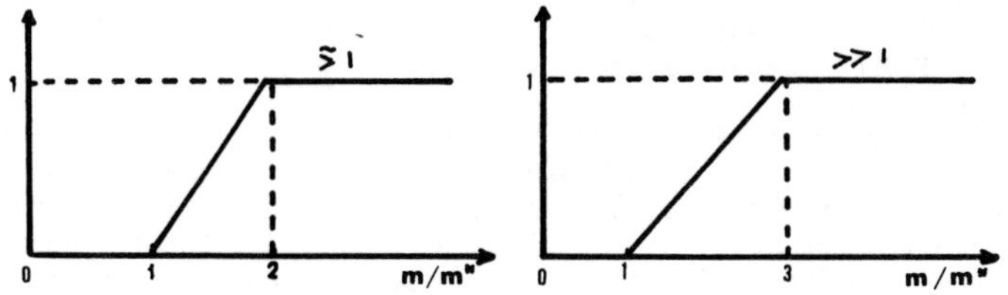

Fig. 5 - Fuzzy sets used in rules $R_{3,1}$ and $R_{3,2}$.

$R_{3,2}$: IF $(m^*/m) \gg 1$
THEN $\forall x \in VAR(\phi)\ [\langle \gamma_U(\phi,x), \mu_{3,2} \rangle]$

When the number of tuples in the relation is much greater than the number of samples covered by ϕ, it is possible that, during a join, some object has been accounted for more than once (the objects have different names in the joined formulae). The definition of ">> 1" is given in Fig. 5 (b).
The knowledge base K3''' contains currently 12 rules.

The strategy for using K3 is the following. The queries which obtain a global evaluation above 0.8 are all applied and those with a global evaluation less than 0.5 are discarded. If none, among those of the first group, succeeds, then those with evaluation between 0.5 and 0.8 are applied in sequence, until one is found which succeeds. If no query succeeds, the formula ϕ is abandoned.

REFERENCES

Arbab B., Michie D. (1985). "Generating Rules from Examples", Proc. IJCAI-9 (Los Angeles, CA), pp. 631-633.

Birman K. P. (1982). "Rule Based Learning for more Accurate ECG Analysis", IEEE Trans. on Pattern Analysis and Machine Intelligence, PAMI-4, 369-380.

Brooks R. (1983). "Model Based Three-Dimensional Interpretations of Two-Dimensional Images", IEEE Trans. on Pattern Analysis and Machine Intelligence, PAMI-5, 140-150.

Buchanan B., Mitchell T. (1978). "Model-Driven Learning of Production Rules", in 'Pattern-Directed Inference Systems', D. Waterman & F. Hayes-Roth (Ed.s), Academic Press (New York), pp. 297-312.

Carbonell J., Michalski R., Mitchell T. (1983). "An overview of Machine Learning", in 'Machine Learning', R. Michalski, J. Carbonell. T. Mitchell (Ed.s), Tioga Publ. Co. (Palo Alto, CA), pp. 3-23.

De Mori R., Giordana A., Laface P., Saitta L. (1984)."An Expert System for Mapping Acoustic Cues into Phonetic Features", Information Sciences, 33 , 115-155.

Hayes-Roth F. and McDermott J. (1978). "An Interference Matching Technique for Inducing Abstractions", Comm. ACM, 21, 401-411.

Lee H. S., Thakor N. V. (1984). "Frame Based Understanding of ECG Signals",

Proc. First Conference on Applications of Artificial Intelligence (Denver, CO), pp. 624-629.

Lesmo L., Saitta L., Torasso P. (1985). "Evidence Combination in Expert Systems", Int. J. of Man-Machine Studies, 22, 307-326.

McKeown D.M., Harvey W.A., McDermott J. (1985). "Rule Based Interpretation of Aerial Imagery", IEEE Trans. on Pattern Analysis and Machine Intelligence, PAMI-7, 570-585.

Michalsky R. S. (1983). "A Theory and Methodology of Inductive Learning", Artificial Intelligence, 20, 111-161.

Michalski R., Carbonell. J., Mitchell T. (1983). 'Machine Learning', Tioga Publ. Co. (Palo Alto, CA).

Mitchell T. (1982). "Generalization as Search", Artificial Intelligence, 18, 203-226.

Mostow D. J., Hayes-Roth F. (1978). "A Production System for Speech Understanding", in 'Pattern Directed Inference Systems', D.A. Waterman and F. Hayes-Roth (Ed.s), Academic Press (New York), pp. 471-481.

Nandhakumar N., Aggarwal J. K. (1985). "The Artificial Intelligence Approach to Pattern Recognition - A Perspective and an overview", Pattern Recognition, 6, 383-389.

Nazif A.M., Levine M.D. (1984). "Low Level Image Segmentation: An Expert System", IEEE Trans. on Pattern Analysis and Machine Intelligence, PAMI-6, 555-577.

Nii H. P., Feigenbaum E.A. (1978). "Rule Based Understanding of Signals", in 'Pattern Directed Inference Systems', D.A. Waterman and F. Hayes-Roth (Ed.s), Academic Press (New York), pp. 483-501.

Prade H. (1985). "A Computational Approach to Approximate and Plausible Reasoning with Applications to Expert Systems", IEEE Trans. on Pattern Analysis and Machine Intelligence, PAMI-7 , 260-283.

Quinlan J. R. (1983). "Learning efficient classification procedures and their application to chess and games", in 'Machine Learning', R. Michalski, J. Carbonell. T. Mitchell (Ed.s), Tioga Publ. Co. (Palo Alto, CA), pp. 463-481. 463-481.

Shepherd B. A. (1983). "An Appraisal of a Decision Tree approach to Image Classification" Proc. IJCAI-8, pp. 474-475.

Vere S. A. (1980). "Multilevel Counterfactuals for Generalizations of Relational Concepts and Productions", Artificial Intelligence, 14 , 139-164.

Weber S. (1983). "A General Concept of Fuzzy Connectives, Negations and Implications based on t-norms and t-conorms", Fuzzy Sets and Systems, 11 , 115-134.

Yager R. R. (1985). "Reasoning with Uncertainty for Expert Systems", Proc. International Joint Conference on Artificial Intelligence (Los Angeles, CA), pp. 1295-1297.

Zadeh L. A. (1983). "A Computational Approach to Fuzzy Quantifiers in Natural Languages", Computer and Mathematics with Applications, 9, 149-184.

Use of Fuzzy Logic in a Rule-based System in Petroleum Geology

J. LEBAILLY*, R. MARTIN-CLOUAIRE** and A. PRADE**

**GAIA, Elf Aquitaine, Tour ELF 12G38, La Defense, 92078 Courbevoie Cedex 45, France*
***Langages et Systèmes Informatiques, Université Paul Sabatier, 118 route de Narbonne, 31062 Toulouse Cedex, France*

ABSTRACT

This paper describes the continuing development of the system SPII (here is the version 2) which is a simple backward chaining inference engine equipped with powerful fuzzy logic capabilities. Fundamentally, SPII-2 is able to accommodate both imprecision and uncertainty in the homogeneous framework of possibility theory. More specifically, in addition to evaluating the certainty of fixed hypotheses (which is about all what most present approximate reasoning systems can do) SPII-2 can take into account judgemental expertise about problems which require computation as well as reasoning on numerical quantities that may be pervaded by fuzziness.

Beside presenting SPII-2 under various aspects (knowledge representation, techniques for approximate reasoning and computation, functioning issues), this paper discusses an application to an important petroleum geology problem that is the one of prospect appraisal.

KEYWORDS

Knowledge-based systems ; knowledge representation ; imprecision ; uncertainty ; possibility theory ; petroleum geology.

INTRODUCTION

Beside medical sciences, geology is one of the leading fields for application of knowledge-based system technology. Good examples of such systems include PROSPECTOR [DUD 79] that helps in evaluating the mineral potential of an exploration site, the DIPMETER ADVISOR [SMI 83] which has been developed for commercial well-log interpretation, LITHO [BON 83] that is concerned with interpretation of various oil-well measurements, ELFIN [MAR 85a] and its predecessor SIMMIAS [PER 84] that reproduce geologists' reasoning for finding migration paths that hydrocarbons may have taken in the subsurface.

The application side of this paper deals with some significant parts of the prospect appraisal problem in a petroleum geology setting. Traditional approaches focus on the use of numerical methods. Among these, some avoid explicit treatment of inherent uncertainties through strongly deterministic models (see, for instance, [WEL 84]) while others [BIS 84] [SLU 84] rely on probabilistic approaches using statistical or pseudo-statistical data and Monte Carlo simulations when arithmetic processing is needed.

Numerical methods presuppose the existence of algorithms. When no algorithm is readily usable but yet sparse knowledge (in the form of chunks or granules of information) is available, the expert system methodology, that is more flexible, provides a possible alternative. On the one hand, in a program implementing an algorithm, the solving procedure is fully described via arithmetic and logical instructions interconnected through control instructions. On the other hand, an expert system keeps the domain knowledge separated from a general enough interpretation mecanism and therefore makes it possible to modify (add, correct or delete) the components of this knowledge. Moreover, since the interpreter is based on associative access (pattern matching) the solving procedure is context reactive. This aspect is very suitable when the issue of the addressed problem depends on a large number of parameters (and events) that need not be considered exhaustively to reach the conclusions corresponding to a particular situation, and/or that relate to each other only from an empirical point of view. Such empirical associations are precious judgemental knowledge that, practically, can be appropriately embedded in "if-then" rules. Several other advantageous features of expert systems (see, for instance, [HAY 83] [FAR 85]) make them suitable for tackling problems normally thought to require human specialists for their solution. It is important to note that such systems may operate calls (via "if-then" rules) to algorithmic procedures and thus do not prevent the use of numerical methods when these are available. Moreover, there are problems where the application of the appropriate algorithm depends on the recognition of some particular situation patterns; in general, such a recognition process may require some symbolic reasoning for which expert systems are good at.

In the prospect appraisal problem, the cooperation of numerical and symbolic treatments is necessary. This characteristic and the fact that uncertainties often pervade geologists' expert knowledge are the major factors behind the specific approach we have taken about this problem. Thus, the main features of the system built for this purpose are that :

- the problem resolution is performed via a process which combines reasoning tasks together with numerical calculus,
- imprecision and uncertainty contained in knowledge and data involved in the problem are dealt with explicitly, through a possibility theory- based technique.

The inference engine SPII-2[1] used in this application is an improved and extended version of SPII-1 [MAR 85c] previously developed by two of the authors. SPII-1 is equipped with powerful fuzzy logic capabilities that allow it to accommodate both imprecision and uncertainty in facts and rules. Basically, imprecision affects the content of a proposition (involving vague categories) while uncertainty pertains to its truth. In other words, a proposition is imprecise if the parameter it aims to describe is incompletely specified. It is uncertain when one cannot definitely state if it is true or false [DUB 85a]. SPII-2 permits to use more sophisticated kinds of rule. Besides, SPII-2 is provided with abilities to perform basic arithmetic operations.

This paper has two major parts. First, the various aspects of SPII-2 are presented in detail. Knowledge representation questions, techniques for approximate computation and reasoning and, finally, functioning issues (inference and control) are dealt with successively. Second, the application of SPII-2 to the prospect appraisal problem is discussed. In Appendix1, the basic background material about possibility theory is provided. Appendix 2 contains a sample of the knowledge base corresponding to the exhibited application.

1 SPII is an acronym for "Système de Propagation de l'Imprécis et de l'Incertain".

PRESENTATION OF SPII-2

1 Representation of imprecise and/or uncertain information

1.1 Unconditional statements : facts

1.1.1 Canonical form

In an expert system, the fundamental primitives for information modelling in the data base (as well as in the rule base) are propositional statements of the form : "a given attribute of a given object has a particular value". Any such a statement can be represented by the symbolic structure (attribute object value) which in turn may be reduced into the canonical form "X is A" where X is a variable that stands for the attribute of the object and A is its current value. For instance, to express that John is 55 years old we write (age John 55) or equivalently "X is 55", where X is John's age. Any proposition "X is A" that belongs to the data base is called a fact.

1.1.2 Imprecise facts

The fact or the proposition "X is A" is imprecise as soon as A does not exactly reduce to one element of the domain U_X (or universe of discourse) of the variable X. In such a case, A is the set of mutually exclusive possible values for X as, for example, in the fact "X is over 50" where X is John's age again. An imprecise proposition "X is A" has to be understood as "X is in A".

Besides and more generally, in the imprecise proposition "X is A" the set A may not have sharp boundaries as, for instance, in "X is old". Then A is what Zadeh [ZAD 65] has named a fuzzy set and "X is A" is said to be a fuzzy or vague statement. A fuzzy set, say A, is described by means of a membership function μ_A, that is, a function from the domain U_X to the interval [0,1]. 0 stands for non-membership, 1 for full membership and any intermediate degree corresponds to partial membership. Thus, the imprecise proposition "X is A" signifies that the possibility distribution π_X [ZAD 78] (i.e. the fuzzy set of possible values which X may take in U_X) is concretely given by the membership function of A. Therefore "X is A" may be interpreted as the possibility assignment equation [ZAD 78]

$$\forall\ u \in U_X,\ \pi_X(u) = \mu_A(u)$$

which means : the possibility that X may take u as its value is nothing but the membership degree of u in A. The fuzzy set A that encodes a vague restriction on the possible values of X may be seen as a fuzzy predicate [ZAD 79]. The domain U_X that is supposed to cover all the possible values of X may either be continuous (e.g. be a part of the real line as in the above example where U_X may safely be taken as [0,150]) or discrete (ordered or not). Note that a precise information corresponds to the case where π_X is equal to 0 everywhere except in one point where it is equal to 1, this point being the precise value. An imprecise but non-fuzzy information is such that $\forall\ u \in U_X, \pi_X(u) \in \{0,1\}$. The complete absence of information about the value of X is represented by $\pi_X(u)=1, \forall\ u \in U_X$.

Practically the identification of a possibility distribution can be relatively qualitative since the possibility theory is not very sensitive to slight variations in possibility degrees. Actually what is important in such a distribution is the order it induces on the domain and not the exact degree associated to any element of the domain. Fundamentally, what matters is to determine the set of completely possible values (i.e. where π_X is equal to 1) and the set of completely impossible values (i.e. where π_X is equal to 0) ; the remaining part of U_X corresponding to gradual transitions between 1 and 0 or 0 and 1. From a pragmatic point of view, these transitions can often be assumed linear when the universe of discourse is ordered. For instance, in the context we are considering, the possibility distribution π_X involved in the fact "X is old" may be given by the function sketched in Figure 1. Since U_X has been taken to cover all conceivable values X may take, there exists at least one element u_o completely possible (i.e. which is such that $\pi_X(u_o)=1$). In this case π_X is said to be normalized. Note that possibility distributions can be drawn from statistical data when available [DUB 83].

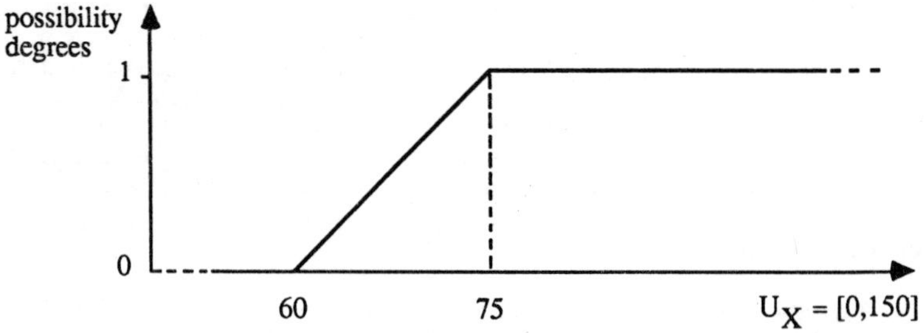

Figure 1.

1.1.3 Uncertain facts

Any precise or imprecise fact may be uncertain. Assume that A in "X is A" is an ordinary (non-fuzzy) subset of U_X. Such a fact is uncertain if one is not sure that the real value of X is indeed in A. To represent our confidence in the truth of a fact we qualify it by a numerical degree η in the unit interval. η is a degree of necessity or certainty (i.e. an estimation of the extent to which it is necessary that X is A). An unqualified fact is assumed to be certain (i.e. such that η = 1). Recalling (see Appendix 1) that the possibility of an alternative is equal to the impossibility (i.e. the complement to 1 of the necessity) of the opposite alternative, the information "X is A", with certainty η means that there is a possibility equal to 1 - η that X takes any value outside A. In other terms,

$$\pi_X(u) = \begin{cases} 1 & \text{if } u \in A \\ 1-\eta & \text{if } u \notin A. \end{cases} \qquad (1)$$

Particularly, when A reduces to the singleton $\{u_o\}$ the relation (1) represents a precise but uncertain piece of information. In the more general case, the possibility distribution

$$\pi_X(u) = \max(\mu_A(u), 1-\eta) \qquad (2)$$

will represent an imprecise and uncertain information. Indeed, there is a possibility equal to 1 - η that the value of X lies outside the support S(A) of A (i.e. $S(A) = \{ u \in U_X / \mu_A(u) > 0\}$) and a certainty equal to η that X takes his value in S(A). Moreover, the possibility distribution induces an ordering over the values whose possibility degree is greater than 1 - η.

Remark that π_X defined by (2) can be seen as the membership function of a fuzzy set **A** ; the information "X is **A**" can be interpreted as a fuzzy default statement about the value of X [PRA 85b]. Note that "X is A" with certainty 0 is equivalent to "X is U_X" (i.e. the value of X is completely indeterminate).

1.2 Conditional statements : rules

Roughly speaking a rule is composed of two parts usually called antecedent and consequent ; a causal relation is supposed to hold between them. Antecedents and consequents are, in general, conjunctions of triples of the form (attribute object fuzzy_set_of_values). In other words, we consider rules that are of the form

"if X_1 is A_1 and... and X_n is A_n then Y_1 is B_1 and ... and Y_m is B_m"

where $A_1,\dots,A_n$, $B_1,\dots,B_m$ are fuzzy or non-fuzzy sets on different universes of discourse.

From now on, for the sake of clarity, we shall deal with single condition and single conclusion rules unless otherwise specified (especially when we are explicitly interested in studying conjunction- related problems).

In the following, we distinguish between rules containing only non-fuzzy statements in their antecedent (i.e. condition) parts and the others. In any case, the value components involved in the consequent part may either be precise or imprecise (fuzzy or not), pervaded or not by uncertainty.

1.2.1 Rules with non-fuzzy conditions

By non-fuzzy conditions we mean that the value component of the triples constituting the condition part (i.e. the A_i's) corresponds either to a precise value or to an ordinary subset of values. The condition part may contain negative triples. Among rules with non-fuzzy conditions there are those having :

- purely uncertain conclusions
- fuzzy but certain conclusions.

In order to describe a causal link between two propositions, p and q pertaining respectively to the variables X and Y, with the former kind of rule we need to know to what extent it is sufficient that p be true for having q true and to what extent it is necessary that p be true for having q true as well. The necessity estimation can be seen as the degree to which it is sufficient to have p false in order to have q false. Let s be an estimate of the sufficiency of having p true for concluding q true. Then 1 - s is an estimate of the possibility of having q false while p is true. Assuming that p="X is A" and q="Y is B", then the rule "if p then q with sufficiency s" is equivalent to the rule "if X is A then Y is **B**" where the characterization of **B** is nothing but $\mu_{\mathbf{B}}(v) = \max(\mu_B(v), 1\text{-}s)$. Similarly, let n be an estimate of the necessity of having p true for concluding q true. Then the rule "if p then q with necessity n" is equivalent to "if X is $\neg$A then Y is $\mathbb{B}$" where $\mathbb{B}$ is defined by : $\mu_{\mathbb{B}}(v) = \max(\mu_{\neg B}(v), 1 - n)$ where $\mu_{\neg B}(v) = 1 - \mu_B(v)$ which defines the complementation operation in fuzzy set theory.

A rule of the form "if X is A then Y is B" where B is a bounded-support fuzzy set, can be viewed as a partial and rough specification of a mapping expressing a dependency between the variables X and Y. In other words, this rule means that whatever value the variable X takes in A the corresponding value of Y is restricted by the possibility distribution μ_B (and in any case we are certain that the value taken by Y is in S(B)). If B is fuzzy, some values in S(B) are more possible for Y than others when X is A.

In general, the causal link between X and Y is described by means of several rules. Let us consider, for example, two such rules "if X is A_1 then Y is B_1" and "if X is A_2 then Y is B_2". A natural consistency condition between these two rules is the following :

$$A_1 \cap A_2 \neq \emptyset \text{ implies } \operatorname{hgt}(B_1 \cap B_2) = 1$$

where $\operatorname{hgt}(B_1 \cap B_2) = \sup_{v \in U_Y} \min(\mu_{B_1}(v), \mu_{B_2}(v))$.

This condition means that if a value of X belongs both to A_1 and A_2, then there must be at least one completely possible value for Y (provided that there always exists a value for Y corresponding to a particular value of X).

1.2.2 Rules with fuzzy conditions

In this subsection, three kinds of rule are considered. First, the rules with fuzzy but certain conclusions, second those with purely uncertain conclusions, third a special kind of rules of the form "the more X is A, the more certain the conclusion q".

A rule of the form "if X is A then Y is B" where A and B are fuzzy sets and S(B) is bounded will be understood as follows : if the value of X lies in the support of A, then the value of Y lies in the support of B. When the value of X has only a partial membership in A, the associated fuzzy set of possible values for Y keeps the same support as B but is less restrictive in terms of possibility degrees.

A rule of the form "if X is A then q with sufficiency s and necessity n" is understood in a way such that when the value of X has only a partial membership in A the certainty of the conclusion will decrease with respect to the certainty that would correspond to a value of X fully in A.
In the representation of the third type of rule "the more X is A, the more certain q", the greater $\mu_A(u)$, the greater the certainty of the conclusion q. One may equivalently see this rule as "if X is {x} then q with sufficiency=s(x)" where x is a mathematical variable and s(x) is directly related to the degree of membership $\mu_A(x)$. Practically and to be consistent with the overall philosophy of the SPII approach, any rule of this kind may also be considered from the dual aspect of necessity. Thus, the general form of the rules expressing such a relationship between the value of a variable X and the certainty of a proposition q is

"if X is {x} then q with sufficiency=s(x) and necessity=n(x)"

where s and n are mappings from U_X to [0,1]. Strictly speaking, any rule of the above type subsumes the following two subrules "the more X is A_1 the more certain q" and "the more X is $\neg A_2$ the more certain $\neg$q" where the membership functions of A_1 and A_2 are taken to be equal to s and n respectively. Note that A_1 may differ from A_2 but for consistency, the following inequality $\forall u \in U_X, \mu_{A_1}(u) \leq \mu_{A_2}(u)$ must be satisfied.

Remark :
As illustrated in our application, SPII-2 is also able to deal with rules of the form "$\forall$ M, if Z is M and X is A then Y is f(M)" where M is any fuzzy set ; such a rule expresses that if a restriction of the possible values of Z is known we are able to compute a rule describing the dependency between the variables X and Y, this so-constructed rule being then of the first type considered in this subsection.

2 Techniques for approximate computation and reasoning

2.1 Approximate computation

In the application, that is presented in the next major part of the paper, we need to perform not only symbolic reasoning but also numerical computation in order to estimate such a variable as the forecast quantity of oil having reached a particular trap. In the following we give the background material needed to perform the addition and the product which are the only two operations we use in our application.

An ill-known real-valued quantity X can be represented by a possibility distribution $\pi_X : \mathbb{R} \to [0,1]$ which restricts the more or less possible values that X may take. In other words, $\pi_X(u)$ has to be seen as the possibility that X may take u as its value. In practice, it is sufficient in most cases to use parameterized trapezoidal distributions. Such a distribution can be symbolically written $\pi_X = (a, b, \alpha, \beta)$ where the meaning of a, b, α, β is given in Figure 2.

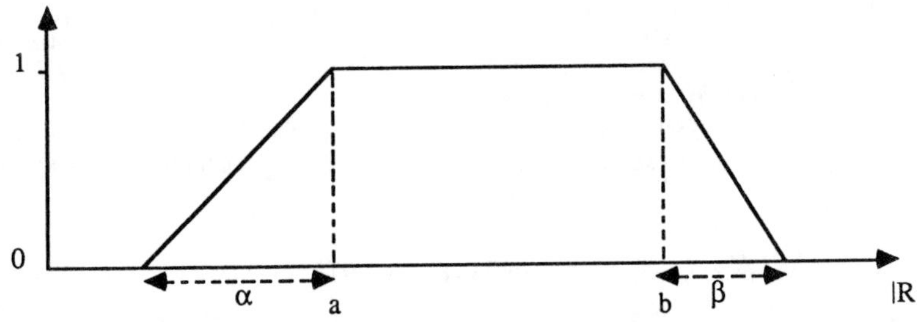

Figure 2.

Such a trapezoidal distribution encompasses the cases of classical intervals and precise values. However results given in the case of trapezoidal distributions can be easily generalized to any unimodal or even multimodal distribution. See [DUB 80]. Given two ill-known quantities X and Y represented by the possibility distributions $\pi_X = (a, b, \alpha, \beta)$ and $\pi_Y = (a', b', \alpha', \beta')$ respectively, one can compute the possibility distribution attached to the quantity X * Y (where * is an arithmetic operation such as the sum or the product) by :

$$\forall w \in \mathbb{R},\ \pi_{X*Y}(w) = \sup_{\substack{u,v \\ u*v=w}} \min(\pi_X(u), \pi_Y(v)) \quad (3)$$

Formula (3) can be justified in a possibility theory framework [DUB 85a]. The expression (3) supposes that X and Y are not interactive, i.e. the possible value of X does not depend on the possible value of Y. In case of trapezoidal possibility distributions, it can be shown [DUB 80] that :

$$\pi_{X+Y} = (a + a', b + b', \alpha + \alpha', \beta + \beta'). \quad (4)$$

When π_X and π_Y reduce to ordinary intervals, formula (4) is nothing but the addition of intervals.

The product of two fuzzy numbers whose supports are completely included in the positive part of the real line (which means here $a - \alpha \geq 0$ and $a' - \alpha' \geq 0$) can be thoroughly approximated using the following formula :

$$\pi_{X \cdot Y} \cong (aa', bb', a\alpha' + a'\alpha - \alpha\alpha', b\beta' + b'\beta + \beta\beta') \quad (5)$$

For justifications and other results pertaining to arithmetic operations on fuzzy numbers, see [DUB 80] [DUB 85a].

2.2 Approximate reasoning

2.2.1 Fuzzy pattern matching [CAY 82]

Given a fact "X is A′" and a condition statement "X is A" appearing in a rule we can estimate to what extent the condition is satisfied by the fact (i.e. to what extent "X is A" is true). This estimation is expressed through necessity and posibility degrees defined by :

$$\mathrm{Nec}(A\,;A') = \inf_{u\in U_X} \max(\mu_A(u), 1-\mu_{A'}(u)) \quad (6)$$

$$\mathrm{Pos}(A\,;A') = \sup_{u\in U_X} \min(\mu_A(u), \mu_{A'}(u)) \quad (7)$$

Note (see Appendix 1) that $\mathrm{Nec}(A\,;A') = 1 - \mathrm{Pos}(\neg A\,;A')$ (8)
and $\mathrm{Nec}(A\,;A') \le \mathrm{Pos}(A\,;A')$. (9)
When A is not fuzzy, we either have
$\mathrm{Nec}(A\,;A') \ge 0$ and $\mathrm{Pos}(A\,;A') = 1$ or $\mathrm{Nec}(A\,;A') = 0$ and $\mathrm{Pos}(A\,;A') \le 1$. (10)
When $\mathrm{Nec}(A\,;A') \ge 1 - \mathrm{Pos}(A\,;A')$, one can say that the condition is rather satisfied whereas in the other case it is rather unsatisfied. In case A is fuzzy, only the equality (8) and the inequality (9) hold, but (10) is no longer true.
The comparison of a compound condition "X_1 is A_1 and... and X_n is A_n" with a collection of fact "X_i is A'_i" i=1,...,n is estimated in terms of necessity and possibility degrees by means of

$$\mathrm{Nec}(A_1 \wedge \ldots \wedge A_n\,; A'_1 \wedge \ldots \wedge A'_n) = \min_{i=1,\ldots,n} \mathrm{Nec}'(A_i\,; A'_i) \quad (11)$$

$$\mathrm{Pos}(A_1 \wedge \ldots \wedge A_n\,; A'_1 \wedge \ldots \wedge A'_n) = \min_{i=1,\ldots,n} \mathrm{Pos}'(A_i\,; A'_i) \quad (12)$$

where $\mathrm{Nec}'(A_i\,;A'_i)$ and $\mathrm{Pos}'(A_i\,;A'_i)$ are respectively equal either to $\mathrm{Nec}(A_i\,;A'_i)$ and $\mathrm{Pos}(A_i\,;A'_i)$ if A_i is non-fuzzy or to

$$1 - \frac{1-\mathrm{Nec}(A_i; A'_i)}{\max(1-\mathrm{Nec}(A_i\,;A'_i), \mathrm{Pos}(A_i; A'_i))} \quad \text{and}$$

$$\frac{\mathrm{Pos}(A_i; A'_i)}{\max(1-\mathrm{Nec}(A_i\,;A'_i), \mathrm{Pos}(A_i; A'_i))} \quad \text{if } A_i \text{ is fuzzy.}$$

The above normalization (that will be used again in (20)) ensures that the necessity and possibility degrees of the compound condition satisfy a relation equivalent to (10).

2.2.2 Generalized modus ponens

The generalized modus ponens is an approximate reasoning pattern introduced by [ZAD 79] that permits to conclude from the two premises
X is A′
and if X is A then Y is B
that Y is B′
where the membership function of B′ is computed from those of A′, A and B as follows

$$\forall v \in V,\ \mu_{B'}(v) = \sup_{u\in U_X} \min(\mu_{A'}(u), \mu_A(u) \rightarrow \mu_B(v)) \quad (13)$$

$$\text{where } \mu_A(u) \rightarrow \mu_B(v) = \begin{cases} 1 & \text{if } \mu_A(u) \le \mu_B(v) \\ \mu_B(v) & \text{otherwise.} \end{cases} \quad (14)$$

The choice of the implication connective function underlying (14) is linked to the choice of the "min" operator as the conjunction operator. However, other choices of implication are possible provided that, in (13), we simultaneously use the correct associated conjunctive operation instead of "min". For instance, if one wants to use Lukasiewicz implication (that is defined by $\mu_A(u) \rightarrow \mu_B(v) = \min(1, 1 - \mu_A(u) + \mu_B(v))$), the operator $\max(0, x + y - 1)$ is to be employed instead of $\min(x, y)$ for performing the conjunction of $\mu_{A'}(u)$ and $\mu_A(u) \rightarrow \mu_B(v)$. See [PRA 85a] [DUB 84] [DUB 85a] for details and justifications. When A′ is included in or equal to A (i.e. $\forall u \in U_X,\ \mu_{A'}(u) \le \mu_A(u)$) B′ is equal to B and therefore the above reasoning pattern

together with (13) embodies a generalization of the usual modus ponens.
It can be proved (see [MAR 84a] [DUB 84]) that

$$\mu_{B'}(v) = 1 \text{ if } \mu_B(v) = 1 \text{ and } \mu_{B'}(v) = \Theta(A\,;A') \text{ if } \mu_{B'}(v) = 0$$

$$\mu_{B'}(v) \geq \max(\Theta(A\,;A'), \mu_B(v)) \text{ in any case} \qquad (15)$$

where $\Theta(A\,;A') = \sup_{t \in D} \mu_{A'}(t) = 1 - \mathrm{Nec}(S(A)\,;A')$ (16)

given that $D = \{u \in U_X \,/\, \mu_A(u) = 0\}$.

When A is non fuzzy, A´ being normalized, (15) reduces to

$$\forall v \in U_Y,\ \mu_{B'}(v) = \max(\Theta(A\,;A'), \mu_B(v)) \qquad (17)$$

The equality (17) expresses that as soon as a significant part of A´ is not included in A (i.e. it is possible to the degree $\Theta(A\,;A')$ that the value of X does not satisfy the condition "X is A" at all) a uniform level of indetermination $\Theta(A\,;A')$ appears in the conclusion. This means that in such a case one cannot be fully confident in the information "Y takes its value in the set S(B).

As already mentioned, it is generally necessary to use several rules "if X is A^k then Y is B^k" k=1,...,r to describe the link between X and Y. In that case it can be proved [DUB 85b] that B´ is obtained by replacing $\mu_A(u) \to \mu_B(v)$ by $\min_{k=1,\dots,r} \mu_{A^k}(u) \to \mu_{B^k}(v)$ in Formula (13).

In other respects, the antecedent part of a rule may be constituted by a conjunction of several elementary conditions as in "X_1 is A_1 and...and X_n is A_n". In such a case, $\mu_A(u)$, in (13) and (14), has to be replaced by $\min_{i=1,\dots,n} \mu_{A_i}(u_i)$ where u_i is an element of the domain U_{X_i} of X_i, i=1,...,n.

Let us now consider the particular case of rules having non-fuzzy conditions and purely uncertain conclusions (see Subsection 1.2.1). The generalized modus ponens expressed by (13) can be applied to this particular case. It can be shown [MAR 85c] that this inference technique provides a result equivalent to the one obtained from the following pattern of reasoning.

if p then q with sufficiency=s and necessity=n
necessity that p is true = Nec(p)
possibility that p is true = Pos (p) with max (Pos(p), 1 - Nec(p)) = 1
———————————————————————————— (18)
Nec(q) = min (Nec(p), s) Pos(q) = max (Pos(p), 1 - n).

Note that we have max (Pos(q),1 - Nec(q)) = 1. Strictly speaking, the above pattern of reasoning is valid only if the proposition p = "X is A" is non-fuzzy (which guarantees the satisfying of the normalization condition max (Pos(p), 1 - Nec(p)) =1). Nec(p) and Pos(p) can be computed, in practice, from the evidence "X is A´" as Nec(A ; A´) and Pos(A ; A´), by means of formulas (6) and (7) respectively.

The behaviour of the generalized modus ponens pattern of reasoning is fully consistent with the desired interpretation (given in Subsection 1.2.1) of rules having non-fuzzy conditions. Moreover, when the condition part of a rule is fuzzy and the conclusion part is fuzzy but certain (i.e. B has a bounded support) we again feel that the generalized modus ponens behaves properly. However, there are other kinds of rule where the strict application of the generalized modus ponens does not lead to suitable results, as discussed in the next subsection.

2.2.3 Additional patterns of approximate reasoning

In this section, we deal with two patterns of reasoning that involve rules with fuzzy conditions and purely uncertain conclusions and pairs of rules of the form "the more X is A_1, the more certain q" and "the more X is $\neg A_2$, the more certain $\neg$q".

Let us consider a rule "if X is A then Y is B" where A is fuzzy and B is an ordinary set. Assume "X is A´ " with $A'=\{u_o\}$. Whatever the membership degree of u_o in A (provided it is strictly greater than 0) the generalized modus ponens yields that B´ is exactly B. In other words, the generalized modus ponens does not take into account the fact that the value u_o may be not completely compatible with the condition "X is A" in this case. This behaviour may or may not meet the interpretation we wish for the rule. Indeed, if we consider that as soon as we are sure that the value of X is in the support S(A) of A, we should conclude that the value of Y is in the support S(B) of B (recall that here S(B)= B) the result given by the generalized modus ponens is acceptable. Contrastedly, if we considerer that the value of X must belong to A with degree 1 in order to conclude with complete certainty that "Y is B" then the generalized modus ponens (at least the one based on the "min" conjunction operator) is no longer appropriate in the case where A is fuzzy and B is an ordinary set. Since the second interpretation is better in our application we use the following pattern in this case.

$$\frac{\begin{array}{l}\text{if X is A then q with sufficiency=s and necessity=n}\\ \text{necessity that p is true} = \mathrm{Nec}(A\,;A') = \alpha\\ \text{possibility that p is true} = \mathrm{Pos}(A\,;A') = \beta\end{array}}{\mathrm{Nec}(q) = \min(\alpha', s) \qquad \mathrm{Pos}(q) = \max(\beta', 1 - n)} \tag{19}$$

where A is fuzzy, q = "Y is B" and B is an ordinary set and where

$$\alpha' = 1 - \frac{1 - \alpha}{\max(1 - \alpha, \beta)} \qquad \beta' = \frac{\beta}{\max(1 - \alpha, \beta)} \tag{20}$$

The normalization obtained via formula (20) is performed in order to have $\max(\beta', 1 - \alpha') = 1$.

It can be checked that when $A'=\{u_o\}$ (note that in this case $\mathrm{Pos}(A\,;A') = \mathrm{Nec}(A\,;A')$), if $\mathrm{Pos}(A\,;A') \leq 0.5$, then the value concluded for Y is completely indeterminate. This characteristic conforms to intuition since in such a situation the degree of matching of A´ with A is less than the one of A´ with $\neg$A (the complement of A). Note that the pattern (19) is nothing but the pattern (18) up to the normalization transformation.

Let us consider now pairs of rules of the form "the more X is A_1, the more certain q" and "the more X is $\neg A_2$, the more certain $\neg$q". In this case, the certainty of q is directly related, first, to the extent to which the fact "X is A´ " fits the condition "X is A_1" and, second, to the extent to which this fact departs from the condition "X is $\neg A_2$". These two pieces of information are obtained, here, through the respective quantities $\mathrm{Nec}(A_1; \mathrm{core}(A'))$ and $\mathrm{Pos}(A_2; \mathrm{core}(A'))$ where $\mathrm{core}(A') = \{u \in U_X \,/\, \mu_{A'}(u) = 1\}$. This is a heuristic choice which, in practice, is satisfying in the application discussed later. Practically, from "X is A´ " and the pair "the more X is A_1, the more certain q", "the more X is $\neg A_2$, the more certain $\neg$q" we infer that

$\mathrm{Nec}(q) = \min(\gamma, \alpha')$ and $\mathrm{Pos}(q) = \max(1 - \gamma, \beta')$ where $1 - \gamma$ expresses the level of indetermination (uncertainty) of the fact "X is A´ " (assuming this fact belongs to the kind of evidence discussed in Subsection 1.1.3) and α', β' are computed by (20) in which $\alpha = \mathrm{Nec}(A_1 \,;\, \mathrm{core}(A'))$ and $\beta = \mathrm{Pos}(A_2 \,;\, \mathrm{core}(A'))$. Keeping in mind the equivalent way of viewing these pairs of rules (as noticed in Subsection 1.2.2) one can verify that this inference is still consistent with the spirit of patterns (18) and (19).

2.2.4 Combining information items related to the same variable

When several rules have conclusion parts which concern the same variable (i.e. the same attribute of the same object), we need to synthesize the information (see, for instance, [MAR 85b]). Each piece of information obtained for Y can be represented as a possibility distribution on U_Y. Two possibility distributions π_Y^1 and π_Y^2 can be combined with the following formula :

$$\forall v \in U_Y, \quad \pi_Y(v) = \frac{\min(\pi_Y^1(v), \pi_Y^2(v))}{\sup_{v \in U_Y} \min(\pi_Y^1(v), \pi_Y^2(v))} \tag{21}$$

The conjunctive operation "min" is preferred here since it is the only one that is idempotent. When the value of the denominator in (21) is not equal to 1, it indiquates that the two pieces of information are somewhat conflicting. By using Formula (21), the normalization of the result is restored but the conflict is occulted. In the particular case where the two pieces of information to be combined reduce to the pairs ($\mathrm{Nec}^1(q)$, $\mathrm{Pos}^1(q)$) and ($\mathrm{Nec}^2(q)$, $\mathrm{Pos}^2(q)$) the formula (21) is equivalent to (see [PRA 85c]) :

$$\mathrm{Nec}(q) = 1 - \frac{1 - \max(\mathrm{Nec}^1(q), \mathrm{Nec}^2(q))}{\max[\min(1-\mathrm{Nec}^1(q), 1-\mathrm{Nec}^2(q)), \min(\mathrm{Pos}^1(q), \mathrm{Pos}^2(q))]}$$

$$\mathrm{Pos}(q) = \frac{\min(\mathrm{Pos}^1(q), \mathrm{Pos}^2(q))}{\max[\min(1-\mathrm{Nec}^1(q), 1-\mathrm{Nec}^2(q)), \min(\mathrm{Pos}^1(q), \mathrm{Pos}^2(q))]} \tag{22}$$

3 Functioning issues

The fundamental techniques described in Section 2 have been embedded and implemented in a simple inference engine, called SPII, that is controlled by a backward chaining mecanism (i.e. any particular rule is invoked according to its ability to produce a desired conclusion). Version 2 of the LE_LISP (a dialect of LISP) program of SPII is running on a VAX-750 under VMS as well as on a 512K Macintosh.

Basically, the user can ask about the value the attribute of an object takes and/or the certainty of a proposition expressed in terms of triples of the form (attribute object (fuzzy)_set_of_values). In order to answer a user's query, SPII-2 develops a reasoning process by chaining rules as any inference engine does. With the knowledge base used in our application, once the reasoning is done, the chained rules constitute an inference network which is an AND/OR graph without any cycle (an OR node corresponds to rules concluding on the same variable; an AND node corresponds to a conjunction of conditions).

Five different kinds of operation may have to be performed when a rule is used. They are successively discussed in the remaining part of this section.

i) The pattern matching phase.
This phase may itself require several different treatments.
First, SPII-2 looks for the triple corresponding to the attribute of the object involved in the elementary condition whose satisfying is to be evaluated. In case such a triple does not exist in the factual data base, rules able to produce it are considered by the backward chaining mecanism that may or may not succeed in this task.
Second, as discussed in Subsections 2.2.2 and 2.2.3, there are rules whose firing require to know to what extent an elementary condition is satisfied. Then, we have to use the fuzzy pattern matching procedure described in Subsection 2.2.1 (Formulas (6) and (7)).
Third, some conditons may only be partially specified in the sense that the value component of such a condition is a variable. The role of the pattern matching phase in such a case is to instantiate (if possible) the variable.

ii) The evaluation of compound conditions.
According to (11)-(12), this process makes use of the "min" operator for combining, on the one hand the degrees of necessity and on the other hand the degrees of possibility that each elementary condition is satisfied. The elementary evaluations which are combined, are obtained via fuzzy pattern matching using (6)-(7).When the generalized modus ponens pattern of reasoning is used under the form (13) (i.e. when a rule with a fuzzy but certain conclusion part is dealt with) the fuzzy pattern matching step is modified, since we are then interested in the quantity $\Theta(A\ ;A') = 1 - \mathrm{Nec}(S(A)\ ;A')$. Clearly, in case of a compound condition $\Theta(A\ ;A')$ must be replaced by $\max_{i=1,\ldots,n} \Theta(A_i\ ;A_i')$ in (15) and (17).

iii) The propagation of uncertainty and imprecision along a rule.
This propagation is performed using the patterns of reasoning (13)-(17), (18) or (19)-(20) depending on the rule being considered ; (18) is used for rules with non-fuzzy conditions and purely uncertain conclusions. The rules having a fuzzy but certain conclusion part are treated by means of the generalized modus ponens, i.e. (13)-(17). An efficient procedure [MAR 84a] computes the possibility distribution defined by (13) when the condition part is fuzzy. As explained in Subsection 2.2.2, in the case of several rules "if X_1 is A^k and ... and X_n is A^k then Y is B^k" $k=1,\ldots,r$, a preliminar combination of them should, in principle, be performed before applying the generalized modus ponens. For some reason (e.g. computing time efficiency) it may be better to use the above rules separately and combine the partial results B'^k with the "min" operator afterwards. As shown in [DUB 85b] [MAR 85b], this latter way of acting is still valid but may produce more imprecise conclusions than those issued from the other method. Nevertheless, even if the rules "if X is A^k then Y is B^k" are applied separately to the fact "X is A′", it can easily be checked that if A′ is included in $A^j \cap A^k$ (where A^j and A^k appear in the j-th rule and the k-th rule respectively), then the global outcome
$B' = B^j \cap B^k$ is obtained. However, the similar result where the intersection is replaced by the union only holds if the rules have gone through the preliminary combination stage.

iv) The combination phase.
This operation is performed using (21) when the partial conclusions to combine are imprecise and (22) when these conclusions are purely uncertain.

v) The numerical combination phase.
Numerical quantities may have to be computed from fuzzy data in order to obtain the approximate value of some variables, which the user is interested in or which are needed in the reasoning process. This computation is performed using the results on fuzzy arithmetic operations which are recalled in Section 2.1. Besides, as it has been pointed out at the end of Subsection 1.2.2, our application example includes rules of the form :

"∀ M, if Z is M and X is A then Y is f(M)" where X, Y and Z are real-valued variables. The functions f we have been using are such that f(M) can be obtained from M by adding a fuzzy quantity to M (in other words, f(M) is obtained via a fuzzy translation from M).

APPLICATION OF SPII-2 TO THE PROSPECT APPRAISAL PROBLEM

1 Introduction to the prospect appraisal problem

Basically, hydrocarbons (oil and gas) are generated in organic-rich source rocks. These are resulting from transformation of kerogen (a solid organic substance) in the deep subsurface under the influence of both relatively high temperature and geologic time. After some period of maturation, hydrocarbons may be expelled from source rocks to migrate along carrier beds and other conduits (eg. faults). Eventually, a particular migration flow has been stopped by a natural obstacle--a sort of porous and permeable rock (a reservoir) that is topped by a perfectly impermeable rock (a seal)--closing a volume where hydrocarbons can be trapped and accumulated.

The aim of prospect appraisal is to obtain an estimate of the recoverable hydrocarbon volumes in an exploration prospect before drilling. This problem is not an easy one because, despite late progresses in several fields of earth sciences we still lack complete theoretical understanding of petroleum formation mechanisms. For a long time, exploration thinking for prospect appraisal was based on the so-called descriptive geologic analog method which consists in making detailed geological studies of drilled and, thus, known areas and conjecturing that similar undrilled settings would be comparable in terms of oil and gas accumulations. More recently, massive gathering and analysis of data as well as progress in geochemistry and advances in understanding the basic process controlling generation, migration, accumulation and retention of hydrocarbons have made it possible to take into consideration the intricate way these processes interact with each other in space and time domains. Consequently, new methods for evaluating the presence and the quantity of hydrocarbons a particular prospect may contain have emerged. Some of these propositions, made in response to the demand for more effective exploration tools, are gathered in a 1984 memoir [DEM 84].

2 Involved knowledge and scope of our application

From a geological/geochemical point of view, our own approach has been influenced by the one of Sluijk and Nederlof [SLU 84] reported in the above-mentioned memoir. Basically, our evaluation technique follows relatively closely the development of a natural process that may be broken into four phases : generation, expulsion, migration and retention in a trap. In each of these phases, the most important geochemical/geological parameters having a bearing on the outcome are dealt with. Among these parameters, some (those for which the value cannot be deduced from other parameters) must be accessible for estimation before drilling. If in some particular situation such an estimation is not readily available the system can conclude however (thanks to the fact that the system can represent complete indetermination about the value of a variable and complete uncertainty about a statement).

A sample of the knowledge base that we developed for the prospect appraisal problem is given in Appendix 2 (it includes the rules mentioned in the remaining part of this section for illustrative purpose). As we said, the knowledge that is dealt with here involves numerical and non-numerical parameters. The numerical ones are : yield fraction attached to the process of going from primary to secondary migration, thickness of the source rock, thickness of the intermediary section, yield fraction of the secondary migration, surface of the drainage area, quantity of oil expelled from the source rock, quantity of oil having reached the trap. The values associated to these numerical parameters may be fuzzy. Such values, denoted by strings starting with the ~ character, are represented by four-tuples defining trapezoidal distributions of the kind shown in Figure 2. Variables (in the mathematical sense) appearing in rules are denoted by strings starting with the character "?". Most rules of the knowledge base (e.g. r2, r25) are used according to the patterns (18) and (19)-(20). The sufficiency and necessity degrees involved in such rules immediately follow the three components (attribute object value) that describe a particular conclusion. Note that some of these degrees are preceded by a "-" mark (e.g. r25) that signifies that the associated conclusion is the negation of what is specified by the triple (for instance, r25 says that if its conditions are satisfied then there is evidence that no oil is present). Negative conditions are triples headed by "non" (for instance, r32 contains a negative condition). Some value components in condition triples are sets (e.g. the second condition of r25). Such a condition is satisfied as soon as the value component of the corresponding fact belongs to the set in question. Rule like r32 and r34 involve computation of, eventually, fuzzy values in their conclusion part. The rule r37 is of the kind described in the remark closing Subsection 1.2.2. The firing of such a rule goes through a two step process. In the first one, the value component of the conclusion is computed (the fuzzy translation to be performed has to be defined in the knowledge base) ; in the second one, the inference is done according to (13)-(17). The rule r40 is an example of the prototypical conditional statement that we have previously discussed under the general form "if X is {x} then q with sufficiency=s(x) and necessity=n(x)". In such a case, the s and n functions (which are specific to the rule) are defined as step functions and attached to the rule.

However, since the present application is still in its early development stage (partly because the prospect appraisal problem, if considered in a general setting, is quite large in terms of knowledge required for solving it), our approach has some temporary limitations, the most important of which are that the trap retention phase is not taken in consideration and gas estimation cannot be done (only oil). Consequently, in its actual form, our system is capable of providing answers to two questions :

- how certain is the fact that some oil has reached the trap ?
- what is the quantity of oil that may have reached the trap ?

3 Example

The user begins by volunteering her or his field observations and measures together with their necessity and possibility degrees. An example of what may be entered is given next (this information may be loaded from a file) on the left hand side of the page. Some comments are provided on the right hand side.

```
(setq f1 '(lith sr clay))
(setq f2 '(nature mig1 contiguity))
(setq f3 '(thickness sr ~60-200))
(setq f4 '(exist tr_fault ok))
(setq f5 '(sensfv res ok))
(setq f6 '(area drainage ~50-150skm))
(setq f7 '(evaluation %ppr ~medium))
(setq f8 '(evaluation ppr 13.5))

(setq ~60-200   '(60 200 20 100))
(setq ~50-150skm  '(50 150 10 20))

(defprop f1 (1 1) cert)
(defprop f2 (.7 1) cert)
(defprop f3 (.6 1) cert)
(defprop f4 (.8 1) cert)
(defprop f5 (0 .5) cert)
(defprop f6 (1 1) cert)
(defprop f7 (.7 1) cert)
(defprop f8 (.8 1) cert)

(setq bf '(f1 f2 f3 f4 f5 f6 f7 f8))
```

Any fact is a LE_LISP atom (e.g. f1) whose value is a list of the form (attribute object value). Any value component that is fuzzy must be specified as an atom starting with the ~ character (see, for instance, f1, f6 or f7). The value of such an atom is a four-member list representing a possibility distribution as shown in Figure 2. Note that the user may have to provide the definition (if not already in the knowledge base) of some of the fuzzy values used in the facts. Here, for instance, the geologist has to specify what she/he means by 'approximately between 60 and 200' (i.e. ~60-200) and 'approximately between 50 and 150 square kilometers' (i.e. ~50-150skm). Any fact has a necessity -possibility pair attached to it via the LE_LISP property denoted 'cert'. Recall that when the necessity degree of a fact having a fuzzy value component is less than 1 (e.g. f3) the real possibility distribution of the attribute of the object (e.g. the thickness of the source rock in f3) is of the kind expressed by formula (2) in which μ_A is the value component of the fact and η is the necessity degree.

bf represents the factual base.

To ask SPII-2 to establish the presence of oil (i.e. with what certainty) or the quantity of oil that may have reached the trap, the user issues either the request (apropos '(presence oil ok)) or the request (apropos '(quantity ohrt ?v)).
The deduction system SPII-2 hypothesizes the desired conclusion (note that, actually, the second one is only partially specified since its component value is to be established by the system ; this component appears as the variable ?v in the request). Thereupon, SPII-2 uses the appropriate if-then rules to work backward toward the facts that support or contribute to the user request. When the facts are reached the associated uncertainty degrees and the values catched in the pattern matching phase are propagated forward, using the previously presented techniques. In the following, we give a slightly edited version of the transcript of a run made on the above factual base. The character ">" (which is the LE_LISP prompt) indicates the user's inputs. The character "=" appearing along the left margin indicates that what follows is the result of the LE-LISP processing of the last user input. The request about the quantity of oil that may have reached the trap causes the production of five facts, i.e. f101 to f105 (some of which are not pertinent to the request). For each fact, two properties are of interest : the one describing its certainty (the pair of necessity-possibility degrees) which is denoted "cert" in our system and the one keeping information about its origins (i.e. which rules have produced it, with what certainty and, eventually, what are the value components contributed by these rules). The latter property is called "provient" in our system. The fuzzy value ~indetermine means complete indetermination. Some more comments are provided on the right hand side of the transcript.

```
>(apropos '(quantity ohrt ?v))
certitude = (1 1)
?v = ~9
= t

>bf
= (f1 f2 f3 f4 f5 f6 f7 f8
   f101 f102 f103 f104 f105)

>f101
= (quantity oesr ~1)
>~1
= ( 16.2 243 9.72 238.95)
>(get 'f101 'cert)
= ( .6 1)
>(get 'f101 'provient)
= ((r34 ~1 .6 1))

>f102
= (yield mig2 ~2)
>~2
= ( 12 42 6 6)
>(get 'f102 'cert)
= ( .5 1)
>(get 'f102 'provient)
= ((r32 ~2 .5 1))

>f103
= (quality entrance ok)
>(get 'f103 'cert)
= ( .6 1)
>(get 'f103 'provient)
```

Processing the request induces the printing of, first, the certainty pair (i.e. necessity, possibility) deduced for it and, second, the instantiation of the variable standing as value component in the requested triple. Here ?v is instantiated by a fuzzy value ~9 which could have been examined just as response of its evaluation (in the Lisp sense). Actually, ~9 is a discrete possibility distribution (it is a fastiduous list of abscissa-degree pairs).
At this point, bf which represents the factual base evaluates to a list containing five more elements (i.e. f101 to f105) than the factual base in its initial state (see previous page).
A certain number of additional information items are readily available for each deduced fact. Consider for example the first one. Typing f101 causes the corresponding (attribute object value) triple to be typed in response. The value component of f101 (i.e. ~1) evaluates to a four-member list that represents a parameterized continuous possibility distribution as shown in Section 2.1 of the presentation of SPII-2. One can ask about the certainty of the fact f101 and where this latter comes from. In the first case, the system (that is built on top of LE_LISP) answers a pair of necessity-possibility degrees (i.e (.6 1))while, in the second one, it returns a list composed of the name of the rule (i.e. r34) having produced f101, the value component of f101 and the certainty degrees contributed by this rule. Recall that r34 (see Appendix 2) involves the computation of numerical quantities in its conclusion part. Therefore ~1 is obtained through a repeated use of Formula (5). The

```
= ((r2  .6  1))

>f104
= (yield  mig1  ~not_v_good_not_zero)
>(get 'f104 'cert)
= ( .6  1)
>(get 'f104 'provient)
= ((r2 ~not_v_good_not_zero  .6  1))

>f105
= (quantity ohrt ~9)
>(get 'f105 'cert)
= (1 1)
>(get 'f105 'provient)
= ((r35  ~4  1  1) (r36 ~indetermine 1  1)
   (r37 ~indetermine  1  1) (r38 ~8  1  1))
```

certainty pair (.6 1) comes from the application of Formula (18) in which Nec(p) (resp. Pos(p)) is obtained as the minimum of the necessity (resp. possibility) degrees of the facts matching the conditions (i.e. f3, f6, f7, f8).

CONCLUDING REMARKS

The SPII-2 inference engine presented in this paper provides an homogeneous treatment of imprecise and uncertain information, in the possibility theory framework. Moreover, SPII-2 is also able to exploit eventually imprecise functional-- by opposition to rule-based--expressions of the dependency (expressed in terms of sums and products) between a variable Y and a set $\{X_1,...,X_n\}$ of variables. It would be possible to introduce more complete numerical treatment capabilities in SPII by implementing the available results about other arithmetic operations and the ranking of fuzzy-valued quantities [DUB 85a]. Possibility theory offers a suitable framework for approximate reasoning as well as numerical computation with fuzzy data ; the models which are proposed are always computationally tractable. The merits of possibility theory as a tool for the representation of imprecise and uncertain knowledge are discussed elsewhere [DUB 85a] [PRA 85a] [PRA 85c].

So far, the experimental results obtained in our application to the prospect appraisal problem are satisfying. From a practical point of view, an important lesson drawn from the development (that is still going on) of the associated knowledge base is that the tuning phase required for adjusting the different numerical degrees conveying uncertainty is in no way a difficult task (as it may be in other approaches, e.g. PROSPECTOR [DUD 79]).

It is worth-noticing that the use of a possibilistic rather than a probabilistic modelling enables us to avoid the use of simulation methods for the computation of numerical quantities pervaded with imprecision or uncertainty.

Finally, it is interesting to point out the trade-off between imprecision and uncertainty. The modeller may prefer imprecise but certain pieces of information, while the user is more attracted by precise conclusions, sometimes forgetting that they are uncertain.

REFERENCES

BIS 84 BISHOP, R.S., GEHMAN, J., YOUNG, A. (1984) Concepts for estimating hydrocarbon accumulation and dispersion. In [DEM 84], 41-52.

BON 83 BONNET, A., DAHAN, C. (1983) Oil-well data interpretation using expert system and pattern recognition techniques. Proc. 8th Int. Joint Conf. Artificial Intelligence, Karlsruhe, Aug. 8-12, 185-189.

CAY 82 CAYROL, M., FARRENY, H., PRADE, H. (1982) Fuzzy pattern matching. Kybernetes, 11, 103-116.

DEM 84 DEMAISON, G., MURRIS, R.J. Eds. (1984) Petroleum Geochemistry and Bassin Evaluation. Memoir 35 of The American Association for Petroleum Geologists.

DUB 80 DUBOIS, D., PRADE, H. (1980) Fuzzy Sets & Systems. Theory and Applications. Academic Press, New York.

DUB 83 DUBOIS, D., PRADE, H. (1983) Fuzzy sets and statistical data. Int. Rep. n° 174, LSI, Univ. P. Sabatier, Toulouse. To appear in J. of Operational Research (1986)

DUB 84 DUBOIS, D., PRADE, H. (1984) Fuzzy logics and the generalized modus ponens revisited. Cybernetics & Systems, 15, n°3-4, 293-331.

DUB 85a DUBOIS, D., PRADE, H. (1985) Théorie des Possibilités. Application à la Représentation des Connaissances en Informatique. Masson, Paris. English version to be published by Plenum Press.

DUB 85b DUBOIS, D., PRADE, H. (1985) The generalized modus ponens under sup-min composition. A theoretical study. In Approximate Reasoning in Expert Systems, (M.M. Gupta, A. Kandel, W. Bandler, J.B. Kiszka, eds.), North-Holland, 217-232.

DUD 79 DUDA, R., GASCHNIG, J., HART, P; (1979) Model design in the PROSPECTOR consultant system for mineral exploration. Expert Systems in the Micro-Electronic Age, (D. Michie, ed.). Edinburgh Univ. Press, 153-167.

FAR 85 FARRENY, H. (1985) Les Systèmes Experts--Principes et Exemples, Cepadues, Toulouse.

HAY 83 HAYES-ROTH, F., WATERMAN, D.A., LENAT, D.B. Eds. (1983) Building Expert Systems. Addison Wesley, Reading, Massachusetts.

MAR 84a MARTIN-CLOUAIRE, R. (1984) A fast generalized modus ponens. BUSEFAL, n° 18, L.S.I., Univ. Paul Sabatier, Toulouse, 75-82.

MAR 84b MARTIN-CLOUAIRE, R., PRADE, H. (1984) Managing uncertainty and imprecision in petroleum geology. Proc. Int. Colloq. "Computer in Earth Sciences for Natural Resources Characterization", (J.J. Royer ed.). Nancy, April 9-13, 85-98.

MAR 85a MARTIN-CLOUAIRE, R. (1985) Un système expert capable de raisonnement spatial : l'approche ELFIN développée pour un problème de géologie pétrolière. Proc. 5ème AFCET "Congrès Reconnaissance des Formes & Intelligence Artificielle". Grenoble, Nov. 27-29, 955-962.

MAR 85b MARTIN-CLOUAIRE, R., PRADE, H. (1985) On the problems of representation and propagation of uncertainty in expert systems. Int. J. Man-Machine Studies, 22, 251-264.

MAR 85c MARTIN-CLOUAIRE, R., PRADE, H. (1985) SPII-1 a simple inference engine capable of accommodating both imprecision and uncertainty. To appear in "Computer Assisted Decision Making", (G. Mitra ed.), North-Holland.

PER 84 PERROT, A., LEBAILLY, J., COURTEILLE, J-M. (1984) The ELFIA project at Elf Aquitaine. Pattern Recognition Letters, 2 (6), 433-437.

PRA 85a PRADE, H. (1985) A computational approach to approximate and plausible reasoning, with applications to expert systems. IEEE Trans. on Pattern Analysis and Machine Intelligence, 7 (3), 260-283. Corrections in 7 (6), 747-748.

PRA 85b PRADE, H. (1985) Reasoning with fuzzy default values. Proc. 15th IEEE Int. Symp. Multiple-Valued Logic, Kingston, On., Canada, 191-197.

PRA 85c PRADE, H. (1985) A quantitative approach to approximate reasoning in rule-based expert systems. To appear in "Computer Expert Systems", (L. Bolc, M.J. Coombs, eds.) Springer Verlag. Also Int. Rep. n° 229, LSI, Univ. P. Sabatier, Toulouse.

SMI 83 SMITH, R.G., BAKER, J.D. (1983) The Dipmeter advisor system. A case study in commercial expert system development. Proc. 8th Int. Joint Conf. Artificial Intelligence, Karlsruhe, Aug. 8-12, 122-129.

SLU 84 SLUIJK, D., NEDERLOF, M.H. (1984) Worldwide geological experience as a systematic basis for prospect appraisal. In [DEM 84], 15-26.

WEL 84 WELTE, D.H., YUKLER, M.A. (1984) Petroleum origin and accumulation in bassin evolution ---a quantitative model. In [DEM 84], 27-39.

ZAD 65 ZADEH, L.A. (1965) Fuzzy sets. Information & Control, 8, 338-353.

ZAD 78 ZADEH, L.A. (1978) Fuzzy sets as a basis for a theory of possibility. Fuzzy Sets & Systems , 1, 3-28.

ZAD 79 ZADEH, L.A. (1979) A theory of approximate reasoning. Machine Intelligence, 9, (J.E. Hayes, D. Michie, L.I. Mikulich, eds.). Elsevier, 149-194.

APPENDIX 1 : BACKGROUND ON POSSIBILITY THEORY

The concept of a possibility measure was introduced by Zadeh [ZAD 78]. A possibility measure Π on a universe U is a set function from $\wp(U)$ to [0,1], where $\wp(U)$ denotes the set of subsets of U, which is such that :

i) $\Pi(\emptyset) = 0$

ii) $\Pi(U) = 1$ (A1)

iii) $\forall A \in \wp(U), \forall B \in \wp(U), \Pi(A \cup B) = \max(\Pi(A), \Pi(B))$.

The axiom iii) shows that a possibility measure completely departs from a probability measure P since for the latter, we have $\forall A \in \wp(U), \forall B \in \wp(U)$, if $A \cap B = \emptyset$, $P(A \cup B) = P(A) + P(B)$ instead of iii). A worth-noticing consequence of (A1) is that

$$\forall A \in \wp(U),\ \max(\Pi(A), \Pi(\neg A)) = 1. \qquad \text{(A2)}$$

(A2) contrast with the probability situation where $\forall A \in \wp(U)$, $P(A) + P(\neg A) = 1$. (A2) ensures that for two opposite events, at least one has a possibility equal to 1 ; however the fact that an event has a possibility equal to 1 does not prevent the opposite event to have a non-zero possibility.

Generally, a possibility measure Π can be built from a so-called possibility distribution π, which is a function from U to [0, 1], in the following way :

$$\forall A \in \wp(U),\ \Pi(A) = \sup_{u \in A} \pi(u). \qquad \text{(A3)}$$

Note that $\Pi(\{u\}) = \pi(u)$. The possibility distribution π can be viewed as a fuzzy restriction on the possible values of a variable X which takes its values in U. Then Π defined by (A3) enables to compute the possibility that X lies in a given subset A of U. Since $\pi(u)=1$, we must have $\sup_{u \in U} \pi(u) = 1$; a possibility distribution such that $\exists\, u_0 \in U, \pi(u_0) = 1$ is said normalized.

A so-called necessity measure N can be built from Π according to the duality expressed by

$$\forall A \in \wp(U),\ N(A) = 1 - \Pi(\neg A). \qquad \text{(A4)}$$

Then N satisfies the dual axiom

$$\forall A \in \wp(U), \forall B \in \wp(U),\ N(A \cap B) = \min(N(A), N(B)) \qquad \text{(A5)}$$

and we have

$$\forall A \in \wp(U),\ \min(N(A), N(\neg A)) = 0 \qquad \text{(A6)}$$

$$\forall A \in \wp(U),\ N(A) = \inf_{u \notin A} 1 - \pi(u). \qquad \text{(A7)}$$

(A4) expresses that the necessity of an event corresponds to the impossibility of the opposite event, which is the usual relationship between possibility and necessity in modal logic. (A6) entails that among two opposite events, at most one has a non-zero necessity measure.

APPENDIX 2 : A SAMPLE OF THE KNOWLEDGE BASE

A SAMPLE OF FUZZY VALUES

~low_thick_sr means "low thickness for the source rock" and is expressed in meters.
~low_thick_is means "low thickness for the intermediary section" and is expressed in meters.
~not_v_good_not_zero means "not very good but still greater than zero" and is expressed (as the other fuzzy values given here) on the [0 100]-scale.

```
(setq ~low_thick_sr '(0 5 0 3))
(setq ~low_thick_is '(0 100 0 20))
(setq ~good '(60 100 10 0))
(setq ~excellent '(80 100 10 0))
(setq ~very_good '(70 90 10 10))
(setq ~rather_good '(40 70 10 10))
(setq ~medium_good '(50 70 10 10))
(setq ~medium_poor '(30 50 10 10))
(setq ~poor_not_zero '(20 40 10 10))
(setq ~poor '(0 40 0 10))
(setq ~medium '(40 60 10 10))
(setq ~not_v_good_not_zero '(20 70 10 10))
(setq ~100% '(95 100 5 0))
```

A SAMPLE OF THE RULE BASE

```
(setq r2 '(((lith sr clay) (nature mig1 contiguity) (thickness sr ~not_low_thick_sr))
        ((quality entrance ok .8 0) (yield mig1 ~not_v_good_not_zero 1 0))))
```

```
(setq r25 '(((quality entrance ok) (nature mig1 (bevel fault contiguity))
            (exist tr_fault ok) (sensfv res ok))
           ((presence oil ok -.8 0))))

(setq r32 '(((yield mig1 ?r) (exist tr_fault ok) (non (sensfv res ok)))
           ((yield mig2 (mult ?r .6) 1 0))))

(setq r34 '(((area drainage ?a) (thickness sr ?e) (evaluation ppr ?p) (evaluation %ppr ?%p))
           ((quantity oesr (mult 1E-5 ?a ?e ?p ?%p) 1 0))))

(setq r37 '(((quantity oesr ?q) (yield mig2 ~excellent))
           ((quantity ohrt (idem ?q)))))
(defprop r37 t floue)    ;means that r37 has to be used with the generalized modus ponens
(df idem (v) (eval (car (cassq v jeu))))   ;idem returns the parameterized distribution associated to v

(setq r40 '(((thickness sr ?e)) ((quality entrance ok (s ?e) (n ?e)))))
(putprop 'r40 '(((1 5) .2) ((5 10) .6) ((10 30) .8) ((30 100) .9) ((100 10000) 1)) 's)
(putprop 'r40 '(((1 10000) 1)) 'n)
```

Rule-based Process Control Using Fuzzy Logic

J. EFSTATHIOU

Department of Electrical and Electronic Engineering, Queen Mary College, Mile End Road, London El 4NS, UK

ABSTRACT

Rule-based techniques for controlling processes have existed for over a decade, anticipating expert systems in their design. This paper will outline the theory behind simple rule-based controllers and describe the self-organising version, which automatically acquires its own control strategy. Some applications of these techniques will be described briefly. The paper concludes by discussing the role and limitations of rule-based methods in process control.

KEYWORDS

Rule-based control; self-organising control; fuzzy logic; expert systems; process control.

INTRODUCTION

Experienced human operators have long been able to control processes which could not be adequately controlled automatically. This is often due to the fact that the behaviour of the process is not sufficiently well understood for it to be possible to create a mathematical model upon which to base an automatic controller. However, the human operators can exercise control over the plant, producing product at an acceptable level of quality, although perhaps not at optimal levels of material consumption and product consistency. This is often evident in the operation of continuously operating plant, run by several human operators who work a shift system. Different operators have slightly different control strategies, which cause noticeable variations in the product and material consumption from shift to shift.

The non-optimality in product and the inconsistency in the control strategy are two reasons for seeking to automate the control of ill-understood processes. If a control strategy could be embedded in an automatic controller, it would lead to its consistent application, whatever the shift. This consistency opens up the possibility of performing experiments on the control strategy, so that it may be tuned up to produce a product of consistent quality at an efficient cost.

However, automation cannot be achieved without the accompanying measurements. The automatic control of some processes has not been possible because of the lack of sensors capable of measuring the variables that the human operators consider important in controlling the plant. Process operators may be controlling a process without even being consciously aware which are the process variables they consider. Not only does this make it almost impossible for them to articulate a meaningful control strategy, it seriously hampers any possibility of installing a suitable set of sensors. Further, human operators are sometimes used precisely because they are able to detect small variations in operating parameters which sensors cannot reliably detect in the often demanding environment of industrial control.

A further identifiable complication in process control, particularly for the basic industries which process raw materials, is that there is little input quality control. When a process relies upon material obtained directly by mining, for example, there is little control that the manufacturer can exert on the properties of the inputs, such as the presence and proportion of trace elements or precise control of the water content.

In these circumstances there are two strategies that may be chosen. The manufacturer may choose to rely upon a well-developed model of the process which can predict the effect of input variations or to use a robust control strategy which accommodates such variations. Reliance upon a model implies again that sophisticated measurements are possible, with a time lag that does not interfere in the production process. If a mathematical model is to be used, the understanding of the physical and chemical processes of manufacture must be well advanced. A robust model, by contrast, need not depend on accurate measurements, but adopts a control strategy that is appropriate to the level of plant disturbances and input variations that normally occur.

But first, the control strategy must be acquired. Overlooking the industrial realtions problems, there are several way of doing this:

1. Observe the human operators at work and copy their actions.

2. The operators teach or show the automatic controller directly what to do.

3. The operators express their control strategy as a collection of If..Then rules.

4. The automatic controller acquires its own control strategy on-line.

The first method is often used by work study psychologists (e.g. Bainbridge, 1974) and knowledge engineers building expert systems. This is a time-consuming method, because of the difficulties in identifying the parameters the operators use to make decisions. Also, it is prone to another shortcoming which also affects the second method. As already stated, the human operators may have differing control strategies and it is also possible that they might make a mistake and teach the automatic controller a faulty action. This method would create a control strategy, djustment later, since it is not guaranteed in any way to be optimal, correct or even as good as the human operators upon whose knowledge it is based.

These criticisms also apply to the third method, which requires the operators to 'verbalise' their control strategy. However, this does at least offer some scope for the discussion of control behaviour amongst the experts before the rules are embedded in the controller, which might go some way to reducing the number of errors built into the automatic controller.

Once the controller has been built and installed, it would be most convenient if the controller could modify itself on-line, adjusting its own strategy to produce better output. This is the fourth method in the list above.

Rule-based controllers were first devised and implemented at Queen Mary College over a decade ago (Assilian, 1974; Mamdani and Assilian, 1975; Mamdani, 1976). A few years later, a self-organising version was developed (Procyk, 1977; Procyk and Mamdani, 1979). This paper will outline the theory behind both versions, the rule-based controller in section 2 and the self-organising controller (SOC) in section 3. Section 4 reviews briefly some applications of these controllers and section 5 concludes with some discussion of the scope and limitations of rule-based techniques in the broader field of process control.

RULE-BASED CONTROL

Rule-based controllers (RBCs) differ substantially from conventional controllers in two main ways.

The first difference to note is the technique used to represent the model of the process, i.e. rules rather than mathematical equations. As a knowledge representation technique, rules are often used in the expert system community, and we shall use these ideas to structure the subsequent discussion of rule-based control. The rule-based controller may be regarded as a simple kind of expert system, in that the inference mechanism is distinct from the knowledge base, in this case the control rules. It is appropriate, therefore, that these two components of the RBC be discussed in these terms below.

The second main difference is that the model uses rules as a convenient way to represent the bahaviour of the operator, rather than that of the process. Essentially, rule-based control models _what_ the operator does, rather than _why_. The knowledge that is used is of a fairly superficial kind, not capable of providing deep explanations of why a particular control action is recommended under certain circumstances. However, this is entirely appropriate since for many processes, no deep knowledge of the process behaviour may be available.

Knowledge Representation

As already mentioned, the control strategy may be stated as If..Then rules of the form:

> If the temperature is high and increasing rapidly, then reduce the oxygen input.

There are three important features of this sample rule. First, it is formulated with respect to a setpoint, i.e. some temperature at which the process should be held. Also, as stated, the rule uses not just the value of temperature, but its rate and direction of change. These would be analogous to the P and D terms of the conventional PID controller. Nothing here is very different from the conventional approach to process control.

The third thing to notice is that the rule is expressed linguistically, using words such as 'high' and 'rapidly', which, although entirely suitable for human operators to use when discussing control strategies, are difficult to implement on a computer. The important point to realise is that when trying to control ill-understood processes, this is as precise a model of how to control the plant as is available.

In order to implement such ill-defined strategies, the original RBCs used fuzzy logic (Zadeh, 1965, 1973). Fuzzy logic was devised to cope with just such problems, based on the premise that much of human decision-making activity was based on sets which did not have the crisp, well-defined boundaries usually associated with mathematical reasoning. Instead, fuzzy logic accommodates elements which are partial members of a set with a grade of membership lying somewhere between 0 and 1.

Using fuzzy logic, it is possible to devise a vocabulary of terms which define on a mathematical scale the linguistic terms used in expressing the control rules. The number of terms required varies, depending on the application, the fineness of the control rules and in particular whether the control rules are to be used to bring the process from rest to the setpoint and hold it there, or just to hold it at the setpoint. At Queen Mary College, seven terms are the norm (see Figure 1). See Sugiyama (1986) for a review of the literature on this topic.

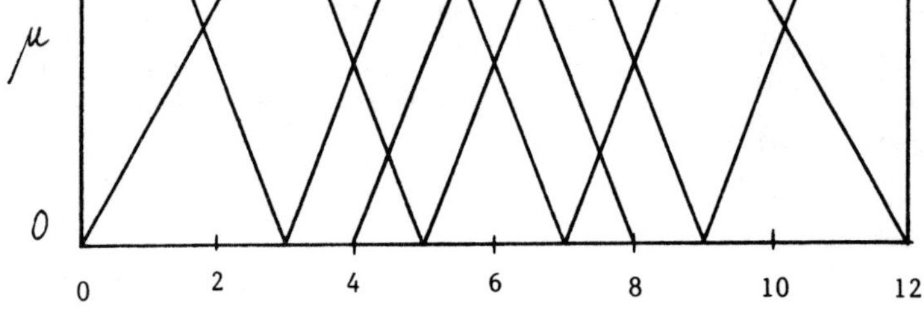

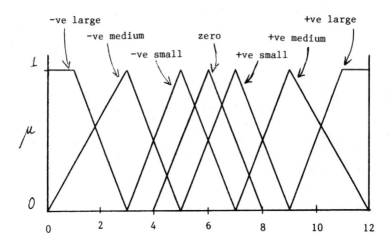

Fig. 1. A vocabulary of linguistic terms defined on a scale.

It is advantageous to express the rule-based controller in as general a form as possible so that it may be easily transferred from one process to another. Part of the generalisation process is to adopt a vocabulary of terms for Error and Change in Error which is not specific to any domain.

The labels used as of the form 'positive big', 'positive medium', 'positive small', 'zero', 'negative small', 'negative medium' and 'negative large', as illustrated in Figure 1.

Each point on the underlying linguistic scale may have a grade of membership in more than one term. From Figure 1, we may see that the point t_1 has a grade of membership in the sets 'positive medium' and 'positive small'. This is a feature of the fuzzy definition and represents the problems in producing sharply defined, mutually exclusive categories. The lack of mutual exclusivity will be important later in determining the recommended control action.

In order to represent the rules compactly, they are mapped onto a quantised scale, where each term may be identified by the point on the scale on which it is centred. This has led to some inadequacies in control, because the quantisation tends to produce some inaccuracy in the control action. This may be overcome in either of two ways. Either the rules are interpolated to produce the control action (Sugiyama, 1986), or a centre of gravity method is used at the defuzzification step (e.g. Yamazaki, 1982).

The control rules, as with all If..Then rules, consist of an antecedent and a consequent. The antecedent (the If part) refers to the observed variables, which might be things like operating conditions and product quality. For each variable, its deviation from the setpoint and rate of change are required. These are usually denoted by E and CE. The consequent of the rule (Then part) applies to all the process variables that may be manipulated directly, such as fuel or material input. These may be stated in terms of the change to the level of input, or the absolute level of input.

The deviation and rate of change of deviation from setpoint, E and CE, define a 'state space' for the process (see Figure 2). The process output should spiral inwards towards the centre of the state space, representing a steady state with no deviation from setpoint. When several controlled variables exist, some compactness of representation may be achieved by grouping the rules into blocks, so that each block only refers to one controlled variable.

The physical representation of the rules, in the case of one observed and one controlled variable, is as a triplet of integers. Each number represents the quantised point upon which the linguistic term is centred. The first two numbers refer to E and CE for the observed variable and the third to the controlled variable. Each extra observed variable is accommodated by adding an extra pair of integers, to describe its values of E and CE. The controlled variables add one more integer to the consequent, or the antecedent of the rule may be duplicated, with the appropriate consequent, in another rule block.

In most implementations of the RBC, the rules are stored as an array, defined in the program. The knowledge base and inference mechanism are not usually stored separately, but this could easily be done. The program executes more quickly if the rules are stored in main memory, and generally

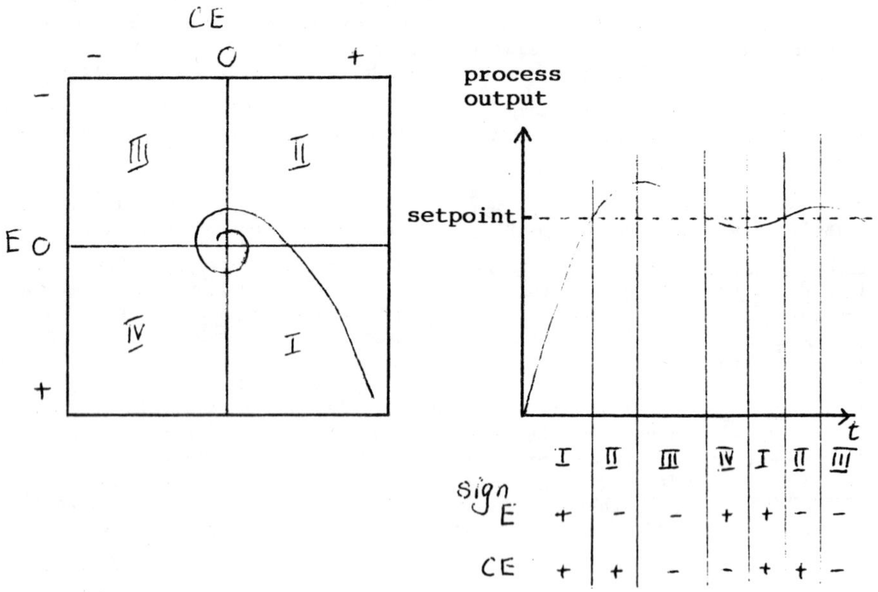

Fig. 2. The state space for a single variable and a sample trajectory.

the number of rules is small enough to make this feasible. In particular, this is desirable because process control applications are required to operate in real time and fast execution is important.

The version of rule-based control described herein is similar to a two-term controller, in that it includes only two of the three possible proportional, differential and integral terms. Sugiyama (1986) has shown how the controller may be extended to the equivalent of a three-term controller, by including a Change in Change in Error term (CCE).

Inference Mechanisms

The inference mechanism is what gives the RBC, or any expert system, its purpose. On its own, the knowledge base is inert. The inference mechanism combines the knowledge with data from the outside world to produce some kind of conclusion. In the case of the RBC, this means data derived from sensors to produce recommended control actions. See Figure 3 for a block diagram of the rule-based controller.

The inference mechanisms required for rule-based control are much simpler than those required for many expert systems. The distinction between controlled and observed variables imposes the simplifying constraint that all chains of reasoning are only one inference long. This is because the conclusion of one rule can never participate in the antecedent of another, thereby limiting the chains of inference. Were other knowledge of the cause-effect behaviour of the process to be included in the knowledge base,

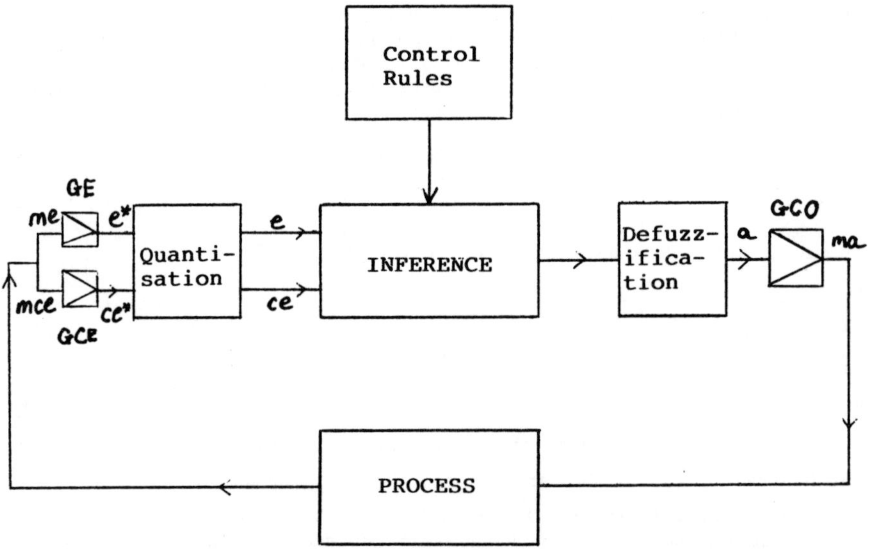

Fig. 3. The block diagram for the rule-based controller.

then longer chains of inference would be required, but so long as the rules are of the form:

If <situation> then <action>

then no extension to the chains of inference is possible.

The next simplification is that for process control, there is no need to generate and test hypotheses, so no backward inference is needed, only forwards, data-driven reasoning. In other words, in normal use, the operator would not ask questions of the type:

For this specified control action, for which possible states of the process would that be the recommendation?

The first stage in the inference process is to map the data onto the quantised scales of the observed variables. This will also require that the readings are multiplied by gains, known as GE and GCE, for the two-term rule-based controller. The settings of these gains is important in determining the response of the controller, but a full explanation is beyond the scope of this paper. See Sugiyama (1986), Yamazaki (1982), Lembessis (1984) for more detailed discussions of these points.

Once the quantised inputs have been obtained, they are compared with each rule in turn. The distinctive feature of rules expressed using fuzzy logic is that they have a region of influence, given by the spread of the fuzzy sets defining the linguistic terms. If a particular input coincides exactly with the antecedent of a rule, then that rule is given a degree of fulfilment of 1. However, if the rule falls off-centre but within the region of influence, then the rule has a lesser degree of fulfilment. All the rules are checked to see if they match the input. Fuzzy rules are not mutually exclusive and more than one rule may contribute at a particular control action. These rules do not define an algorithm or decision tree, therefore, but are instead a declarative description of the control strategy.

This may be written mathematically as follows:

$$d_i = \min(\mu_{E_i}(e), \mu_{CE_i}(ce)) \qquad i = 1,..,n$$

where E_i is a term defined on the Error scale, CE_i is a term on the Change in Error scale. E_i and CE_i are the terms in the antecedent of rule i. d_i is the degree of fulfilment calculated for rule i. e and ce are the scaled measurements on the Error and Change in Error scales. The total number of rules is denoted by n.

Measurements of e and ce will produce non-zero degrees of fulfilment only when the appropriate grades of membership in <u>both</u> E_i and CE_i are non-zero. When a rule has a degree of fulfilment greater than zero, the rule is said to be triggered.

Once each rule has been inspected, the consequent of the triggered rules (i.e. those with a degree of fulfilment greater than 0) is qualified by that rule's degree of fulfilment. Then, the consequents of all the triggered rules are combined together using the union operation of sets. This produces a recommendation which is the combination of the advice of all the rules.

This may be expressed formally as:

$$\mu_{A'}(a) = \max(d_i A_i(a)) \qquad \forall a \in A, \quad i = 1,..,n$$

where A' is the fuzzy set representing the recommended action, a is a point on the linguistic scale of action, A, and A_i is the consequent of rule i.

The outcome of the inference process so far is a fuzzy set, specifying a fuzzy distribution of control action. However, a single action only may be applied, so a single point needs to be selected from the set. This process of reducing a fuzzy set to a single point is known as defuzzification.

There are several possible methods, each of which have advantages and disadvantages. A method which is currently being widely adopted is to take the centre of gravity of the whole set. This has the advantage of producing smoothly varying recommended actions (Sugiyama, 1986; Yamazaki, 1982). Other possible methods concentrate on the action values where the possibility distribution reaches a maximum (Assilian, 1974; Mamdani and Assilian, 1975; Mamdani, 1976), called the mean of maxima or average of maxima methods. The methods are criticised as producing less smooth controller output (Yamazaki, 1982).

This may be written formally as:

$$a' = \frac{\sum a \, \mu_A(a)}{\sum \mu_A(a)} \qquad \forall a \in A'$$

where a' is the recommended, defuzzified control action. We use the summation rather than integral symbol to indicate that the action scale has also been quantised.

This concludes an outline description of the rule-based controller. Many details of the design and implementation of the RBC have been omitted, since they would be beyond the scope of this paper. The interested reader is referred to Procyk (1977), Procyk and Mamdani (1979), Yamazaki (1982) and Lembessis (1984) for more detailed discussion of these points. Other researchers have suggested improvements and refinements to the basic algorithm outlined above (Tong, 1984; Maiers and Sherif, 1985).

SELF-ORGANISING CONTROLLER

The introductory section discussed the various methods of obtaining control rules from human operators. An automatic controller based on the operators' protocol does have the advantage of consistency, but might not be much better in practice than the human operators themselves. Therefore, it is desirable that the controller should be able to improve its performance and produce substantial improvements in process performance. The self-organising controller originally implemented by Procyk (1977, Procyk and Mamdani, 1979) sets out to accomplish this. A block diagram of SOC is in Figure 4.

Looking again at the state space, we see that the ideal trajectory through the state space is a straight line from the outer corner into the centre. This would represent the process rising directly to the setpoint without overshoot. However, this should be accomplished quickly - there is little advantage in avoiding overshoot if the process responds too sluggishly.

The self-organising controller is based on the observation that the ideal trajectory lies on a diagonal path through the state space. Any deviation of the trajectory from this path should be corrected by modifying the rule or rules that were responsible for the undesirable process behaviour. This is implemented by having a 'performance table' which is a table the same shape as the state space. Its entries are not rules, but <u>changes</u> in rules. By applying these corrections to the consequents of the rules, the subsequent passes of the trajectory will be guided back to the desired path.

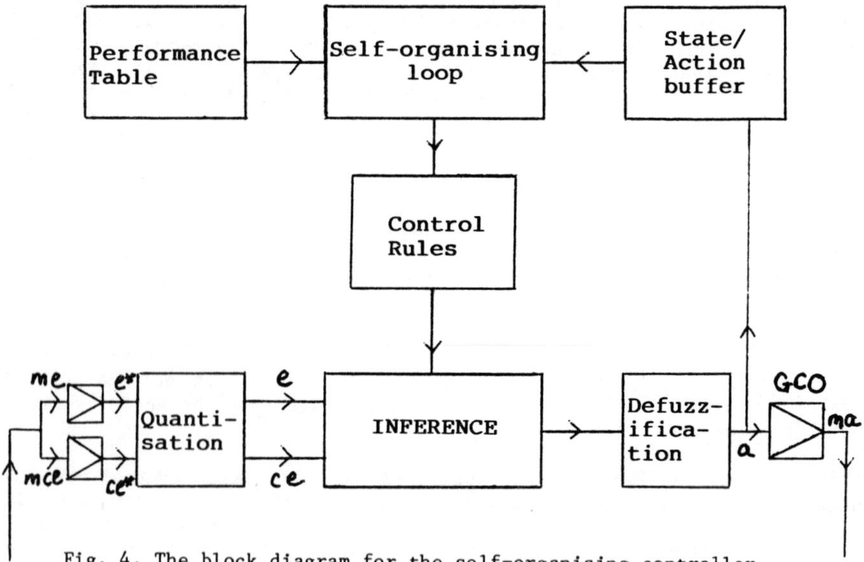

Fig. 4. The block diagram for the self-organising controller.

The performance table consists of a diagonal of zero entries, with entries increasing in absolute value the further away from the diagonal. One half of the entries are positive, the other negative, representing the damping and accelerating effects of the rules. The entries in the performance table are a measure of the desirability of each possible state in the E,CE space. The magnitude and arrangement of the entries have been investigated bu several authors, e.g. Yamazaki (1982). See Fig. 5 for a sample performance table.

	ce*													
		-6	-5	-4	-3	-2	-1	0	1	2	3	4	5	6
	-6	-12	-11	-10	-9	-8	-7	-6	-5	-4	-3	-2	-1	0
	-5	-11	-10	-9	-8	-7	-6	-5	-4	-3	-2	-1	0	1
	-4	-10	-9	-8	-7	-6	-5	-4	-3	-2	-1	0	1	2
	-3	-9	-8	-7	-6	-5	-4	-3	-2	-1	0	1	2	3
	-2	-8	-7	-6	-5	-4	-3	-2	-1	0	1	2	3	4
	-1	-7	-6	-5	-4	-3	-2	-1	0	1	2	3	4	5
e*	0	-6	-5	-4	-3	-2	-1	0	1	2	3	4	5	6
	1	-5	-4	-3	-2	-1	0	1	2	3	4	5	6	7
	2	-4	-3	-2	-1	0	1	2	3	4	5	6	7	8
	3	-3	-2	-1	0	1	2	3	4	5	6	7	8	9
	4	-2	-1	0	1	2	3	4	5	6	7	8	9	10
	5	-1	0	1	2	3	4	5	6	7	8	9	10	11
	6	0	1	2	3	4	5	6	7	8	9	10	11	12

Fig. 5. Sample performance table (Sugiyama, 1986).

The rules are modified according to the following equation:

$$R(t-mT) = A'(t-mT) + PT(t)$$

where t is a point in time, T is the sampling interval, m is the delay in reward parameter, a'(t-mT) is controller output m sampling intervals ago, PT(t) is the performance table entry calculated from e and ce at time t, and R(t-mT) is the rule that was applied m sampling intervals ago. The consequent of the rule is replaced by the right hand side of the above equation.

The principal parameter in the design of the self-organising controller is the distribution of corrections. This may be done by selecting a single rule which was applied at some fixed interval ago and applying all the correction to that rule. Other schemes have favoured a distribution of correction, reasoning that a single control action cannot be held responsible but the actions before and after also deserve some of the blame.

Once the decision has been made between whether a single rule or several rules should be corrected, the next decision is how far back in time to go to select the responsible rule. This is the delay in reward parameter, m in the equation above. The original implementations used an interval equal to the dead time of the process. However, Sugiyama (1986) has recently extended the degree of self-organisation of the controller by suggesting how this parameter may also be selected automatically.

The nature of SOC makes detailed mathematical analysis difficult. It is a heuristic controller, depending for its performance on the performance of the process it is attempting to control. Most of the recent insights on the behaviour of SOC have been obtained through painstaking empirical investigation, but assisted by comparison of SOC with other well-established control paradigms, such as the PID or Model Reference Adaptive Controller. These investigations are shedding light on the interactions between parameters of the controller and leading to better design procedures.

APPLICATIONS AND PERFORMANCE OF RULE-BASED CONTROLLERS

The very first implementation of a rule-based controller was to control a laboratory steam engine, which was a two-input two-output process (Mamdani and Assilian, 1975). The first commercial application was to control cement kilns. This was a well-chosen application because the process was ill-understood and prone to changes in the input material. Control rules had already been formulated to try to provide a consistent control strategy (Peray and Waddell, 1972). Rule-based controllers are now supplied as standard equipment by the Danish cement plant manufacturer FLSmidth.

FLSmidth have found the controllers to be very stable and robust in operation. They have found that the controllers can be installed and made operational within a few hours, since the control rules are the same for every installation and only the gains need some adjustment.

In addition, Japanese manufacturers Fuji and Nippon are producing commercial rule-based controllers. Researchers in the USA and Japan are working on special purpose hardware for implementing fuzzy mathematics, which could lead to great improvements and extensions in the possible domains of fuzzy control.

The self-organising controllers are still undergoing development, although most of the research details are fairly well established. Self-organising controllers have recently been the subject of two collaborative research contracts supported by SERC and industry. One involved writing a controller for a robot arm, the other a controller for a piece of heavy industrial plant. The robot arm was a realistic and demanding application. In use, a robot arm may have to pick up and deposit objects, which causes changes in the dynamics of the arm. Thus, the controller should be able to cope with a continually varying load (Scharf and Mandic, 1984). The other project is awaiting a test bed to be made available by our industrial collaborators, but the controller is being tested on a laboratory water rig.

The rule-based controllers have been found to perform well in practice. For simple processes, their performance is at least equal to that of a PID controller. The self-organising controllers (SOC) are at their best in controlling complex processes, particularly those with dead bands, changing gains or very small or large gains (Sugiyama, 1986). Early versions suffered from the quantisation of the state variables, but various methods have been devised to overcome these problems.

Many other applications of rule-based controllers exist around the world, principally in the USA, Japan, Denmark, China and Eastern Europe. See Tong (1984) and Maiers and Sherif (1985) for reviews of reported applications.

In practice, rule-based controllers have shown themselves to be useful in those domains where a good process model was not available, but human operators could perform adequately. The installation of a rule-based controller has for some of the process industries been the first time when a consistent, automatically applied control strategy was feasible. As a result of the consistency, the management of the plant have been able to observe its long term behaviour with only natural plant disturbances to cope with, freed from the variations created by the differing control strategies of the shift operators.

As a result of this consistency of approach, two benefits may be obtained. First, the organisation benefits from a more consistent product, providing a marketing edge over their competitors. Secondly, the consistency of process input means that experiments may be performed showing up behaviour of the process that was previously masked by the variations in performance of the human operators.

The installation of a rule-based controller may be viewed, therefore, as a first step in the application of automatic control. The consistency of control, where none was available before will help the management refine through experiment their control strategy. It may be possible that rather than a collection of separately defined, overlapping rules, a straightforward lookup table of recommended actions for every situation may be derived. Eventually, the control algorithm may bear little resemblance to the rule-based controller originally installed, but improved performance is the criterion of success.

In this way, a rule-based controller may be regarded as a means of formalising the heuristic control behaviour of human operators, derived from their experience. Applied consistently, this may be further refined, possible losing thereby its original character as a fuzzy logic, rule-based controller. Since improved control is the goal, this is an acceptable development. Where a process is well enough understood for an optimal control policy to be derived, one would not usually recommend a rule-based controller, since it cannot outperform what is known to be optimal. But its strength is that it can help capture, use and refine the vague and ill-defined knowledge that for some process may be all that is available.

The important point to realise is that all these developments have not in any way deviated from the original conception of a rule-based controller. The use of fuzzy logic to provide the inference mechanism was also unique in its time and marks a convincing applications of fuzzy mathematics. The idea of a collection of rules to control a plant has proved to be especially powerful. Recently, expert systems have been devised to perform similar functions in different domains, but rule-based controllers were designed and implemented before the term 'expert system' was coined. Nowadays, the idea of using rule-based techniques does not seem so strange.

CONCLUDING REMARKS

In the previous section, we reviewed the performance of rule-based controllers so far. Generally, they have been useful and successful in the control of complex and ill-understood processes. This also represents an application of artificial intelligence (AI) in the industrial domain. It is instructive to look at the other techniques AI can offer to see if any others could enhance the scope of rule-based control.

As pointed out earlier, the inference mechanisms used in rule-based control are very simple. Backward chaining is unlikely to provide anything else, but the technique of induction could yield some insights. Induction takes a collection of rules and looks for more general rules, i.e. reasoning from the particular to the general. This could be useful for improving the compactness of the rule base for an individual piece of plant. Further, if induction were applied to the rules generated for a collection of similar pieces of equipment, trends might be detected which might be useful in the early detection of abnormal process behaviour for particular items of plant.

The limitation of rule-based control is that it is applied at the level of an individual piece of plant. There is no information on how one component is connected to others, and an expert system has no knowledge of anything that is not explicit in its knowledge base. Therefore, rule-based controllers are good for handling process complexity, but are not well suited to plant complexity. This is because as a knowledge representation technique, rules are not adept at handling exceptions, novel cases and complex antecedents. However, this is not to say that rule-based controllers are incompatible with plant controllers which are much more complex in nature, based on frames to represent knowledge and with a host of complex and interesting inference techniques. See Mamdani, Efstathiou and Sugiyama (1984) for further discussion on this topic.

Rule-based controllers represent a useful application of fuzzy logic and approximate reasoning to a difficult and useful part of industry.

ACKNOWLEDGEMENTS

Thanks are due to colleagues in the Knowledge Engineering Applications Group at Queen Mary College, in particular Tim Chau, Mukta Krishnamurthy, Agelos Lembessis, Abe Mamdani, Nick Mandic, Eric Scharf, Kenji Sugiyama, Ricardo Tanscheit and Kasa Yamazaki. Thanks too to our industrial collaborators for their down to earth assessments, and the SERC for financial support.

REFERENCES

Assilian, S. (1974). Artificial Intelligence Techniques in the control of real dynamic systems. PhD thesis, Queen Mary College, University of London.

Bainbridge, L. (1974). 'Analysis of verbal protocols from a process control task'. In Edwards and Lees (Eds.), The Human Operator in Process Control, Taylor & Francis Publishers, London.

Lembessis, E. (1984). Dynamic learning behaviour of a rule-based self-organising controller. PhD thesis, Queen Mary College, University of London.

Maiers, J. and Y.S. Sherif (1985). Applications of fuzzy set theory. IEEE Transactions on Systems, Man and Cybernetics, SMC-15, 175-189.

Mamdani, E.H., and S. Assilian (1975). An experiment in linguistic synthesis with a fuzzy logic controller. International Journal of Man-Machine Studies, 7, 1-13.

Mamdani, E.H. (1976). Advances in the linguistic synthesis of fuzzy controllers. International Journal of Man-Machine Studies, 8, 669-678.

Mamdani, E.H., H.J. Efstathiou, and K. Sugiyama (1984). Developments in Fuzzy Logic Control. IEEE Proceedings of 23rd Conference on Decision and Control, Las Vegas.

Peray, K.E. and J.J. Waddell (1972). The rotary cement kiln. Chemical Publishing Co, New York.

Procyk, T.J. (1977). A self-organising controller for dynamic processes. PhD thesis, Queen Mary College, University of London.

Procyk, T.J. and E.H. Mamdani (1979). A Linguistic Self-Organising Process Controller. Automatica, 15, 15-30.

Scharf, E.M. and N.J. Mandic (1984). Development of learning algorithms for applications in control of robot arms. Internal report, Knowledge Engineering Applications Group, Dept of Electrical and Electronic Engineering, Queen Mary College, University of London.

Sugiyama, K. (1986). Analysis and synthesis of the rule-based self-organising controller. PhD thesis, Queen Mary College, University of London.

Tong, R.M. (1984). A retrospective view of fuzzy control systems. Fuzzy Sets and Systems, 14, 199-210.

Yamazaki, T. (1982). An improved algorithm for a self-organising controller and its experimental analysis. PhD thesis, Queen Mary College, University of London.

Zadeh, L.A. (1965). Fuzzy Sets. Information and Control, 8, 338-353.

Zadeh, L.A. (1973). Outline of a new approach to the analysis of complex systems and decision processes. IEEE Transactions on Systems, Man and Cybernetics, SMC-3, 28-44.

Diagnosis Based on Subjective Information in a Solar Energy Plant

A. ASSE*, A. MAIZENER**, A. MOREAU*
and D. WILLAEYS*

**Laboratoire Automatique Industrielle et Humaine UA, CNRS 1118, Université de Valenciennes, 59326 Valenciennes, France*
***Direction des Etudes et Recherches Electricité de France, 6, Quai Watier, 78400 Chatou, France*

ABSTRACT

In the case of malfunctioning of industrial installations, symptoms appear, which take the form of noise, vibrations, smoke...

Taking into account this "subjective" information (for it is supplied by human operators supervising these installations) is going to increase rapidity in detecting causes of malfunctionning which involves a decrease in breakdow time costs. In this article we present a system of computer aided diagnosis which is based on the theory of fuzzy sets and we develop the knowledge acquisition procedure and man-machine communication.

GENESIS OF THE PROBLEM

This study results from the search for solutions to diagnosis problems after a malfunction in an industrial installation has been taken into account. When a malfunction occurs the amount of information submitted to the operator for analysis may be very large. Confronted with the different indications he should make the right decision as to what action should be taken, which depends on how the operator evaluates the state of the installation. In effect, his judgement may be hampered by the imprecision, or the possible irrelevance of the information provided and by the oversimplication of the functionnal model followed, an oversimplication resulting from the complexity of the controled process. We then decided to look at several ways of detecting defects.

We studied various methods prepared for use during system exploitation : statistical diagnosis method (PAU, 1975), determinist estimative method (DUHAMEL ; RAULT, 1975), probabilities estimation method, topological or taxonomical methods.

The methods which seemed more promising to use were the FMEA method, the cause/consequence method and the methods for early detection of a defect based on the comparison between the reference model and the actual parameters and the method using the fuzzy sets theory.

The fuzzy set theory may seem an abstract concept which means little to the operator of a power station, but we nevertheless selected it for our study. Methods based on FMEA or early defect detection have conceptual and practical limits due for example to the high number of factors to be taken into consideration (several tens of thousands for a nuclear power station). Establishing a defect tree is then a tedious and costly job. Moreover these installations are going to be modified structurally or by changing components. These modifications make it necessary to adjust the cause/consequence tree structure, which is quite difficult. We also discovered that a significant number of the sensors were not adapted to diagnosis. After studying we came to the conclusion that whatever method you choose, you still have to establish a functionning model either in the form of a tree, a physical model or a knowledge base. We drew up a list of the attributes which this model should have in order to make a correct diagnosis.

Exhaustivity

The functionnal analysis must reflect the every facet of the behaviour of the installation.

Validity

The model, once established must be confronted with the actual state of the installation. In practice the adaptation of the model is not always easy, on the one hand the physical models are valid in a functionning interval and do not cover the whole range of the system, on the other hand several critical defects will never appear during the life of the installation and hence it is difficult to check the behaviour of the model in these circumstances.

Access to the information

Establishing diagnosis rules for large system is often hampered by the difficulty of gainning access to certain information. A variable which was analysed while establishing the theoretical defect tree may be found to be inaccessible because the corresponding instrumentation does not exist or because this instrumentation is momentarily not working. On the other hand a great deal of the information directly depends on the sensorial perception of the operators (heat, noise...). This kind of information cannot be quantified, but should be taken into account.

Quality of the information

The information provided is often imprecise due to the quality of the sensors used or due to a possibly imperfect functionning of the sensors.

To be properly used the information should be previous by checked either through duplicating the sensors or through functionnal validation algorithms.

Versatility of the model

The set of hardware components of an industrial installation is in constant evolution. Some machinery may be added or taken away, circuits may be adaptated to new control specifications...

A good model building technique should enable one to easily modify the initial structure.

The above mentioned considerations on the selection criteria of a model may explain why we decided to study fuzzy techniques, in fact these methods :

- allow one to use many non quantifiable pieces of information which are impossible to take in account by other methods. This information is of the kind directly related to the operators' perception like heat, colour, noise...

- allow one to add a dimension of "incertainty" to the processed information and to the diagnosis made which is of interest when it is impossible to have direct access to a piece of information but when the operator may propose an estimation of its value.

- allow one to compensate for the incompleteness of the model. The less detailed parts are represented in the model in a more "fuzzy " way.

- allow one progressively to add refinements to the model in a relatively simple way and to adjust it in case of a modification of the functionning principles changes.

Naturally, the importance of the role of the operator in controling and checking a power station led us to study techniques which are able to reflect his behaviour as closely as possible.

EXPERIMENTAL INDUSTRIAL SITE

The experimental site was power station Themis which is a solar power station with a tower. A 201 heliostats field with movable, slightly concave mirrors, catches solar radiation and sends it back in a focal plan situated at the entry of the solar boiler implanted at the top of a tower.

The heat is transmitted to a fluid wich is a melted eutectic salt, in order to be stocked or to produce steam.

The remaining ports of the site, genereting electricity are classical with the exception of an air driven condensor.

Figure n°1 illustrates the plant functionning.

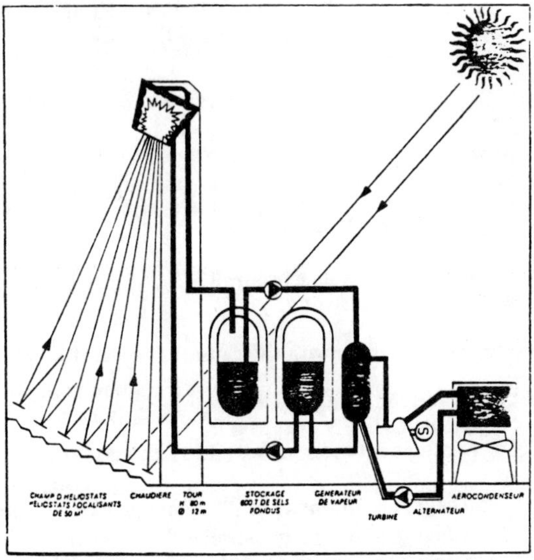

Fig. 1. General view of Themis power station functionning (EDF documentation)

In order to make a model of the functionning, the power station has been split into functionnal systems as shown in figure 2.

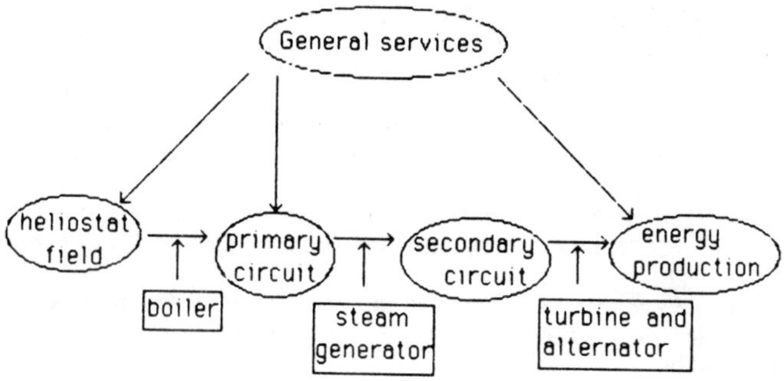

Fig. 2. Principal functions of the power station.

To illustrate how our algorithm works, we chose to make a system to diagnosis leaks. The problem of leaks is a permanent problem of the power stations because it is, in this field, impossible to foresee all the necessary instruments. The role of the operator in detection of a leak is thus fondamental and this problem is quite suitable to a fuzzy model. The exemple of the application in Themis is quite important in so far as in this particular case, the nitrogen leak detection is important for security reasons. We can now describe the diagnosis method.

FUZZY DIAGNOSIS

Diagnosis and more precisely medical diagnosis has been one of the first fields of application of fuzzy set theory. In fact, ZADEH (1969), himself was the first to suggest the use of this concept for medical diagnosis.

The way of representing medical knowledge with fuzzy relation has been described by SANCHEZ (1977). Industrial diagnosis is very similar to medical application as illustrated by the studies of TSUKAMOTO et TERANO (1977) who use fuzzy relation between causes and symptoms. These fuzzy relations illustrate the link between the malfunctionnings of the system and the possible symptoms. In fact the way process works may be described in the following terms :

IF such malfunctionning of the system occurs THEN one may observe that
Symptom 1 is weak, Symptom 2 is strong, ...

This type of rule can be formalized with the causality model (fig. 3)

Let : A the set of malfunctionning causes
B the set of symptoms likely to appear
R the set of relations between causes and symptoms

where $B(j)$ is a degree of intensity of jth symptom likely to appear
$R(i,j)$ is a degree of intensity between i^{th} cause and j^{th} symptom
$A(i)$ is degree of possiblility of ith cause

The causality model can be formalized by the MAX-MIN composition.

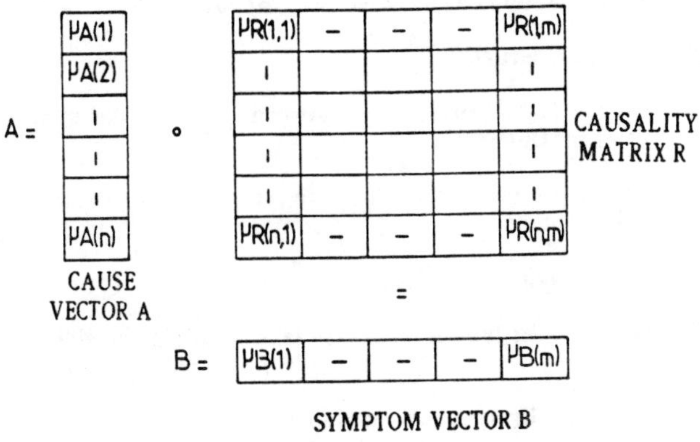

Fig. 3. Causality model

The fuzzy diagnosis consists of starting form an objective or subjective perception of a set of symptoms by the operators and then finding the set of all the possible causes for their occurence.

Thus to make a fuzzy diagnosis means to make the inversion of fuzzy relation equations. As inversion of fuzzy relation equations algorithm we can quote, in chronological order of their publication :

SANCHEZ's algorithm (1976), TSUKAMOTO and TERANO's algorithm (1977), PEDRYCZ's, CZOGALA's, DREWNIAK's algorithms (1982) and TOGAI and WANG's algorithm (1982). In order to take into account, on one hand, the time factor for a system which must deal with several hundreds of causes/symptoms relations we have developped an inversion method which is efficient for computing time and allowing one at the same time to evaluate subjective information in the form of quantifications intervals therely helping an operator to express his subjective perception with greater ease (ASSE A. ; MANGIN P. ; WILLAEYS D., 1985).

We can now present the knowledge acquisition procedure.

KNOWLEDGE ACQUISITION PROCEDURE

The method to establish the relation matrix is based on the same principle as that used to establish the knowledge basis of an expert system by holding interviews with experts.

To secure a fruitful dialogue with the experts, we have carefully analysed the process which then allowed us to prepare preliminary documents explaining the principles of the method and establishing a priliminary list of possible causes for malfunctions (MAIZENER A. ; ZWINGELSTEIN G. ; and co-workers, 1983).

To make the discussion easier the different causes have been grouped according to the following criteria :

. criteria 1 related to system configuration

. criteria 2 related to supposed by defective function

. criteria 3 related to security

. criteria 4 related to the differences between parts of the system containing different fluids

. criteria 5 related to the fluid exchange (the risk of contamination of one fluid by another)

. criteria 6 related to the technology

. criteria 7 related to the type of leaks (salt leak toward the outside, leaks toward the inside,...)

An abstract of the causes list is shown on figure n° 4 the discussion with the experts was on the subject of the correctness and completeness of the proposed list of causes and symptoms and on the fuzzy relations linking causes and symptoms.

Description criteria							Description of causes	
1	2	3	4	5	6	7		
X							Nitrogen leak on nitrogen stocking frame	1
X				X			Nitrogen leak on depressurisation station 7 bars	2
X							Nitrogen leak on nitrogen stock	3
				X			Nitrogen leak on depressurisation station SES	4
			X				Nitrogen leak on salt stock	5
		X	X				Nitrogen leak on gilotherm stock	6
			X				Nitrogen leak on feeding tank	7
			X				Nitrogen leak on steam generator	8
		X					Nitrogen leak on distributing circuit	9
			X				Nitrogen leak on aircondensor tank	10
		X	X				Nitrogen leak on superheated water expansion tank	11

Figure 4 : Preliminary list of causes

The dialogue with the experts using this method has proved to be easy, thanks to the relative simplicity of the method formulating knowledge. These discussions with the experts allowed us to collect very quickly the pieces of information useful for the diagnosis and also to encourage uniformity in the description of causes and symptoms and of perception quantification. The interviews have to be held with special care because of the important correlation which takes place between the validity of the collected pieces of information and the quality of the future diagnosis.

Group techniques may help to make the interviews successful in particular nominal group techniques.

Necessary informations for building dialogues
/ASSE, MANGIN, WILLAEYS, 1985/

As our industrial aided diagnosis is closely linked with the observation and quantification of symptoms, it involves a particular examination of the information related to these symptoms.

We have then pointed out headings which may be associated to symptoms. The information quoted above are going to facilitate symptom observation and also to increase the certainty of registered symptoms.

In practice, to facilitate the observation of symptoms corresponds, at the system level, to give main characteristics of symptoms to human operators. So, the observation will be done with a greater accuracy by the operators, and will better agree with the knowledge Base of Experts.

Headings for symptoms : There are two classes of headings which may be associated to the symptoms, that associated to the whole set of symptoms and that which is specific to each symptom.

The division into two classes is achieved to avoid reiteration of data enquiry from experts when buiding the knowledge basis.

Headings common to several symptoms

Let us examine the not exhaustive list of headings common to several symptoms.

Geographical area of symptom appearance

We must keep in mind that industrial aided diagnosis is designed for large sized installations.

The geographical area may be indicated :

- by cardinal points (North, South, East....)
- by a text locating the appearance area in relation to a masterpiece of the installation (for example : near coolers)

Nature of symptoms

As second heading, we find the nature of symptoms.By nature, we mean the kind of apparent sign which can be :

- vibrations
- smoke
- flames
- noise
- smell

Elementary systems on which the symptoms appear

The installation are divided into a certain number of blocks or functional systems and the association of observable symptoms with elementary systems on which they appear, facilitates the man-machine communication.

Labels associated to elementary systems

This information may be the siglum associated to the designation of elementary system. It may be represented in the form of initials used by operators, in order not to change their language habits.

Elementary sub-systems on which the symptoms appear

We step down in the division of installations into functional blocks, with the same objective mentioned in elementary systems.

Labels associated to elementary sub-systems

It is the same way than labels for elementary systems.

Operational contexts

This type of information may be very important in as far as there are several production stages and observable symptoms depend on a particular stage.

Evaluation of symptoms location easiness

This information is usefull for the man-machine interactivity for the choice of the symptoms to observe preferentialy by operators.

The symptom location easiness may be evaluated by using language variables like :

- very easy
- easy
- rather easy
- little easy
- not easy

Evaluation of symptoms accessibility

As in above, this information is used for man-machine interactivity to choose symptoms to be preferentialy observe. Taking into account this information which can be evaluated by the use of linguistic variables, as before, is to avoid sending operators towards difficult access areas or dangerous areas.

Headings specific to each symptom

Symptom designation

The langage terms used to quantify symptom perception

It appears necessary to keep the operators vocabulary to quantify their perception, which makes it possible to minimize misunderstanding risks between operators, and on the other hand, to increase the credibility of perceived information. Of course, numerical values are associated to language terms for computer treatment.

Subjective reference linked with the symptom

The standards or objective references such as meter, gram... have been established to facilitate comparison and communication between men.

So, it appears interesting to us that the operator can standardize his perception in relation to a reference. This reference is said to be subjective for it is made of subjective and suggestive information facilitating the communication of sensations between persons located in the same environment.

As an illustration, let us take a water leak. In an electrical power station, considering a water leak in a aero-condenser (cooler), the term "very important" will refer to a water leak having the flow of a small stream. On the other hand, considering a water leak of a turbine, the same term "very important" will refer to a thin trickle of water. The subjective reference is described by a text written by experts who suggest to the operator the highest intensity of the symptom likely to appear. As a consequence, operators, during the quantification stage of their observations, can adjust their quantification in relation to the subjective reference.

Headings linked with causes : After the phasis of the diagnosis establishment, it is desirable to give information on causes in order to ensure the link with maintenance departments and minimize the intervening time.

Headings common to several causes

A - Geographical areas of causes

B - Elementary systems of causes

C - Labels associated to elementary systems

D - Elementary sub-systems of causes

E - Labels associated to elementary sub-systems

Headings linked with causes are similar to those of symptoms.

Headings specific for each cause

Cause designation

We have, now, only one specific heading ; others heading are possible, for exemple :

- dismentle procedure
- repare procedure
- intervention procedure

This is the expert who can enrich the list of headings.

MAN-MACHINE COMMUNICATION

The large volume of informations necessary to our diagnosis system leads to the conception of dialogues which would aid experts in the work of building the knowledge base and, also, operators for the task of information handling.

Those dialogues must be not forbidding and easily usable by a non specialized population with computers.

In our system, the expert dialogue and the operator dialogue are built by hierarchical screen-pages with multiple choice.

Presentation of some screen-pages

We are going now to visualize the different screen pages which are displayed to the operator when he starts the diagnosis procedure, with, as an illustration, a simulation for troubleshooting.

A) SCREEN-PAGE OF COMMON HEADING

In this page, the operator chooses the heading to which he can provide an answer

```
SYSTEM OF INDUSTRIEL AIDED DIAGNOSIS
MENU OF COMMON HEADINGS

1-Geographical area
2-Nature of symptom
3-Elementary system
4-Label for elementary system
5-Elementary subsystem
6-Label for elementary subsystem

Answer 1                      Command V

Answer  Type your choice or 0 if you don't
        know
Command V=Validation          C=Correction
        F=Dialogue end        A=Aid
```

Page 1 MENU OF COMMON HEADINGS

B) SELECTION OF HEADING CONTENT
The operator chooses the contents of the heading

```
SYSTEM OF INDUSTRIEL AIDED DIAGNOSIS
SELECTION OF HEADING CONTENT

Here is the content of heading
      Geographical area

1-Energy production
2-Mirror field
3-Cooler
4-Pumps

  Answer 1                    Command V

Answer  Type your choice or 0 if you don't
        know
Command V=Validation          C=Correction
        F=Dialogue end        A=Aid
```

Page 2 SELECTION OF HEADING CONTENT

The operator has observed a symptom in the energy production area

C) SYMPTOM DISPLAY
The operator chooses the symptom that he has observed

```
SYSTEM OF INDUSTRIEL AIDED DIAGNOSIS
SYMPTOMS DISPLAY

S(1) Frequent change of Z frame
S(2) Considerable consumption of Z FCH
S(3) Lower pressure in salt circuit

  Answer 1                    Command V

Answer  Type your choice or 0 if the
        symptom does not appear on the list
Command V=Validation             C=Correction
        L=List of all symptoms  A=Aid
        R=Return to "Common heading" menu
```

Page 3 : SYMPTOMS DISPLAY

D) QUANTIFICATION OF SYMPTOMS

The operator quantifies the intensity of the observed symptom using the subjective reference

SYSTEM OF INDUSTRIEL AIDED DIAGNOSIS

QUANTIFICATION OF SYMPTOM

For the symptom **Frequent change of Z frame**

Here is the subjective reference
The change of Z frame is very frequent
if the needle varies of 3 positions
in less than one minute

Language Term	Quantification Low	Quantification High
1-Little change	0	03
2-Rather frequent	03	06
3-Frequent change	06	08
4-Very frequent change	08	1

Answer : **3** [1]

Enter quantification
Low - High -

Command : F [2]

Command : **V**

Answer : Type your choice or 0 if term is absent of the list

Command V=Validation C=Correction
M=Return to symptom menu . A=Aid
F=Dialogue end

Page 4 : QUANTIFICATION OF SYMPTOMS

Part 1 is displayed if there are some linguistic variables associated to the symptom

Part 2 is displayed if there is no linguistic variables or if operator needs to define an other quantification

E) ESTABLISHMENT OF DIAGNOSIS

The system determines malfunctionning possible causes which are displayed to the operator in the following way

SYSTEM OF INDUSTRIAL AIDED DIAGNOSIS

MALFUNCTIONING POSSIBLE CAUSES

Highly possible causes

1-Default groupe motopompes SES •••
2-Important consumption D by another systems that SES ••
3-Obstruction piping tracage •

Possible causes

4 - .... •••
5 - .... ••
6 - .... •

Lowly possible causes

7 - .... •••
8 - .... ••

Command : P

Command P = Pursuit of diagnosis procedure
F = Dialogue end A = Aid
B = Idea box

Page 5 : Establishment of diagnosis

The operator has decided to continue the procedure in order to innove diagnosis

F) MAN-MACHINE INTERACTIVITY

This page presents the best symptoms to observe in order to reduce the number of possible causes

SYSTEM OF INDUSTRIAL AIDED DIAGNOSIS

SYMPTOMS TO OBSERVE PREFERABLY

S(1) Lower pressure in salt circuit

S(2) important nitrogen consumption

S(3) Lower pressure in gilotherm circuit

Answer 1 Command V

Answer Type your choice for having
precisions or 0 if you don't want

Command V=Validation F=Dialogue end
C=Correction A=Aid
P=Pursuit of diagnosis procedure

Page 6 LIST OF SYMPTOMS TO OBSERVE PREFERABLY

G) INFORMATIONS ABOUT SYMPTOMS

The operator can dispose of some precisions that will facilitate his task when he will research the symptoms on the process

SYSTEM OF INDUSTRIAL AIDED DIAGNOSIS

INFORMATION ABOUT SYMPTOMS

For the symptom **Lower pressure in salt circuit the informations attached to it are:**

Geographical area	: Energy production
Nature of symptom	Abnormal greatness (P,T...)
Elementary system	Heliostats field, boiler
Label for elementary system	F
Elementary sub-system	Hot and cold salt stocking
Label for elementary sub-system	FCH

Command M = Return to symptom menu
P = Pursuit of diagnosis procedure
B = Idea box
F = Dialogue end A = Aid

Page 7 INFORMATIONS ABOUT SYMPTOMS

CONCLUSION

The feasability study which is doing on the site, will permit to us to evaluate the performance of our system, on the both side of reliability and aid provided to the operators.

Nevertheless, we can mention that the possibility, for the diagnosis system, to take into account subjective informations, is very appreciated by the operators.

REFERENCES

ASSE A., MANGIN P., WILLAEYS D. (1982)
Assisted diagnosis using fuzzy information.
Congrès NAFIP 1 - LOGAN U.S.A. - June 1982

ASSE A., MANGIN P., WILLAEYS D. (1983)
Assisted diagnosis using fuzzy information.
Congrès NAFIP 2 - 29-30 June and 1er July 1983
SCHENECTADY - NEW YORK

ASSE A., MANGIN P., WILLAEYS D. (1984)
Assisted diagnosis using fuzzy information.
Realization of interactivity in a system of assisted diagnosis based on fuzzy information.
Naples meeting on "the matemactics of fuzzy systems"
NAPOLI - ITALIE - June 1984

ASSE A., MANGIN P., WILLAEYS D. (1984)
Assisted diagnosis using fuzzy information.
Method of inverting equations of fuzzy relation with fuzzy sets.
FIP 84 Conference - HAWAIIAN ISLANDS - June 1984
Article à paraître dans le livre édité par BEZDEK "The analysis of fuzzy information" - CRC Volumes

ASSE A., MANGIN P., WILLAEYS D. (1985)
Method of inverting equations of fuzzy relation with fuzzy sets.

ASSE A., MANGIN P., WILLAEYS D. (1985)
Design of subjective dialog for computer aided diagnosis.
Article à paraître au Congrès IFSA - MAJORQUE - ESPAGNE - July 1985

CZOGALA E., DREWNIAK T., PEDRYCZ (1982)
Fuzzy relation equation on a finite set.
Fuzzy sets and systems 0165114

DUHAMEL, RAULT (1979)
Automatic test generation techniques for analog circuits and systems. A review.
IEEE Transactions on circuits and systems - Vol. Cas 26 N°7 - pp. 411-440

MAIZENER A., ZWINGELSTEIN G., MANGIN P., WIART D., WILLAEYS D.
Diagnosis aid system by fuzzy techniques : Diagnosis aid system using fuzzy theory feasability stucy on a solar power station.
3rd Symposium of IMEKO Technical committee
4-6 October 1983 - USSR

PAU (1975)
Diagnostic des pannes dans les systèmes.
Editions Cepadues 1976

SANCHEZ E. (1976)
Resolution of composite fuzzy relation equations.
Information and control 30, 1 - pp. 38-48

SANCHEZ E. (1977)
Solutions in composite fuzzy relation equations : application in medical diagnosis in Brouwerian logic fuzzy automata and decision processes.
North Holland Publi - pp. 221-234

TOGAI M., WANG P. (1982)
The upper and lower bounds of fuzzy inverse problem.
Duke University - Department of Electrical Engineering
DURHAM N.C. 27706 U.S.A.

TSUKAMOTO Y., TERANO T. (1977)
Failure diagnosis by using fuzzy logic.
Proc IEEE Conf. Décision Control - NEW ORLEANS
pp. 1390-1397

ZADEH L.A. (1965)
Fuzzy sets.
Information and control 8 pp. 338-353

ZADEH L.A. (1969)
Biological application of the theory of fuzzy sets ans systems.
Biocybernetics of the Central nervous system - L.D. Proctor Edition - pp. 199-212

Diagnostics of Faulty States in Complex Physical Systems Using Fuzzy Relational Equations

J. KITOWSKI and M. BARGIEL

Institute of Computer Science, Academy of Mining and Metallurgy, 30-059 Cracow, Poland

ABSTRACT

The paper presents a method for diagnostics of physical system failures based on the fuzzy relational equation with the max-min composition. The heuristic algorithm for inverse problem solving is briefly described. Since proper description of the plant properties is significant to increase efficiency of the diagnostics two versions of the relationship matrix extension are proposed. The first one considers different directions of failure and symptom deviations from their nominal values. The second one deals with on-line extensions of the relationship matrix in a case of unexpected failure occurrence. Finally the diagnostic system with some elements of fuzzy logic is discussed in order to improve man-machine communications. For test purposes the systems have been applied for failure analysis of the THTR-300 nuclear power plant modelled by a computer code.

KEYWORDS

Fuzzy relational equations; failure diagnostics; fuzzy logic; nuclear power plant diagnostics; max-min composition.

1. INTRODUCTION

Control and diagnostics of complex industrial processes is usually a difficult task due to their non-linear, time varying behaviour, uncertainty and poor quality of available measurements. In many cases a human operator can control the complex process more efficiently than automatic systems designed by modern control techniques. The operator, usually trained on the process simulator, often decides on control strategies or on diagnostic patterns heuristically. The decision is made on his own experience and knowledge of the plant under study. Usually it has a linguistic character, based on intuition. However, such vague conclusions are of very useful value.

Human reliability may be affected by various factors, physical, psychological, environmental, etc. There are many types of uncertainties involved in safety analysis or risk assessment. They may be divided into two major categories: the uncertainty related to randomness and that related to fuzziness. Methods of expressing strategies of the human operator using the fuzzy set theory have been proposed elsewhere. The fuzzy set theory being a theory about vagueness and uncertainty is applied in a wide class of so-called ill-defined systems (Zadeh, 1975a) in order to perform operations on imprecise information in a mathematically strict sense (Dubois and Prade, 1979). This theory seems to be essential for safety analysis of man-machine systems or complex systems such as nuclear power plants in which human factor would play an important role.

Characteristic properties of a modern nuclear power plant could be stated as follows (Mogilner, Skomorokhov and Shvetsov, 1981):

a) number of different physical processes in the plant,
b) imprecise, stochastic and correlated nature of the processes,
c) a very complicated construction of the reactor,
d) control systems have a great number of control instruments and operating modes,
e) the overall control system has usually a hierarchical structure,
f) a human factor is very significant for control and diagnostic processes.

The properties mentioned above determine difficulties of the nuclear power plant control and diagnostics. Due to complexity of the plant various kinds of numerical analysis are used for its control, optimization and diagnostics. Typical methods are: the classical and modern control theory (e.g. Ebert, 1982; Friedrich, 1974; Wade and Terney, 1971), statistical analysis (e.g. Oguma, 1982; Wakabayashi and Fukumoto, 1981) and methods using elements of artificial intelligence (e.g. Brunet and Dubuisson, 1983; Gonzalez, Fry and Kryter, 1974; Hoshino, 1972; Kitowski and Mościński, 1979; Kitowski, Mościński and Cebula, 1982; Macdonald and Koen, 1975; Mogilner, Skomorokhov and Shvetsov, 1981). The fuzzy set theory is also used for those purposes (e.g. Bubak, Mościński and Jewulski, 1983; Nishiwaki and others, 1985; Shahinpoor and Wells, 1980).

The aim of the paper is to present and to discuss a system for fuzzy diagnostics of the primary loop of the THTR-300 nuclear power plant, thus it deals with detection of the deviation from a designated operation point of the plant and estimation of the causes. The main argument in favour of failure and diagnostic analysis is to improve safety of plant operation. The economical aspect is also important due to limited amount of nuclear resources.

The nuclear system considered in this paper consists of a high temperature, pebble bed reactor, a steam generator, reactor-generator thermal connections and classical control systems (see Fig. 1). The loop is simulated by a high accuracy computer code (Petersen, Kujawski and Wu, 1980). For the diagnostic purposes the plant properties are represented by a fuzzy relational equation with the max-min composition. Despite disadvantages of the composition it is widely used in practical applications - for instance fuzzy controllers (e.g. Kickert and van Nauta Lemke, 1976), medical diagnostics (e.g. Sanchez, 1979) and technical diagnostics (e.g. Shahinpoor and Wells, 1980; Tsukamoto, 1979; Tsukamoto and Terano, 1977). The operator is easy in interpretations and implementations (Zadeh, 1975c; Zimmermann, 1976).

In the following section fuzzy diagnostics based on the fuzzy relational equation solving is introduced together with a brief description of a heuristic algorithm used for that purpose. The next sections are devoted to studies dealing with the relationship matrix, namely to consideration signs of failure changes and to dynamical extension of the matrix in cases while the existing failure has properties for which the matrix is not appropriate chosen or the failure has not been expected to occur. An application of fuzzy logic elements to the diagnostics is presented in the rest of the paper. Finally some conclusions of the investigations are formulated.

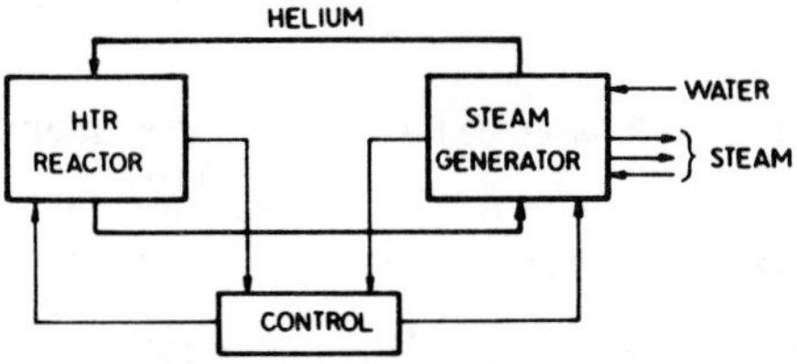

Fig. 1. Model of the nuclear power plant.

The present study is based on previous papers (Kitowski, 1985, 1986), considerations of the signs of failure changes and the relationship matrix extension have been discussed briefly in (Kitowski and Bargieł, 1985, 1986).

2. FUZZY DIAGNOSTICS PRINCIPLES

In the language of fuzzy diagnostics let X and Y be the universal sets of kinds of failures and symptoms respectively: $X=\{X_i \mid i=1,...,m\}$, $Y=\{Y_j \mid j=1,...n\}$, where m and n are numbers of different failures and symptoms. A_i and B_j being defined in X_i and Y_j are fuzzy sets of the i-th failure and the j-th symptom. They can be specified linguistically as for example $A_i \triangleq$ "i-th kind of failure takes place" and $B_j \triangleq$ "j-th symptom is observed (Shahinpoor and Wells, 1980; Tsukamoto, 1979). Their membership functions $\mu_{A_i}(x_i)$ and $\mu_{B_j}(y_j)$ depend on values of the physical parameters x_i and y_j, where subscripts 'i' and 'j' represent respective kinds of failures and symptoms. In general $\mu_{B_j}(y_j)$ depends on the observation or perception of the j-th symptom by the operator rather than on the objective existence of the symptom. Therefore the statement "A_i implies B_j" is more fuzzy than that defined on X_i and Y_j.

For a current diagnostic stage the parameters have fixed deterministic values $\{x_i^* \mid i=1,...,m\}$ and $\{y_j^* \mid j=1,...,n\}$, thus it may be noted: $\mu_A(i)=\mu_{A_i}(x_i^*)$ and $\mu_B(j)=\mu_{B_j}(y_j^*)$. The membership functions $\mu_A(i)$ and $\mu_B(j)$ represent failures and symptoms fuzzy sets A and B respectively (Shahinpoor and Wells, 1980; Tsukamoto and Terano, 1977). For example $\mu_A(i)=0.3$ and $\mu_B(j)=0.8$ at the current diagnostic stage imply the partial occurrence of the i-th failure and the certain observation of the j-th symptom (with degrees 0.3 and 0.8).

The fuzzy relational equation takes a form:

$$B = A \circ R \qquad (1)$$

with a fuzzy relation R expressing the relationship between A and B. For convenience failure and symptom vectors are defined (Shahinpoor and Wells, 1980; Tsukamoto and Terano, 1977):

$$\mu_A = [\mu_A(1), \ldots, \mu_A(i), \ldots, \mu_A(m)] \tag{2}$$

$$\mu_B = [\mu_B(1), \ldots, \mu_B(j), \ldots, \mu_B(n)] \tag{3}$$

The fuzzy relation R is represented by a matrix $\mu_R \triangleq \{\mu_R(i,j)\}$ which states the causal connection of the i-th failure with the j-th symptom. Eq. (1) can be rewritten using the membership functions:

$$\mu_B(j) = \bigvee_{i=1}^{m} [\mu_A(i) \wedge \mu_R(i,j)] \qquad \text{for } j=1,\ldots,n \tag{4}$$

$\vee$ and $\wedge$ denote the max and min operators.

The fuzzy diagnostics is based on the inverse problem of the fuzzy relational equation, i.e. having obtained μ_B and given μ_R one is able to solve eq. (4) in respect to μ_A. There are many algorithms existing in literature (e.g. Higashi and Klir, 1984a; Pappis and Sugeno, 1976; Sanchez, 1976; Tsukamoto, 1979; Tsukamoto and Terano, 1977) for the inverse problem solving.

In practice the symptom vector μ_B is defined on the plant operator perception of available measurements. The relationship matrix is constructed either heuristically by experienced plant managers (involving their knowledge of plant properties, cf. Shahinpoor and Wells, 1980; Tsukamoto, 1979; Tsukamoto and Terano, 1977) or identified mathematically with different kinds of compositions (Higashi and Klir, 1984b; Pedrycz, 1984; Sanchez, 1976, 1979). According to complexity of the problem the algorithms for inverse problem of eq. (4) solving may fail in applications. To make the diagnostics realizable practically the fuzzy relational equation is relaxed to the following one:

$$B \subseteq A \circ R \tag{5}$$

The diagnostics system works on two levels: firstly it makes an identification of the plant properties and next it formulates a result of the failure diagnostics. The identification is performed using the Sanchez's α operator (Sanchez, 1976, 1979) with vectors $\mu_A{}^{\vee}$ and $\mu_B{}^{\vee}$ known at a current plant state. Then the greatest relationship matrix from those fulfiling eq. (1) is obtained:

$$\mu_R{}^{\vee}(i,j) = \mu_A{}^{\vee}(i) \;\alpha\; \mu_B{}^{\vee}(j) \qquad \text{for } i=1,\ldots,m;\; j=1,\ldots,n \tag{6}$$

where $\vee$ means a current number of the identification experiment. The α operator is defined as follows. Let a and b be defined in [0,1], then:

$$a \;\alpha\; b = \begin{cases} 1 & \text{if } a \leq b \\ b & \text{if } a > b \end{cases} \tag{7}$$

Dealing with eq. (1) the cumulate experience from the identification experiments at a current plant state is represented by intersection of fuzzy relations obtained from every identification experiment (eq. (6)). Such an approach is no longer appropriate while the fuzzy relational equation is relaxed to eq. (5). In that case the cumulate experience from the identification experiments at a current plant state is represented heuristically by (Kitowski, 1985; Kitowski and Bargieł, 1985; Kitowski and Ksiązek, 1985):

$$\mu_R(i,j) = \bigvee_{\nu=1}^{\nu_m} \mu_R^{\nu}(i,j) \qquad \text{for } i=1,\ldots,m \quad j=1,\ldots,n \tag{8}$$

where ν_m is a number of experiments carried out for the identification purpose.
The nuclear power plant is a dynamical object thus the failure vectors depend on time. Consequently the relationship matrix is determined successively for every interval of T=20s. The overall cumulate experience obtained from the identification is a set of the relationship matrices defined for the separated time intervals.

In order to failure recognition at a current plant state the following equation is solved:

$$\mu_B(j) \leq \bigvee_{i=1}^{m} [\mu_A(i) \wedge \mu_R(i,j)] \qquad \text{for } j=1,\ldots,n \tag{9}$$

The Tsukamoto's algorithm (Tsukamoto, 1979; Tsukamoto and Terano, 1977) is one of the best known methods for the inverse problem solving. Dealing with eq. (4) it is often used in practical applications, however relatively high cpu-time and memory requirements are its drawback.

The heuristic algorithm concerns the relaxed fuzzy relational equation (9). Thus it gives practical diagnostic results also in a case in which no algebraic equality in eq. (9) is satisfied. It consists of a main procedure and a solution modification section with two kinds of modifiers (Kitowski, 1985, 1986). In the main procedure the ω and $\bar{\omega}$ operators are applied (Tsukamoto, 1979; Tsukamoto and Terano, 1977), which for real a and b defined in [0,1] give:

$$a\,\omega\,b \triangleq \begin{cases} b & \text{if } a > b \\ [b, 1] & \text{if } a = b \\ \emptyset & \text{if } a < b \end{cases} \tag{10}$$

$$a\,\bar{\omega}\,b \triangleq \begin{cases} [0, b] & \text{if } a > b \\ [0, 1] & \text{if } a \leq b \end{cases} \tag{11}$$

where $\emptyset$ stands for the empty set. Matrices U={u(i,j)} and V={v(i,j)} are determined:

$$u(i,j) \triangleq \mu_R(i,j)\ \omega\ \mu_B(j) \tag{12}$$

$$v(i,j) \triangleq \mu_R(i,j)\ \bar{\omega}\ \mu_B(j) \tag{13}$$

for $i=1,\ldots,m$; $j=1,\ldots,n$.

In the Tsukamoto's algorithm a set of W^k matrices is formulated using the U and V matrix elements. Next the set $\{W^k\}$ is applied for solution determination.

In contrast to the Tsukamoto's algorithm, in the heuristic approach row variants of the W matrix are built up and work out separately. Consequently, variants for every $\mu_A(i)$ are obtained independently. The failure vector is formulated subsequently using a heuristic approach. If there is a possibility existing to get the algebraic equality in eq. (9) the algorithm determines the greatest solution of the inverse problem. Otherwise the solution modification section is involved for solution improvement, which uses some geometrical properties of vectors. In that case the smallest failure vector fulfiling eq. (9) is taken as a diagnostic result. Convergence of the heuristic solution to the Tsukamoto's one was proved for the case in which the last one existed (Kitowski, 1986). Due to the heuristic method applied the algorithm may fail in exceptional cases.

In the paper number of failures is m=6 and number of symptoms n=13. This order of magnitude (from 10 to 20) is typical at present in technical applications, including diagnostics of car and marine engines (Tsukamoto, 1979; Tsukamoto and Terano, 1977) or that of nuclear power plants (Shahinpoor and Wells, 1980; Wakabayashi and Fukumoto, 1981).

For test purposes deviations of the plant parameters from their nominal values are taken as the failures. The universal sets of kinds of failures and symptoms applied for test purposes are characteristic for nuclear power plants (Friedrich, 1974; Kitowski, 1985; Kitowski and Ksiązek, 1985; Wakabayashi and Fukumoto, 1981). Since quality of the algorithm will be discussed in respect to the failure vectors obtained, the set of kinds of failures is presented in Table 1.

TABLE 1 Universal Set of Kinds of Failures

i	X_i
1	jump change of the water mass flow in the secondary loop
2	jump change of the helium mass flow in the primary loop
3	exponential change of the helium mass flow in the primary loop
4	exponential change of the water mass flow in the secondary loop
5	jump change of the feed water pressure
6	jump change of the reheater inlet temperature of helium

Sample kinds of symptoms are: helium outlet temperature of the reactor, live steam pressure of the steam generator, reactor power, average fuel temperature, steam generator power, etc. Since the symptom vector and the relationship matrix are defined for the time intervals of T=20s, the diagnostics is made separately for each of them. An example of the failure recognition with the heuristic algorithm is presented in section 6.

3. RECOGNITION OF SIGNS OF FAILURES

The diagnostics presented in this section deals with additional recognition of changes in the physical plant parameters. Since the changes are taken as parameter deviations from their nominal values, indication of their signs (increase or decrease of values of respective parameters) would be of high importance. The term 'recognition of failure signs' will refer to this feature. The diagnostics discussed below is supplemented with such a kind of recognition. The similar feature called 'signs of symptoms' concerns symptom properties.

In the study the dimensions of both the failure and the symptom vectors are doubled in comparison with the approach discussed in section 2. Every pair of the odd-even coordinates stands for the same kind of failure. The same arrangement concerning coordinates of the symptom vector is adopted. Each odd vector coordinate represents increase of the corresponding parameter value while the even one indicates value decrease. Analogously every element of the relationship matrix $\mu_R(i,j)$ for $i=1,...,m$; $j=1,...,n$ is replaced by four elements with coordinates respectively: $(2i-1, 2j-1)$, $(2i-1, 2j)$, $(2i, 2j-1)$, $(2i, 2j)$. According to the plant properties the only two cross-lying elements from the four ones (representing failure-symptom relationship) can take on values greater than zero. Values of the elements are determined with the identification experiments using approach similar to eqs. (6,8).

For such extended relationship matrix and the symptom vector the heuristic algorithm with the solution modifier is used in order to solve the inverse problem (eq. (9)) with doubled dimensions 2m, 2n (see sample results in section 6). The approach described above can be applied for such symptom and failure sets only for which possibility of sign indication exists. For the rest of cases the unextended forms of the relationship matrix and of the symptom and failure vectors should be used.

4. RECOGNITION OF UNEXPECTED FAILURES

This section outlines a method of dynamical extension of the relationship matrix in cases while the existing failure has properties for which the matrix is not appropriate chosen or the failure has not been expected to occur. In the approach this feature is represented by addition of a new row to the relationship matrix or by modification of one of the previously added rows. Thus two functions complement the diagnostic system operation: detection of the unexpected failure occurrence and proper modification of the relationship matrix. For the inverse problem solving (see eq. (9)) the heuristic algorithm with the solution modification section (briefly described in section 2) is used.

Verification of the Failure Recognition

In extension of the diagnostic system two heuristic criteria are used for verification whether the failure recognition is satisfactory in practice. Each solution of the inverse problem is verified in respect to the criteria as follows:

a) performance index

$$s = \sigma/\epsilon \qquad (14)$$

where

$$\sigma = \{\frac{1}{m-1} \sum_{i=1}^{m} [\mu_A(i)-\epsilon]^2\}^{1/2} \qquad (15)$$

and

$$\epsilon = \frac{1}{m} \sum_{i=1}^{m} \mu_A(i) \qquad (16)$$

The greater is s value the more clear is system response.

b) distance between the symptom vector $\mu_B(j)$ and its approximation $\mu_B^+(j)$. The approximation $\mu_B^+(j)$ is obtained using the max-min composition to the calculated failure vector and the relationship matrix. The distance is represented by (e.g. Dubois and Prade, 1980):

$$d = \{ \sum_{j=1}^{n} [\mu_B(j) - \mu_B^+(j)]^2 \}^{1/2} \tag{17}$$

where:

$$\mu_B^+(j) = \bigvee_{i=1}^{m} [\mu_A(i) \wedge \mu_R(i, j)] \qquad \text{for } j=1,\dots,n \tag{18}$$

Results of the failure recognition are accepted if $s \geq s^*$ and $d \leq d^*$ where s^* and d^* are given threshold values. Approval of the results indicates that one or more of expected failures occur. If those conditions are not fulfiled (i.e. $s < s^*$ or $d > d^*$) it means that the unexpected failure takes place. Since in such a case the relationship matrix is extended or modified, the matrix can be divided in two parts: the main one containing rows obtained during the plant identification stage (see section 2) and the secondary one containing those rows which have been added dynamically during the stage of the failure recognition.. The main part of the matrix remains unaltered during the system operation. The extended realtionship matrix can be noted as follows (Kitowski and Bargieł, 1986):

$$\mu_R = \{\mu_R(i, j)\} \qquad \text{for} \quad i=1,\dots,m,\dots,m+k \quad j=1,\dots,n \tag{19}$$

where $\mu_R^1 = \{\mu_R(i,j)\}$ for $i=1,\dots,m$; $j=1,\dots,n$ represents the main part and $\mu_R^2 = \{\mu_R(i,j)\}$ for $i=m+1,\dots,m+k$; $j=1,\dots,n$ the second part of the matrix respectively. Due to the extension of the matrix, the failure vector is extended as well:

$$\mu_A = [\mu_A(1),\dots,\mu_A(i),\dots,\mu_A(m), \mu_A(m+1),\dots,\mu_A(m+k)] \tag{20}$$

For the diagnostic purposes the only one part of the relationship matrix is used and consequently the equation:

$$\mu_B(j) \leq \bigvee_{i} [\mu_A(i) \wedge \mu_R(i, j)] \tag{21}$$

is solved for $j=1,\dots,n$ and $i=1,\dots,m$ or $i=m+1,\dots,m+k$ independently. Choice of the appropriate part depends on the actual plant state represented by a state vector. For sake of simplicity the actual symptom vector is taken as a state vector of the plant:

$$\Theta = [\mu_B(1),\dots,\mu_B(j),\dots,\mu_B(n)]^T \tag{22}$$

The state is classified to one of the state classes existing in respect to a heuristic criterion. On a base of computer experiments the criterion consisting in the cosine of angle between the state vector and the centre of the class has been adopted:

$$E_l(\Theta) = \cos\ (c_l, \Theta) \qquad \text{for } l \in L \tag{23}$$

where L is a set of classes. The centre of the l-th class is represented by:

$$c_l = [c_l(1),\dots,c_l(j),\dots,c_l(n)]^T \tag{24}$$

The state belongs to the class with the greatest cosine value, i.e.:

$$\Theta \in \ell \mid E_\ell(\Theta) = \max_{l \in L} E_l(\Theta),\ E_\ell(\Theta) \geq E^* \tag{25}$$

If the cosine values for all classes are less than a chosen threshold E^* ($E_l(\Theta) < E^*$ for $l=1,\ldots,lm$) the actual state vector defines a new class centre ($c_{lm+1}=\Theta$). On the other hand if the state vector is included to the ℓ-th state class the class centre coordinates are modified as follows:

$$c_\ell^x(j) = \frac{c_\ell(j) \cdot n_\ell + \mu_B(j)}{n_\ell + 1} \qquad \text{for } j=1,\ldots,n \tag{26}$$

where $c_\ell^x(j)$ and $c_\ell(j)$ represent new and old j-th coordinates of the ℓ-th state class and n_ℓ is cardinality of the class. In addition the set of state classes is divided into two exclusive subsets L^1 and L^2 ($L=L^1 \cup L^2$). State classes containing the states for which the solution of eq. (21) calculated with the main part of the relationsip matrix (μ_R^1) is satisfactory in practice (criteria (14) and (17) hold) belong to the subset L^1. The rest of classes for which the main part of the relationship matrix is not a good representation stands for the subset L^2. If the actual state belongs to one of the classes from the first subset ($\ell \in L^1$) then the main matrix part (μ_R^1) is used for diagnostic purposes otherwise the secondary part (μ_R^2) is applied. Summarizing the relationship matrix is divided into the main and the secondary parts. With each part of the matrix a subset of the state classes is associated.

Stages of the Approach

The presented approach consists of three stages:

a) determination of the main part of the relationship matrix (μ_R^1) with the α operator applied to a training set of failures and symptoms (see eqs. (6-8)).

b) preliminary construction of the diagnostic system memory which consists of initial determination of the plant state classes and the first rows of the secondary matrix part (μ_R^2). Since this feature is similar to the dynamical extension or modification of the matrix it is described later on together with the plant diagnostics.

c) on-line failure recognition reduced to the inverse problem of eq. (21) with the main or with the secondary matrix part (μ_R^1 or μ_R^2) chosen in respect to the actual state of the plant. This stage can be realized independently of a) and b).

In a case of unsatisfactory solution with the part μ_R^2 this part is modified or extended if necessary. Thus the system experience is continuously enlarged with regard to possible on-line extension of the matrix. This feature warrants ability for indication that unexpected or unknown previously failure takes place. At the beginning of the diagnostics the necessary condition of the solution existence is verified for μ_R^1 and μ_R^2 separately:

$$\mu_B(j) \leq \bigvee_i \mu_R(i,j) \qquad \text{for } j = 1,\ldots,n \quad i = \begin{cases} 1,\ldots,m \\ m+1,\ldots,m+k \end{cases} \tag{27}$$

If this condition is not fulfiled for any matrix part the diagnostics is performed after the matrix modification. The modification and the extension of the secondary matrix part is described below. The idea is restricted to cases of single kind of unknown failure occurrence. Assume that the actual number of rows in the part μ_R^2 is k. Each row is associated with a state class from the second subset L^2, i.e.:

$$i = f(l) \qquad \text{for } i=m+1,\ldots,m+k;\ l \in L^2 \tag{28}$$

where f is a mapping function.

Cases of the Diagnostic System Operation

Consider the following cases of the diagnostic system operation according to classification of the actual plant state Θ to the state classes:

a) Θ is classified to ℓ' from L^1 or there is no such a l-th state class from L ($L=L^1 \cup L^2$) for which $E_l(\Theta) \geq E^*$. If the solution of the inverse problem (with μ_R^1) is satisfactory then the ℓ'-th class centre is modified (for $\ell' \in L^1$) according to eq. (26) or a new class is defined in L^1, otherwise the secondary part of the matrix is taken into considerations. For μ_R^2 taken the class ℓ'' is found ($\ell'' \in L^2$) for $E_{\ell''}(\Theta) \geq E^*$ and case b) is involved. If there is no such ℓ'', case c) is considered.

b) Θ is classified to ℓ'' from L^2. The ℓ''-th class centre is modified in respect to eq. (26). If the necessary condition of the solution existence (see eq. (27)) is not fulfiled or the solution of the inverse problem (with μ_R^2) is not satisfactory the experience of the diagnostic system is enlarged by modification of the respective row of μ_R^2:

$$\mu_R^x(m+i_2, j) = \mu_R(m+i_2, j) \vee \mu_D(j) \qquad \text{for } j=1,\ldots,n \tag{29}$$

where

$$i_2 = f(\ell'') \quad , \quad \ell'' \in L^2 \tag{30}$$

and ^{x} means the modified values.
The values $\mu_D(j)$ are calculated with:

$$\mu_D(j) = \mu_A(m+i_2) \ \alpha \ \mu_B(j) \qquad \text{for } j=1,\ldots,n \tag{31}$$

$\mu_A(m+i_2)$ is taken to be equal to 1 in respect to the occurrence of the $(m+i_2)$-th failure assumed. The inverse problem is solved again with new μ_R^2 considered and its solution is treated as a final result.

c) involved from case a) only. A new class is defined in L^2. If the necessary condition of the solution existence (eq. (27)) is not fulfiled or the solution of the inverse problem (with μ_R^2) is unsatisfactory a new kind of failure is assumed, i.e. $k^x=k+1$ and the experience of the diagnostic system is extended by addition of a new row to the matrix:

$$\mu_R(m+k^x, j) = \mu_A(m+k^x) \ \alpha \ \mu_B(j) \qquad \text{for } j=1,\ldots,n \tag{32}$$

Similar to case b) $\mu_A(m+k^x)$ is equal to 1 and the inverse problem solving is repeated for extended μ_R^2. The solution obtained stands for a final result.

5. APPLICATIONS OF FUZZY LOGIC ELEMENTS TO DIAGNOSTIC PURPOSES

In this section we consider a simplified approach to applications of fuzzy logic principles to the diagnostic problem, which is based on the approach mentioned in the literature (Tsukamoto, 1979; Tsukamoto and Terano, 1977). Using propositions:

$A_i \triangleq$ "i-th kind of failure takes place"
$B_j \triangleq$ "j-th kind of symptom is observed"
$R_{ij} \triangleq$ "X_i is causally related to Y_j"

one is able to consider the following compound statements:

$P_j \triangleq$ "if the j-th symptom is observed then at least one from among the failures related to the j-th symptom takes place", i.e.:

$$P_j \triangleq \text{"}B_j \rightarrow R_{ij} \cap A_i\text{"} \qquad \text{for } i=1,\ldots,m;\ j=1,\ldots,n \tag{33}$$

$T_{ij} \triangleq$ "if the i-th kind of failure causally related to Y_j takes place then the j-th symptom is observed", i.e.:

$$T_{ij} \triangleq \text{"}R_{ij} \cap A_i \rightarrow B_j\text{"} \qquad \text{for } i=1,\ldots,m;\ j=1,\ldots,n \tag{34}$$

The aim of the method is to find lower and upper bounds of the failure vector coordinates:

$$\mu_A(i) = [\hat{\mu}_A(i), \check{\mu}_A(i)] \tag{35}$$

Using the α-level set definition:

$$F^{\alpha} \triangleq \{x \mid \mu_F(x) \geq \alpha\}, \qquad \alpha \in [0,1] \tag{36}$$

where F is any fuzzy set, one is able to transform the coordinate interval into the linguistic truth value. Consequently the diagnostic results can be formulated linguistically. For determination of the interval represented by eq. (35) the algorithm has been presented in the literature (Tsukamoto, 1979; Tsukamoto and Terano, 1977). The algorithm deals with the α-level sets and relations $P_j{}^{\alpha}=[\mu_P(j),\ 1]$, $T_{ij}{}^{\alpha}=[\mu_T(i,j),\ 1]$, $R_{ij}{}^{\alpha}=[\hat{\mu}_R(i,j),\ \check{\mu}_R(i,j)]$, $B_j{}^{\alpha}=[\hat{\mu}_B(j),\ \check{\mu}_B(j)]$, $A_i{}^{\alpha}=[\hat{\mu}_A(i),\ \check{\mu}_A(i)]$ and with the fuzzy implication resulting from the Łukasiewicz logic (Dubois and Prade, 1980):

$$\mu_{Q\rightarrow S}(q,s) \triangleq [1-\mu_Q(q)+\mu_S(s)] \wedge 1 \tag{37}$$

where Q and S are any propositions with numerical truth values $\mu_Q(q)$ and $\mu_S(s)$. For problem solving the ϵ and $\bar{\epsilon}$ operators are introduced (Tsukamoto, 1979; Tsukamoto and Terano, 1977):

$$[p,q]\,\epsilon\,[r,s] \triangleq \begin{cases} [r,1] & \text{if } [p,q]\cap[r,s]\neq\emptyset \\ [r,s] & \text{if } p>s \\ \emptyset & \text{if } q<r \end{cases} \tag{38}$$

and

$$[p,q]\,\bar{\epsilon}\,[r,s] \triangleq \begin{cases} [0,1] & \text{if } p\leq s \\ [0,r] & \text{if } p>s \end{cases} \tag{39}$$

for [p,q] and [r,s] defined in [0,1]. Using those operators U and V matrices are determined in a similar way as shown in eqs. (12-13). Then a set $\{W^K\}$ is formulated for determination of the solution lower bound. The upper bound of the solution is defined with the application of the ϵ-operator as well (Tsukamoto, 1979). In the simplified approach proposed in the paper the following assumptions are considered:

a) elements of the relationship matrix take binary values from {0,1} and

$$\mu_R(i,j) \triangleq \hat{\mu}_R(i,j) = \check{\mu}_R(i,j) \qquad \text{for } i=1,\dots,m \quad j=1,\dots,n \tag{40}$$

b) symptoms are defined with their numerical truth values and

$$\mu_B(j) \triangleq \hat{\mu}_B(j) = \check{\mu}_B(j) \qquad \text{for } j=1,\dots,n \tag{41}$$

c) linguistic truth value of the proposition P_j is *completely true*

$$\mu_P(j) = 1 \qquad \text{for } j=1,\dots,n \tag{42}$$

In that case the solution upper bound is equal to:

$$\check{\mu}_A = \bigwedge_{j=1}^{n} \{[\mu_B(j)+1-\mu_T(i,j)] \wedge 1\} \qquad \text{for } i=1,\dots,m \tag{43}$$

It can be shown (Kitowski, 1985) that with those assumptions considered the lower bound of the solution can be determined on a base of μ_R and μ_B with ω and $\bar{\omega}$ operators (see eqs. (10,11)). Thus there is a possibility existing for the application of the heuristic algorithm (described in section 2) to the inverse problem solving.

As mentioned before (eqs. (33, 34, 40, 43)) two matrices are introduced for the solution determination. The first one is the relationship matrix μ_R whose values are now from {0,1} and the second one - the truth matrix μ_T of values from [0,1]. The values of μ_R give the information if there is any relationship between the j-th symptom and the i-th failure and μ_T shows the grade of this relationship. A set of the truth matrices is obtained with identification experiments (see comments to eq. (8)). Every element of the relationship matrices is defined according to:

$$\mu_R(i,j) = \begin{cases} 1 & \text{if } \mu_T(i,j) \geq \mu^* \\ 0 & \text{if } \mu_T(i,j) < \mu^* \end{cases} \tag{44}$$

where μ^* is a given threshold. In the paper the following linguistic truth values are applied (Baldwin, 1979):

$$\mu_\tau(v) = v \qquad \text{for } \tau = \textit{true} \tag{45}$$

$$\mu_\tau(v) = 1-v \qquad \text{for } \tau = \textit{false} \tag{46}$$

where v is a numeric truth value. According to Zadeh (1975b) the hedges are introduced:

$$\mu_{\textit{very}\ \tau}(v) = [\mu_\tau(v)]^2 \tag{47}$$

$$\mu_{\textit{rather}\ \tau}(v) = [\mu_\tau(v)]^{1/2} \tag{48}$$

Using this approach the proposition: "i-th kind of failure takes place" can have linguistic truth values from among the values mentioned above. If $\check{\mu}_A \neq 1$ or $\hat{\mu}_A \neq 0$ then the value is an intersection of the fuzzy sets representing the linguistic truth values mentioned above. Assume for example that $\mu_A(i)=[0.8, 1]$ then for $\alpha_1=0.8$ $\tau_1=$*true* and the linguistic truth value of the proposition is *true*. For other levels $\alpha_2=0.9$ and $\alpha_3=0.6$ the linguistic truth values are approximated by *rather true* and *very true* respectively. The higher is the value of α the lower is the linguistic truth value.

Since the results can be presented in the linguistic form (using the linguistic truth values) the reliability of the diagnostic system is improved in respect to more human oriented man-machine communication.

6. SAMPLE RESULTS

The nuclear power plant is a dynamical object thus the diagnostics is performed for every interval of T=20s.

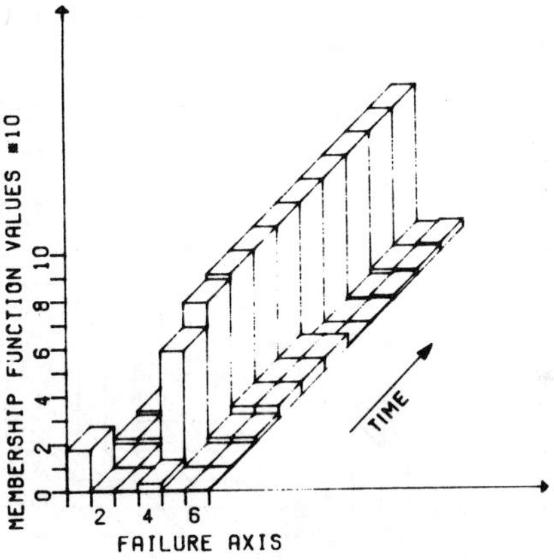

Fig. 2. Recognition of the exponential change of the water mass flow in the secondary loop with the basic version of the algorithm.

In Fig. 2 recognition of the exponential change of the water mass flow in the secondary loop of the plant is presented. The diagnostics is made with the basic version of the heuristic algorithm briefly described in section 2. The expected value of $\mu_A(4)$ in the steady state is equal to 0.74, while the value of 0.61 is obtained from the diagnostic system. Result understating in 10÷20% is a common feature of the heuristic algorithm due to the form of eq. (8), however time dependency of the failure is recognized sufficiently usually. The kind of failure is pointed out clearly with no contribution of the others. For some kinds of failures the basic version of the heuristic algorithm gives less clear results than above (see Fig. 3a).

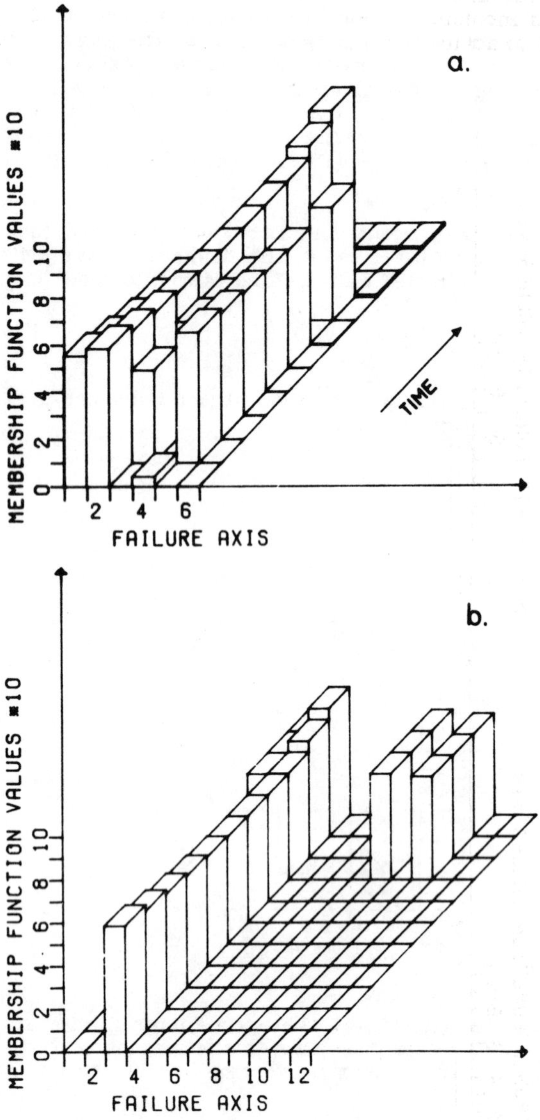

Fig. 3. Recognition of jump change of the helium mass flow in the primary loop with basic (a) and advanced (b) versions of the algorithm.

The application of the more advanced algorithm with the recognition of the failure signs (see section 3) improves quality of the analysis (cf. Fig. 3b) in respect to more detailed construction of the relationship matrix. This feature is observed especially at the beginning of the failure occurrence. Since in Fig. 3b the highest value is detected for the third (i.e. odd) coordinate of the failure vector, the increase of the helium mass flow is recognized. Thus inclusion of the failure signs into the diagnostcs makes it more flexible in practice. The expected value of $\mu_A(2)$ is equal to 0.57 (in Fig. 3a).

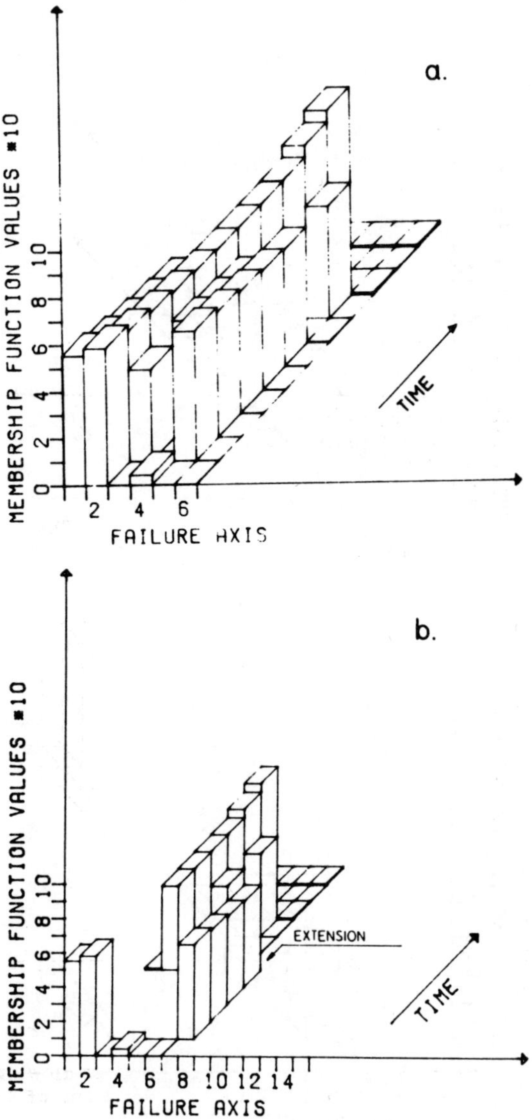

Fig. 4. Results for diagnostics without (a) and with extension (b) of the matrix.

Diagnostic performance with the dynamical extension of the relationship matrix included is presented in Fig. 4 and Fig. 5 with reference to the same kind of failure as shown in Fig. 3. Results obtained with the extended version of the algorithm (see section 4) indicate its advantage over the basic algorithm. This feature is observed especially for extremely low membership function values (cf. Fig. 5) and for the beginning periods of the failure

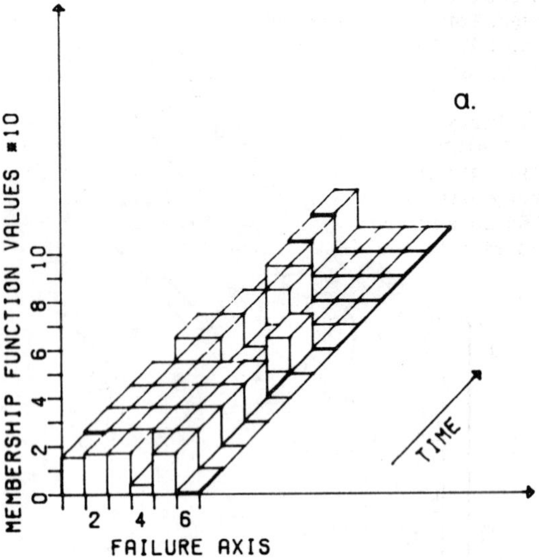

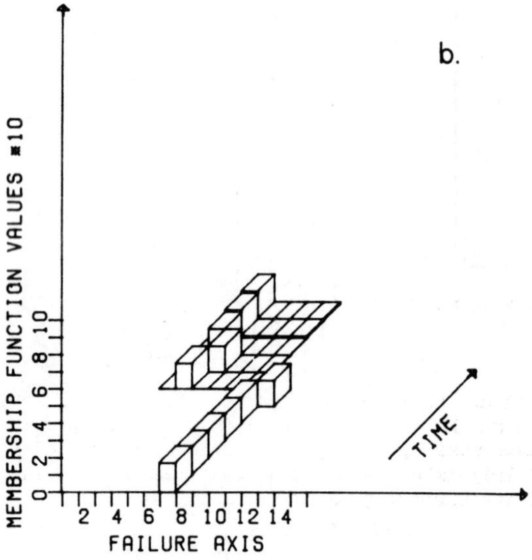

Fig. 5. Results for diagnostics without (a) and with extension (b) of the matrix for extremely low membership function values.

occurrence. For those periods of time the relationship matrices have not been determined properly (the solutions of the inverse problem have not been sufficient in practice) thus occurrence of a new kind of failure is pointed out (see Figs. 4b and 5b). Obviously physical meaning of such a new kind of failure should be identified by the personnel of the plant, but in the test case considered it is known to be the same as the second one. From the results it follows that the matrix has been extended properly and quality of the results improved. For the experiment presented above the threshold values are: $E^*=0.9$, $s^*=1$ and $d^*=0.2$, the expected values of $\mu_A(2)$ are equal to 0.57 and 0.23 (in Figs. 4a and 5a) respectively.

Sample results of fuzzy logic application for the diagnostic purposes are presented in Fig. 6 with reference to the same kind of failure as shown in Figs. 3 and 4. Each group of bars represents the respective kind of the failure, while every bar shows a range of the specific failure vector coordinate (see eq. (35)) in succeeding time periods. For the second failure kind the highest linguistic truth value is observed. For example for $\alpha=0.5\div0.6$

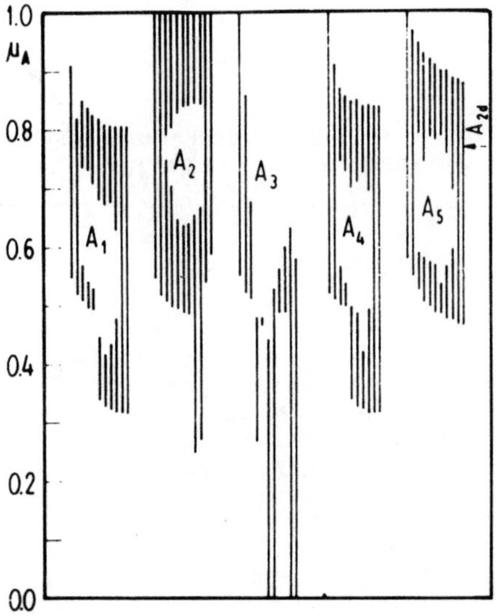

Fig. 6. Ranges of the failure vector coordinates in the method with fuzzy logic elements.

this value is equal to *true*, while the rest of failures has lower linguistic truth values. The threshold $\mu^*=0.1$ has been adopted. The advantage of the method is the possibility of linguistic interpretation of the failure occurrence. High linguistic truth values for the rest of failures besides the second one are a drawback of the method.

7. CONCLUSIONS

In the paper the advanced versions of the fuzzy diagnostic system have been presented and sample results of their applications to failure recognition of the nuclear power plants shown. All versions have some advantages over the basic heuristic algorithm with the solution modifier. The kind of deviation of plant physical parameters (parameter increase or decrease) can be detected with inclusion of failure signs to the diagnostic system. The unexpected and previously unknown failures can be recognized with the relationship matrix extension performed on a base of the heuristic verification if the solution of the inverse problem is satisfactory in practice. Using the two versions, quality of the results is improved in comparison with failure recognition obtained with the basic heuristic algorithm. The reliability of the diagnostic system is improved with elements of fuzzy logic applications to the algorithm in respect to more human oriented man-machine communication, however quality of the failure recognition is lower in that case.

The presented results confirm possibility of wide applications of the proposed diagnostic system in practice.

It would be interesting in future to apply other forms of the fuzzy relational equation (e.g. with the max-product operator) and to introduce some elements of learning for proper determination of not extended relationship matrix.

8. ACKNOWLEDGEMENT

The authors are grateful to Professor Jacek Mościński from the Academy of Mining and Metallurgy (Cracow) for his kind interest during the investigations.

9. LITERATURE

Baldwin, J. F. (1979). Fuzzy logic and approximate reasoning for mixed input arguments. *Int. J. Man-Mach. Stud.*, 11, 381-396.

Brunet, M., and B. Dubuisson (1983). Pattern recognition techniques applied to acoustic detection of liquid-metal fast breeder reactor cooling defects. *Nucl. Sci. & Eng.*, 84, 373-379.

Bubak, M., J. Mościński, and J. Jewulski (1983). A fuzzy logic approach to HTR nuclear power plant model control. *Ann. nucl. Energy*, 10, 467-471.

Dubois, D., and H. Prade (1979). Outline of fuzzy set theory. In M. M. Gupta, R. K. Radage, and R. R. Yager (Eds.), *Advances in Fuzzy Set Theory and Applications*, North Holland, Amsterdam.

Dubois, D., and H. Prade (1980). *Fuzzy Sets and Systems*, Academic Press, New York.

Ebert, D. (1982). Practicality and benefits from the applications of optimal control to pressurized water reactor maneuvers. *Nucl. Technol.*, 58, 218

Friedrich, K. (1974). Die Regelung des Thorium-Hochtemperatur-Kernkraftwerkes Uentrop. *BBC Nachrichten*, 4, 120-127.

Gonzalez, R., D. Fry, and R. Kryter (1974). Results in the application of pattern recognition methods to nuclear core component surveillance. *IEEE Trans. Nucl. Sci.*, NS-21, 1-8.

Higashi, M., and G. J. Klir (1984a). Resolution of finite fuzzy relational equations. *Fuzzy Sets and Syst.*, 13, 65-82.

Higashi, M., and G. J. Klir (1984b). Identification of fuzzy relation systems. *IEEE Trans. Syst., Man & Cybern.*, SMC-14, 349-355.

Hoshino, T. (1972). In core fuel management optimization by heuristic learning technique. *Nucl. Sci. & Eng.*, 49, 59-71.

Kickert, W. J., and H. R. van Nauta Lemke (1976). Application of a fuzzy controler in a warm water plant. *Automatica*, 12, 301-308.

Kitowski, J. (1985). Applications of fuzzy relational equations and fuzzy logic elements in diagnostics of complex systems. *Sci. Bull. of the*

Academy of Mining and Metallurgy s. Automatica, 37, Cracow. (in polish).
Kitowski, J. (1986). Heuristic resolution of the fuzzy relational equations. submitted to *IEEE Trans. Syst., Man & Cybern.*
Kitowski, J., and M. Bargieł (1985). On the failure diagnosis in applications to complex physical systems. *First IFSA Congress Abstracts*, vol. III. Universitat de Palma de Mallorca.
Kitowski, J., and M. Bargieł (1986). Applications of fuzzy diagnostics to failure analysis of industrial complex plants. *Comput. Phys. Commun.*, 41, (in press).
Kitowski, J., and E. Ksiązek (1985). Fuzzy logic applications for failure analysis and diagnosis of a primary circuit of the HTR nuclear power plant. *Comput. Phys. Commun.*, 38, 323-327.
Kitowski, J., and J. Mościński (1979). Computer simulation of heuristic reinforcement-learning system for nuclear power plant load changes control. *Comput. Phys. Commun.*, 18, 339-352.
Kitowski, J., J. Mościński, and M. Cebula (1982). A heuristic approach to the reinforcement learning control of one-dimensional model of a HTR core. *Ann. nucl. Energy*, 9, 45-46.
Macdonald, J. L., and B. V. Koen (1975). Application of artificial intelligence techniques to digital computer control of nuclear reactor. *Nucl. Sci. & Eng.*, 56, 142-151.
Moligner, A., A. Skomorokhov, and D. Shvetsov (1981). On the problem of noise spectra classification in nuclear power plant operation diagnostics. *Nucl. Technol.*, 53, 8-18.
Nishiwaki, Y., M. Muroya, T. Tsunoda, T. Terano, M. Sugeno, and T. Onisawa (1985). Human factors and fuzzy sets theory for nuclear safety analysis. *First IFSA Congress Abstracts*, vol. I. Universitat de Palma de Mallorca.
Oguma, R. (1982). Extended partial and multiple coherence analyses and their application to reactor noise investigation. *Nucl. Sci. & Technol.*, 19, 543-554.
Pappis, C. P., and M. Sugeno (1976). Fuzzy relational equations and inverse problem. *Internal Report*, Queen Mary College, London.
Pedrycz, W. (1984). Identification in fuzzy systems. *IEEE Trans. Syst., Man & Cybern.*, SMC-14, 361-366.
Petersen, K., E. Kujawski, and T. Wu (1980). User's manual for Thermix - a two-dimensional transient thermal-hydraulics code. *Reports of General Electric*, Sunnyvale.
Sanchez, E. (1976). Resolution of composite fuzy relational equations. *Inf. Control*, 30, 38-48.
Sanchez, E. (1979). Inverses of fuzzy relations. Application to possibility distributions and medical diagnosis. *Fuzzy Sets & Syst.*, 2, 75-86.
Shahinpoor, M., and D. J. Wells (1980). Application possibilities for fuzzy failure analysis and diagnosis of reactor plant components and areas. *Nucl. Eng. & Design*, 61, 93-100.
Tsukamoto, Y. (1979). *Fuzzy logic based on Łukasiewicz logic and its applications to diagnosis and control.* Thesis, Tokyo Institute of Technology, Tokyo.
Tsukamoto, Y., and T. Terano (1977). Failure diagnosis by using fuzzy logic. *Proceedings IEEE Conference on Decision Making and Control*, New Orlean, pp. 1390-1395.
Wade, D. C., and W. B. Terney (1971). Optimal control of nuclear reactor depletion. *Nucl. Sci. & Eng.*, 45, 199-217.
Wakabayashi, J., and A. Fukumoto (1981). Simulation study of a system for diagnosis of nuclear power plant operation. *Nucl. Technol.* ,54, 19-30.
Zadeh, L. A. (1975a). The concept of a linguistic variable and its application to approximate reasoning - I. *Inf. Sci.*, 8, 199-249.
Zadeh, L. A. (1975b). The concept of a linguistic variable and its applica-

tion to approximate reasoning - II. *Inf. Sci.*, 8, 301-357.
Zadeh, L. A. (1975c). The concept of a linguistic variable and its application to approximate reasoning - III. *Inf. Sci.*, 9, 43-80.
Zimmermann, H. J. (1976). Description and optimization of fuzzy systems. *Int. J. Gen. Syst.*, 2, 209-215.

Keyword Index